The Common Law
in Colonial America

VOLUME 1

The Chesapeake and New England, 1607–1660

WILLIAM E. NELSON

OXFORD

UNIVERSITY PRESS

2008

OXFORD
UNIVERSITY PRESS

Oxford University Press, Inc., publishes works that further
Oxford University's objective of excellence
in research, scholarship, and education.

Oxford   New York
Auckland   Cape Town   Dar es Salaam   Hong Kong   Karachi
Kuala Lumpur   Madrid   Melbourne   Mexico City   Nairobi
New Delhi   Shanghai   Taipei   Toronto

With offices in
Argentina   Austria   Brazil   Chile   Czech Republic   France   Greece
Guatemala   Hungary   Italy   Japan   Poland   Portugal   Singapore
South Korea   Switzerland   Thailand   Turkey   Ukraine   Vietnam

Published by Oxford University Press, Inc.
198 Madison Avenue, New York, New York 10016

www.oup.com

Oxford is a registered trademark of Oxford University Press

Library of Congress Cataloging-in-Publication Data
Nelson, William Edward, 1940–
The common law in colonial America / William E. Nelson.
   v. cm.
Includes bibliographical references and index.
Contents: v. 1. The Chesapeake and New England, 1607–1660
ISBN 978-0-19-532728-1
1. Law—United States—History.   2. United States—History—Colonial
period, ca. 1600–1775.   I. Title.
KF361.N45 2008
349.7309′031—dc22   2007044063

9 8 7 6 5 4 3 2 1

Printed in the United States of America
on acid-free paper

To John Phillip Reid
Mentor and Friend

ACKNOWLEDGMENTS

Three factors coalesced to induce me to undertake the writing of volume one and what I hope will be three additional volumes of *The Common Law in Colonial America*.

The first is the state of the existing literature. No synthesis grounded in archival sources exists for all thirteen North American colonies for the entire colonial period. Excellent studies do exist for the legal history of some colonies and for particular legal subjects; in addition, historians have produced a wealth of scholarship on colonial political, intellectual, economic, and social history. My hope is to make use of this excellent scholarship in order to provide context for and otherwise supplement what I can extract from the archival sources. Combining archival material with existing scholarship will, I hope, produce the more general synthesis that the field of colonial legal history so far has lacked.

The second factor is the stage of my own career. After four decades of work in archival judicial records, I have developed, for better or worse, an efficient methodology for extracting information from them. It is time to put that methodology to work. In doing so, I have been and will be aided immensely by the efforts of the Genealogical Society of Utah, which has microfilmed most seventeenth and eighteenth-century court records and deposited its films in state archives and in its own archive in Salt Lake City. The Genealogical Society was kind enough to sell me a roll of film of Middlesex County, Massachusetts, records and thereby saved me the time and expense of traveling to Massachusetts. I am most grateful. The Library of Virginia sold me a number of rolls of county records, many of them microfilmed by the Genealogical Society of Utah; I am indebted to both for not having to spend weeks in Richmond, Virginia.

Maryland possesses the most technologically sophisticated state depository: all of its seventeenth-century archival materials that have not been published in seventy-two printed volumes are available on line. I thank the Archives of Maryland for providing me with access as well as the Connecticut State Archives for permitting me to use the original manuscripts of its seventeenth-century judicial records.

The third factor that induced me to attempt a synthesis of colonial legal history is the support of my institution, New York University School of Law. The Filomen D'Agostino and Max E. Greenberg Faculty Research Fund provides generous sabbatical leaves, summer research grants, and support for travel and for purchasing research material; completion of this project would be unimaginable without the Fund's support. I also thank the Committee that administers the Fund for its patience and its faith that my work will eventually find its way into print, even when publication sometimes does not occur until several years after the Committee has provided for my research and writing. Dean Richard Revesz and his predecessors, Deans Norman Redlich and John Sexton, are responsible for the providing the wherewithal that facilitates the Committee's generosity; my colleagues and I owe them a giant debt of gratitude.

I am also grateful to the family of Samuel I. Golieb which, through the Katzenberger Foundation, supports the Legal History Colloquium at NYU. The Colloquium is simply the best seminar in the world for workshopping legal history scholarship, and its members have read some portions of this book in draft as many as three times and the entire draft once. Among the members of the Colloquium whom I thank for their noteworthy contributions to my thinking are Lauren Benton, Richard B. Bernstein, Harold Forsythe, Dan Hulsebosch, Bill LaPiana, and Deborah Malamud.

I am also indebted to the four readers of the manuscript selected by the Oxford University Press—Mary Bilder, James Ely, Peter Hoffer, and David Konig. All four of them provided helpful advice and useful bibliographic suggestions. Konig, in addition, forced me to rethink the analytic structure of portions of the book, while Hoffer helped me to see and articulate more clearly the role that legislation played in the seventeenth-century colonies.

Two librarians who provided all sorts of assistance were Elizabeth Evans of the New York University Law School Library and Jeff Mason of the Hewlett-Woodmere Library. Tom Attanasio and Barbara Kern checked citations in the footnotes for accuracy, and Shirley Gray, as always, efficiently performed innumerable clerical chores. I thank them all.

Chapters 2 and 3 were delivered in an earlier form as the 2002 Kormendy Lecture at Ohio Northern University School of Law and were then published as "Authority and the Rule of Law in Early Virginia," *Ohio Northern University Law Review,* 29 (2003), 305. I am indebted to Dean David Crago and Professor Liam O'Melinn for inviting me to speak. An earlier version of chapters 4 and 5 appeared as "The Utopian Legal Order of the Massachusetts Bay Colony, 1630–1686," *American Journal of Legal History,* 47 (2005), 183. Both articles, as revised, are reprinted here with permission.

I first met John Phillip Reid forty-four years ago as a second-year law student in his legal history class. At the time my ambition was to become a scholar of English legal history. He is responsible for making me an American historian by persuading me that, while the past may have been in England, the future would be in America. He sent me to Harvard to study for a Ph.D. under his mentor, Mark DeWolfe Howe, but there his responsibility ended, when circumstances led me to work instead with Bernard Bailyn, whose work Reid has criticized. Over a decade later, when I was in desperate need of an academic appointment, Reid at long last obtained one for me at NYU. I have rountinely rejected his guidance ever since.

My family—Elaine, Leila, and Greg—is, as always, most responsible for this book. Elaine, at least, is eager for me to retire, but I trust she, Leila, and Greg are geared up for however many years three more volumes will take.

New York, NY
February, 2008

Contents

The Common Law in Colonial America

INTRODUCTION

Half a century ago law professors such as Julius Goebel, George L. Haskins, Mark deWolfe Howe, and Joseph H. Smith were among the leading students of American legal history.[1] Unsurprisingly, the academic milieu in which they worked affected their scholarship. In particular, their history was influenced by the search of their colleagues—Henry M. Hart, Albert M. Sacks, and Herbert Weschler are the most prominent who come to mind—for "an architecture for thinking about a dynamic public law that was nonetheless accountable to the rule of law in a democracy."[2]

Colonial American law appeared to offer a model for that architecture in the story of the reception of the common law. On the one hand, the common law could be seen as a set of fixed principles and procedures by which judicial discretion was constrained, policy choices handed off to other institutions, and the rule of law thereby preserved. On the other hand, reception had occurred as part of a dynamic policy process; the American colonists ended up receiving only so much of the common law as was appropriate to their needs and circumstances.

Except for J. Willard Hurst, all the great mid-twentieth-century legal historians, at one point or another in their careers, set out to examine in detail how the common law came to America. They all devoted considerable effort to studying colonial legal history,[3] "at least prior to 1700, when our jurisprudence had in all important respects taken the pattern that it retained until well after the American Revolution, and to a great degree retains today."[4] The issue of reception was the nub of their work.

In studying the common law's reception, however, this old school of legal history confronted an immense obstacle. The obstacle was this: A historian can never comprehend the law of a past society merely by reading legislation and treatises; particularly in a common law system, it is also necessary to understand how judges and other officials applied law on the ground.[5] To determine whether Americans actually received England's common law, historians accordingly must delve deeply into English as well as American case law. That is a daunting task indeed. Although I have not systematically surveyed England's judicial records and have not yet completed my work in colonial American ones, I know enough to be confident that the source material for sixteenth-, seventeenth-, and eighteenth-century English legal history exceeds the material available for colonial America by many multiples. Sir John Baker tells us, for example, that the plea rolls for the first four decades of the sixteenth century alone are more than twenty-five miles in length; if they were cut and bound in books as colonial court records were, they would amount to some 250 volumes.[6] In contrast, because America was much smaller in population than England and because many American legal records have been lost, I doubt whether that much legal material exists for the entire period from 1607 to 1776 for all thirteen colonies; in Massachusetts Bay prior to 1685, for example, there are only fifteen extant volumes of court records, nearly all in print, covering its fifty-five-year history.

I do not imagine that a single scholar in a single lifetime could write a comprehensive history of sixteenth-, seventeenth-, and eighteenth-century English law; indeed, it is with great trouble that a small, dedicated group is striving collectively to accomplish the task.[7] From this it follows that, if we conceptualize colonial legal history around the issue of reception as Goebel, Haskins, Howe, and Smith did, we cannot write about it comprehensively either.

Making reception the central focus of colonial legal history also presents another difficulty, best illustrated in Paul Reinsch's monograph, *English Common Law in the Early American Colonies*. In view of the dearth of scholarship about colonial law at the time he was writing, his book was truly extraordinary. Reinsch was very perceptive, and he got much right. But his attention to "[t]he first question" of "the influence upon our system of the English common law" misled him. He concluded that the common law had scant influence during the colonial period; in its place, the early colonists adopted a system "of rude, untechnical, popular law."[8] By so misfocusing on reception and assuming that the alternative to common law was the implementation of unsophisticated law, Reinsch failed to study how the law of the early colonies was both a refined product of the social forces within them and a complex instrument affecting the course of their development.

More recent scholars, professionally trained as historians and teaching mainly in history departments, have begun to study the relation of colonial law to society. Several outstanding random monographs that contribute to our understanding of the legal development of particular localities are especially valuable.[9] Meanwhile, many social historians have used colonial legal records, which constitute some of the best source material available to them, in order to reconstruct the life experiences of colonial Americans, particularly members of underclasses such as slaves and women. Their valuable work is one of the foundations on which this and subsequent volumes rest.[10]

Nearly everything known about colonial American law grows out of the work of underclass historians, local historians, and the earlier generation of historians who studied the reception of the common law. But studies of local legal development and of the impact of law on underclasses cannot generate comprehensive hypotheses about the legal structure of society or the workings of the colonial judicial system as a whole, and work on common-law reception necessarily must remain tentative until historians know much more about case law on both sides of the ocean than is currently known. Accordingly, the study of colonial legal history demands a new beginning—a new lens through which to focus on the vast body of source materials that exist.

The key to a new beginning is to ask the right question. As we have seen, an inquiry into how colonial American law developed out of English common law is a poor question, in part because of our lack of knowledge about English law. In contrast, legal historians have devoted significant efforts during the past half century to the study of nineteenth-century American law and have learned a great deal about it.[11] Thus, a good start might be to ask how colonial law developed into post-Revolutionary American law.

This question, in turn, gives rise to a simple hypothesis underlying this and what I hope will be several subsequent volumes. The thirteen mainland American colonies were founded by different groups—indeed, by different nations—for many different purposes. Insofar as law reflects the societal conditions[12] under which it operates, tremendous differences had to exist among the legal systems of the early colonies. As this volume will show, the mid-seventeenth-century colonies functioned under Maryland law, New England law, and Virginia law. After 1800, if not by 1776, in contrast, it became possible to speak of American law, not as a body of perfectly uniform doctrine—there remained significant differences among the laws of the several states, especially in regard to slavery—but as a set of organizing principles around which authors such as St. George Tucker and James Kent could write treatises, teachers such as Tapping Reeve and James Gould could organize lectures, and judges such as John Marshall and Lemuel Shaw could decide cases.

This hypothesis gives rise, in turn, to further questions. How did the law of the early colonies differ? In what ways were the legal systems of all the colonies similar? What impact did various economic, social, political, and religious forces have in promoting similarity and difference? These are the central questions for this first volume, which examines the founding of the Chesapeake and New England colonies. They also will be important in volume two on the founding of the middle colonies and the Carolinas. A third volume will then address a powerful force toward legal convergence—the effort of British authorities to transform the largely independent English provinces of North America and the Caribbean into a coherent empire. A final volume will examine the state of the mainland colonies' law on the eve of the Revolution; it will present a detailed picture of the gestation of an emerging body of national, though far from perfectly uniform, American law even before the birth of a nation-state.

This first volume, as already noted, focuses on how the law of the early Chesapeake colonies differed from the law of early New England, as well as on the differences among the legal systems of the colonies within the two regions. It explores the legal history of the Chesapeake colonies— Virginia and Maryland—and the New England colonies—Massachusetts

Bay, Connecticut, New Haven, Plymouth, and Rhode Island—from their initial settlement until approximately 1660. The choice of this date—the year when Charles II was restored to his throne—is not an arbitrary one. Prior to 1660, the government of England frequently was distracted first by conflicts between the king and parliament, later by Charles I's financial straits resulting from his attempt to rule without parliament, and ultimately by civil war. As a result, the North American colonies were in large part left free to govern themselves. Various holders of power, occasionally in London but usually in the Chesapeake or New England, fought each other to determine the direction each colony would take. Since the individuals and groups that controlled the colonies had different agendas, the legal system of each colony developed in somewhat different directions. Only after 1660, when the crown launched a long-term effort to fashion England's colonies into a coherent empire, did these legal orders begin to converge in the direction of a single common-law system.

By ending this volume in 1660, the initial differences between Chesapeake and New England law emerge with greater clarity than they would if the story were continued to a later date. The choice of 1660 also has another advantage. To the extent there were similarities among the legal orders of the early colonies, and there were many, the 1660 date facilitates analysis of their root causes. Similarities prior to 1660 resulted, this volume claims, from the common social and economic realities that colonists faced as they settled and tamed the continental wilderness. After 1660, another explanatory element—British imperial policy—entered into the picture. Ending this volume in 1660, in short, facilitates separate examination of the impact of local conditions, on the one hand, and imperial policy, on the other, on the development of colonial common law.

The primary thesis of this volume is that the Chesapeake and New England came into being as strikingly different places and that the law in force in each both reflected and contributed to their differences. I start with a verity on which all colonial historians agree—that Virginia was founded primarily for economic profit; New England, primarily to create a religious utopia; and Maryland, primarily to establish a haven for persecuted Roman Catholics. Of course, the profit motive was not absent in Maryland and early New England, and many Virginians cared about God and the church.[13] Nonetheless, the legal order of each of these colonies reflected its founders' primary purposes. The common law was important to Lord Baltimore, the founder of Maryland, from the outset; one author, indeed, has urged that Baltimore granted religious toleration and adopted common-law rules protecting property rights in an effort to create a precursor to a nineteenth-century liberal state, in which minority Catholics could use their wealth to retain lawyers who, in turn, could manipulate the law to protect their clients from the whims of Protestant political majorities. Baltimore, it was suggested, appreciated the power of law to protect minorities who have sufficient wealth to retain lawyers and thereby access the courts, and understood that law protective of wealth and property furthers social stability and thereby ensures that the families and groups who are put at the top of a social order at one point in time are likely to remain at or near the top in future times.[14]

In contrast, as the following chapters will show, the leaders who initially governed Virginia and New England made little use of the common law as an instrument for social control. Virginia's rulers sought to accomplish their main chore, which was to coerce labor out of the local inhabitants, through intimidation and brutality, while New England's leaders strove to create a religious utopia by recourse to the law of God, not the law of England. The English legal heritage of the inhabitants of both Virginia and New England constituted a set of background norms to which they occasionally turned when convenient, but England's common law was not the initial foundation of their legal systems.

What began to push the law of Virginia and New England toward greater, though not complete, convergence was the concept of the rule of law, about which John Phillip Reid has recently written.[15] Although the language "rule of law" was not in vogue in the seventeenth century, Reid documents the prevalence of the idea that society ought to be governed by ascertainable and unchanging rules capable of restraining arbitrary actions by those in power. This rule of law idea was not a unitary one, however; as we shall see, it meant something different in Virginia from what it meant in New England.

The rule of law came to Virginia first. When the Virginia Company, which had founded the colony, proved unable to remain afloat and Virginia's ruling elite needed to coax investment from other sources, the colony's leaders announced that they would govern by English law, and

Virginia adopted elements of its English legal heritage that would provide investors with familiar remedies to recover the funds they had lent. In particular, the colony put into place known and certain common-law procedures by which people who lent money could recover their debts. On balance, these debt-collection mechanisms were somewhat inefficient: creditors who turned to the law often waited a long time to obtain judgment in their favor, and they did not always collect their judgments in full.

But the difficulties that creditors faced did not stop them from lending; the difficulties merely raised the price of loans, typically in the form of higher prices for goods sold on credit. In their lending and borrowing practices, creditors and debtors merely followed what we now know as basic economic theory. When markets are free, as they were after 1625 for trading between England and Virginia, traders will make deals that market conditions warrant as long as they know the background contractual rules and are confident that those rules will not be subject to arbitrary change. Background rules will only affect price: if merchants know, for example, that they will never collect payment for 5 percent of the goods they sell, they will increase their price on all sales by 5 percent; the only times they will not sell are when no mechanisms are in place for securing payment or when the operation of those mechanisms is so uncertain that they cannot estimate collection costs as an element of doing business. By announcing that they would govern by the law of England, Virginia's rulers put known law in place and promised not to alter it arbitrarily. This adoption of the rule of law thereby created the markets that enabled Virginia to thrive, even though the specific law they adopted had no particular facilitative function.

As it functioned after 1625 in Virginia, the rule of law mattered not because the law had particular content, but because its content was known, fixed, and not subject to arbitrary change.

In contrast, the content of the law mattered enormously in colonial New England, where, as we shall see, a key issue was the discretion of magistrates. The magistrates wanted to rule by the law of God, but most of the people in the towns found God's law too ambiguous. Its ambiguity, the people discerned, gave magistrates a broad discretion to resolve legal disputes and other issues however they wished. The townspeople wanted the law enveloped in clearly written codes that everyone could interpret easily and uniformly and that left whatever discretionary power remained in the hands of local communities.

In 1648–1649, the townspeople of Massachusetts won the battle in their jurisdiction. After years of study and work, the Massachusetts legislature in 1648 adopted a code of laws that dealt with the main issues its legal system confronted. The code represented a compromise between proponents of the law of God and proponents of alternative rules, but to the extent the compromise left anyone with discretion, it was not the magistrates. By legislation in 1649 that will be examined in chapter 4, the Massachusetts General Court provided that when a local jury sitting on a case disagreed with magistrates, the case would proceed on appeal to the General Court where the two houses sitting together would resolve it. Since the deputies in the elected lower house outnumbered the magistrates in the upper house by about three to one, the 1649 legislation ensured that Massachusetts would be governed by preexisting, codified law unless the representatives of the local towns who controlled the legislature decided otherwise.

Like the people of Massachusetts, those of the smaller New England colonies—Connecticut, New Haven, Plymouth, and Rhode Island—strove to control their rulers' discretion, especially in matters of criminal law, where people feared interference in their daily lives. Connecticut, as we shall see, codified its penal laws even before Massachusetts did, while Rhode Island refused to prosecute people when no written law could be found prohibiting the conduct in question. New Haven and Plymouth adopted procedural rules protecting their citizens from overreaching by government.

Unlike the rulers of Virginia, the townspeople of the New England colonies did not seek to control the law out of a need to promote the certainty and predictability needed for entrepreneurial investment. New Englanders needed the rule of law to serve the quasi-constitutional function of restraining arbitrary government on the part of their rulers. Similarly, the founding leaders of Maryland needed something more than a content-free rule of law. These Roman Catholics needed a mechanism for protecting their religious liberty when, as they fully appreciated, they would become a minority. Over time, however, religious issues declined in importance, and after 1660, as we shall see, Maryland fell into Virginia's orbit and adopted a conception of the rule of law without particular substantive content, designed only to commit the province to government by clear, unchanging dictates that would guarantee the certainty and predictability needed for entrepreneurial investment.

In sum, this volume will show that the legal orders of the Chesapeake and New England colonies started out on different paths. Between 1607 and 1660, however, they began to converge toward adherence to the rule of law and acceptance of the colonists' English legal heritage, of which the common law was a part. Nonetheless, the social, economic, and political pressures pointing toward convergence were different. As a result, the rule of law took on different meanings in the Chesapeake and in New England. Different segments of the English legal heritage shared by the people of the two regions were emphasized, and the legal orders of the Chesapeake and New England colonies, even as they became more alike, continued to further different goals and to fulfill different functions.

1

LAW IN THE JAMESTOWN SETTLEMENT

The English settlers who arrived in Jamestown, Virginia, in 1607 did not bring the common law with them. It would have contradicted the very purpose of the Virginia Company, the founder and governing entity of the colony, to have done so. Organizing the Virginia Company and planting its colony at Jamestown required enormous and continuing investment, and everything that could be done had to be done to keep investment forthcoming. Profits, if any were to materialize, had to be reserved for investors in England, whose continuing flow of cash was essential to keep the colony from dying. For this reason, the Virginia Company set itself up as a monopolist and adopted three subsidiary policies. First, it decided to retain total control over all assets, including all land, in Virginia. Second, it determined to regulate minutely all economic transactions in the colony so that it, rather than private individuals, would collect the profits. Third, it resolved to require settlers in the colony to labor for the company, not for themselves, and it further decided to obtain their labor through coercive discipline rather than free market inducements.

For the first five years of the colony's existence, there was no private ownership of land whatsoever. In fact, private property would have made no sense because the Virginia Company had been set up as a trade and exploration venture, not as a locus for family farming or the production of a staple crop. As late as 1616, less than a quarter of the colony's men were farmers. In 1613–14, the company did grant every settler a small garden plot of three acres, but these grants did not reflect any change in economic vision. The best guess is that the grants were designed to alleviate food shortages by encouraging the settlers to grow their own and thereby reduce the need for the company to import food from England.[1]

In addition to controlling all means of production in the colony, the Virginia Company regulated all economic transactions minutely. Sir Thomas Dale's *Lawes Divine, Moral and Martial*, the code promulgated in 1611, provided, for example, that no settler could trade with or steal from the Indians, on pain of death. Because of difficulties the colony had experienced with merchants and seamen selling provisions "at unreasonable rates and prices unconscionable," it outlawed all efforts "to bargain, exchange, barter, truck, trade, or sell, upon pain of death, unto any one Landman member of this present Colony, any provisions of what kind soever, above the determined valuations and prices set down and proclaimed." It also prohibited any merchant on land "or keeper of any store" from "sell[ing] or giv[ing] away any thing under his Charge to any Favorite of his, more than unto any other." Then, there were provisions dealing with the maintenance of tools, prohibiting the killing of farm animals, and authorizing suits for the collection of debt in the Marshall's Court, "where the creditor shall have Justice."[2]

With the profit motive and the motive of acquiring land unavailable as devices to induce settlers to labor, the Virginia Company turned to coercion to induce the workforce to work. It may have had little choice given the composition of Virginia's early population, which consisted overwhelmingly of young men, largely recruited from impoverished, uneducated, and undisciplined backgrounds. Because Virginia offered few rewards to settlers, such young men were usually the only people who could be induced or conscripted into migration. Throughout the seventeenth century men outnumbered women by about two or three to one. Available figures for 1625 suggest that 68 percent of all inhabitants over the age of nine were men between the ages of 16 and 34—a percentage that probably would have been even higher at any given time in the previous eighteen years, when almost no children had been born in the colony and fewer men had aged. Women, and hence children and families, rarely migrated to Virginia—on a list of more than 2,000 passengers embarking from London to Virginia in 1635, only 14 percent were female.[3]

Worst of all, the young men who came to Virginia died at an appalling rate. During the first two decades of its existence, the colony was a death trap for most immigrants. Within the first few summers after arriving in Virginia, about 40 percent of all immigrants were killed by disease, although women survived better than men, dying at only half the rate. Between 1625 and 1640, for example, a number in excess of 15,000 people arrived from England, but during that same period the colony's population increased by less than 7,000—from 1,300 to 8,100 inhabitants. Indeed, over the course of the entire seventeenth century, some 120,000 settlers immigrated to the Chesapeake, but the white population in 1700, which included many who had been born in the region, still numbered less than 90,000.[4]

Such demographic conditions did not encourage the men who populated Virginia either to work hard or to obey societal norms. On the one hand, there were few incentives to lead upstanding lives. In the colony's first decade, a man could not amass a landed estate since private property in land did not exist. Most forms of working for profit were outlawed; in particular, it was unlawful for a man to buy something at one price and resell it at a higher one. A few men, perhaps, could save their wages, marry, and raise a family. But, since men outnumbered women by a ratio of more than three to one, marriage was available only to a few.

On the other hand, opportunities for misbehavior were abundant. Sloth was effortless. Beer, cider, and like beverages calmed fears and made hardships temporarily disappear. Opportunities for theft, particularly of company property such as pigs, which could be quickly consumed, were ever present. And why should young men not enjoy sexual pleasure, either with the few women who could be shared or with each other or with animals?

For nearly everyone in early Virginia, life was barbarous, savage, and vulgar. Sir Thomas Dale's *Lawes Divine, Moral and Martial* responded in a harsh, coercive fashion. The code promulgated in 1611 has long epitomized the brutality of Virginia's legal order during the first two decades of the colony's history. Dale's code was, indeed, Spartan. It provided the death penalty for innumerable crimes, as well as whipping, galley service, tongue piercing, the cutting off of ears, and being tied neck and heels together. The laws contained no procedural safeguards; they envisioned "military discipline" and "punishment" that quickly and "without partiality shall be inflicted upon the breakers of the same."[5]

Most extraordinary of all was the substance of the *Lawes*. After making provision for divine worship and for crimes against religion, such as blasphemy, the code addressed such offenses as treason, murder, sodomy, adultery, rape, and perjury, all of which were punishable by death, as were most forms of theft. Next, it provided punishment for anyone who spoke "traitorous words" against the king or "royal authority" or who dared "to detract, slander, calumniate, or utter unseemly and unfitting speeches, either against his Majesty's Honorable Council for this Colony, resident in England, or against the committees [and] assistants unto the said Council," resident in Virginia. The code also set out penalties for those who "detract[ed], slander[ed], calumniate[d], murmur[ed], mutinie[d], resist[ed], disobey[ed] or neglect[ed] the commandments...of...[any] public officer" or who gave "any disgraceful words or commit[ted] any act to the disgrace of any person in this Colony."[6]

The code's health provisions, concerning the dumping of laundry water, the height of beds above the floor, and the requirement that everyone "keep his house sweet and clean," most clearly reflected the need to control a young, raucous male population. More important, though, were the following two sections:

> 26. Every tradesman in their several occupations, trades and functions shall duly and daily attend his work upon his said trade or occupation, upon peril for his first fault and negligence therein, to have his entertainment checked for one month, for his second fault three months, for his third one year, and if he continues still unfaithful and negligent therein, to be condemned to the galley for three years.
>
> 27. All overseers of workmen shall be careful in seeing that performed which is given them in charge, upon pain of such punishment as shall be inflicted upon him by a martial court.[7]

Historians have disagreed about the significance that should be attributed to Dale's *Lawes*. According to David Konig, the historian who has produced the most important scholarship on early Virginia law, the colony's "swift and discretionary justice unbound by common law" and the "stern system of social control" that it produced were not aberrational, but fit readily into the antecedent English and Virginia legal traditions. Before Virginia's settlement, semi-military conciliar justice long had dominated the landscape of England's northern marches, of Wales, and of Ireland. And in Virginia itself, the death penalty had been unmercifully imposed on two occasions prior to Dale's *Lawes*. On the first, the Council had put one of its members to death after convicting him of suspicion of spying for Spain, while on the second, John Smith had been sentenced to death for manslaughter because he had failed to prevent Indians from killing two men under his command. He was saved from capital punishment only by the fortuitous arrival of a vessel from England carrying orders appointing a new Council President.[8]

Not all historians of seventeenth-century Virginia agree, however, with Konig's analysis. While emphasizing the colonists' experimentation with their "richly diverse legal heritage," Warren Billings, for one, argues instead that Englishmen "carried to America" a belief in a "civilized society...governed by rules," specifically the common law—a belief that might have precluded the brutality Konig highlights.[9] One reason these divergent interpretations persist is that historians have been centrally concerned with "trac[ing] institutional inheritances, and...pursu[ing] trails of ideas from old country to new."[10] A new focus not on what law the colonists brought with them, but on how the law of the early colonies differed can turn attention, however, to other matters.

We do not, in fact, know how harshly Dale's laws were enforced in Virginia, although Virginians did complain about their enforcement.[11] All we know for sure is that the code was published in England. Perhaps, its main purpose was not to maintain order or promote discipline on the ground, but merely to reassure English investors that the Virginia Company was doing all it could to secure labor from its workers. Nevertheless, the logic of Dale's laws, which proclaimed that Virginia was organized on a corporate, military model rather than a civilian, free-market one, directed the small group of Virginia Company officials who exercised judicial authority to decide disputes to maximize the company's power, not to do justice between the parties. That logic, in turn, steered them toward obtaining labor at as low a cost as possible by coercing their inferiors to work and imposing mean, nasty, and cruel punishments when they did not. When disputes arose, in short, the raison d'etre of the Virginia Company compelled its officials on the ground to act arbitrarily.

But Sir Thomas Dale's draconian rules remained on the books only for seven years. Beginning in the late 1610s, change started to occur. What drove the change was a transformation of the colony's economy from one based on trade and exploration to one based on agricultural production of a staple crop, tobacco.[12]

The first step occurred when the company offered 50 acres of land to anyone who had subscribed or would subscribe £12.10s to its funds. Then, in 1618 it instituted what became the headright system, whereby anyone who transported himself or another to Virginia received 50 acres for every person transported. During these same years the company also began issuing patents to groups of settlers who proposed to found entire communities.[13]

These early steps toward change emerged as part of a package of reform when the company sent Sir George Yeardley as governor. Upon his arrival in April 1619, Yeardley issued a proclamation freeing all men who had resided for at least three years in the colony "from such public services and labors which formerly they suffered" and authorizing them "to make choice of their dividends of land and…to possess and plant upon them." It also confirmed the abrogation of "those cruel laws" by which Virginia had been governed and provided for future government "by those free laws which his Majesty's subjects live under in England." Finally, the proclamation directed the calling of an assembly so that the inhabitants "might have a hand in the governing of themselves."[14] This distribution of property and commitment to self-government under the laws of England had the obvious purpose of encouraging Englishmen to settle in Virginia.

The process of reform proceeded slowly, however, and did not lead immediately to a free market legal order. Even after the repeal of Dale's *Lawes*, the Virginia Company, and later the royal government of Virginia, continued to regulate the economy extensively. The company, for example, persisted in prohibiting private trade with Native Americans, in setting maximum prices for many commodities, and in forbidding individuals from reselling goods at a price higher than what they had paid. It also developed a scheme for sharing work on farms among those who remained home while most men were marching off on an expedition against the Indians.[15] The subsequent royal government continued to fix prices, as well as to require that "goods be indifferently distributed among the inhabitants without any enhancing of the price or other engrossing" and that no one resell goods purchased from a vessel at anchor at a higher price than he had paid. It also enforced legislation requiring landowners to plant specified amounts of corn. And, as late as 1634, a county court departed from the usual rule that bargains were judicially enforceable when it found a particular "bargain unreasonable, and not fitting to continue."[16]

Indeed, the most pervasive regulatory schemes occurred after the crown had taken control of the colony. For over a decade, the House of Burgesses sought to prevent declines in the price of tobacco by limiting the amount individual planters could grow, setting minimum prices at which crops could be sold, and establishing markets in which sales were to take place. It also sought to fix the charges of millers and prevent the export of scarce commodities such as corn and female cattle.[17]

A second scheme was proposed in a proclamation by Governor Yeardley, when he returned to Virginia in 1626 as the first royal governor. It sought to deal with the problems that arose when "every man" was "left free...to buy what quantity he thought good himself," with the result that "the whole Colony...suffer[ed] by...irregular buying up of commodities into a few men's hands." Yeardley proposed to end these problems by appointing "in every plantation...one sufficient man chosen as merchant or factor to deal and buy for all the people dwelling in the same plantation." This "storekeeper for the common store," as the office would be known in later years, was then required to distribute goods to all people "equally...as near as may be." Pursuant to the proclamation, the corporation of James City appointed a storekeeper, who agreed to take a profit of 12 percent on the goods he acquired and sold.[18]

But Yeardley's proposal was not popular. It was one thing to have a common storekeeper in economic backwaters such as King's Creek and Old Plantation Creek on the Eastern shore, but quite another to tolerate such storekeepers in centers of economic activity along the James River.[19] In the words of one man, "notwithstanding the said proclamation, if he were at James City he would go aboard and buy what commodities he wanted, for I am as free as any man in the country." He was not alone.[20] Although Yeardley's proclamation had been "intended... for the general good of the Colony..., it ha[d] bred great murmurings & discontent both on the part of the merchants, and of the people also." Accordingly, the General Court suspended its operation until the next session of the House of Burgesses could consider it. In the interim, traditional forms of economic control were employed, as ships that unloaded at Jamestown were directed to sell to all inhabitants, who could buy provisions for themselves and their family but not for resale at a higher price. And in the longer run, statutes remained on the books prohibiting forestalling and engrossing.[21]

Harsh, coercive mechanisms for maintaining public order and obtaining labor from settlers also remained in place even after Dale's *Lawes* ceased to be of force in 1618. In that very year, for example, when some citizens of Bermuda Hundred were refusing "to follow their arts to the great prejudice [of the] Colony," Governor Samuel Argall imposed military discipline on the community, with the proviso that the provost marshal he appointed have authority to take into "safe custody all delinquents and prisoners of what nature and quality soever their offenses be" and to put down "all mutinies, factions, rebellions, and all other discords." Labor difficulties in Bermuda Hundred, it appears, thereupon disappeared.[22]

In 1619, the very year in which the Virginia Company announced its reform package, the company also reaffirmed the Spartan nature of the colony's criminal justice system when it instructed the Governor and Council to appoint a master for anyone living in idleness and directed that drunkenness be dealt with by "such severe punishments as the Governor or Council of State shall think fit," including degradation to servile or bond status. Instructions two years later similarly gave the Governor "absolute power and authority... to direct, determine, and punish at his good discretion any emergent business neglect or contempt of authority in any kind or what soever negligence or contempt may be found."[23]

Then there was the 1624 prosecution of Edward Sharpless,[24] the clerk of the Council of State. In that year, the crown sent royal commissioners to Virginia to make an investigation preparatory to revoking the colony's charter and placing it under direct royal control. The Virginia Company and its local officials in Virginia, in an effort to do what they could to resist and obstruct the investigation, did not want company records given to the commissioners, but Sharpless ignored their wishes and handed over some records.

For this, he was hauled before the Governor and Council, which styled itself "A Court...held on the 10th of May 1624." The entry of that date reveals all:

> Whereas it appeared to this Court by sufficient proof & his own confession that Edward Sharpless...has betrayed our counsels and intentions, in giving copies of our writings and letters to the King's Majesty & the Lords of the Privy Council, to some of the Commission out of promise of reward, etc. *This Court has adjudged* that he shall be set upon the Pillory in the market place of James City & there to have his ears nailed to it & cut off.[25]

The bloody penalty was quickly imposed, with no indictment, no jury trial, no appeal, and no sign whether due process had been afforded, on a man who had simply obeyed a lawful royal command.[26]

On the same day, an equally cruel punishment was administered to Richard Barnes, who had given "base & detracting speeches concerning the Governor." Again without indictment, trial, appeal or any other evidence of due process, the Governor and Council sitting as a Court directed that Barnes be disarmed and then punished by having "his tongue bored through with an awl" and being "butted" by each of forty guards, "kicked down & footed out of the fort," and forever "banished out of...the land." Two months earlier Captain Quaile, for his speeches against the Virginia Company's administration of its colony, had been "ignominiously degraded from his degree of Captain, his sword broken, and...sent out of the port of James City with an ax on his shoulder, afterwards to be brought in again by the name of Richard Quayle, carpenter." Upon his return, he was "set on the pillory with his ears nailed thereto & they...to be cut off." As late as the winter of 1625–1626, the General Court sentenced one man "to lose both his ears" and another to be "whipt from the fort to the gallows and from thence to be whipt back again, and be set upon the pillory and there to lose one of his ears," both for criticizing the court's imposition of the death penalty on a third man.[27]

The result was the continuation of an oppressive society in which, it was said, "neither the Governor nor Council could or would do any poor man right, but that they would show favor and wrong the poor." The speaker, who was fined 100 marks on a charge of slandering an individual and held over for further punishment for his seditious speech against the administration, added that "if he were a man of sufficient means yet he would not be one of the Council, because he did not see how they could well discharge their conscience." He explained "that poor men could hardly get any right and that the great men would hold all together, and further said that he did not see that the Governor could do any man right and used some other speeches concerning the authority of the Governor and Council…to punish men."[28]

We need to conclude by asking why the Virginia Company continued to engage in detailed economic regulation and to govern through harsh, coercive law even after proclaiming its 1619 reforms. In part, it acted out of habit "rooted in English and continental experience" and earlier Virginia practice.[29] The explanation also lies, however, in the inconsistencies of the company's post-1619 policies. On the one hand, the company sought to attract settlers by promising them profits and opportunities to better their lives by coming to Virginia. On the other hand, the company remained under an obligation to produce profits for its English investors. Maintaining the company's investment lifeline, which had kept its colony afloat, required the maintenance of conditions on the ground that were at war with the 1619 reforms. Hence, the company proclaimed its reforms while continuing to follow its older, oppressive policies.

A legal order based on private property and self-government, at which the Virginia Company had hinted in its 1619 reforms, simply could not come into existence while the company retained its control of the colony. But that control was destined not to last for long. On May 24, 1624, the Court of King's Bench in London, pursuant to *quo warranto* proceedings begun in the previous year, vacated the charter of the Virginia Company. The next year, on the death of James I, his son and successor, Charles I, incorporated Virginia into the royal demesne. Virginia thereupon became a royal colony, with a governor appointed by the crown.

2

Private Property and the Free Market in Virginia, 1619–1660

The revocation of the Virginia Company's charter ultimately transformed the colony from one in which settlers were coerced into working for an absentee monopolist to one based on the rule of law. This transformation was not, however, a Whiggish one in which Virginians escaped from tyranny in a search for freedom and liberty and a constitution founded on the people's consent.[1] Tyranny, liberty, and consent are the wrong concepts through which to understand why the legal system of seventeenth-century Virginia changed. Although some of the substantive law changes described in this chapter ultimately may have promoted liberty, there is no evidence that such was their purpose. Profit and the accumulation of wealth, not the attainment of liberty, were the highest aspirations of seventeenth-century Virginians and of the Englishmen who invested in Virginia. It was those aspirations and the need to facilitate the investment that would foster them which drove transformation of the colony's law.

The Virginia Company, as we have seen, had been set up to maximize the profits of English investors through exploration and trade. It always was searching for—indeed, its success required—a stroke of good luck, such as the discovery of some precious metal or other valuable commodity. But luck never materialized. Instead, tobacco saved the colony. At the outset of the seventeenth century, smoking was a luxury reserved for wealthy Europeans; no one could produce tobacco cheaply enough and in sufficient quantity to bring its price within reach of the masses. Virginia did. After John Rolfe's first crop proved enormously successful, production rose from 1,250 lb. in 1616, to 400,000 lb. by 1630, and 15,000,000 lb. by the 1660s. At the same time output increased, production costs fell, as did price—from a high of 2s. per lb. in the 1620s to 2d. per lb. in the 1630s and as low as 1d. per lb. in the 1660s. Large quantities and low prices led to development of a mass market for tobacco in Europe, which created a demand for mass production in Virginia. Mass production, in turn, created a huge demand for labor, with the result that immigration increased Virginia's population from only 900 residents in 1620 to 8,000 in 1640 and 25,000 by 1660.[2]

Tobacco cultivation, however, was not of great help to the Virginia Company. It had never intended to engage in large-scale agricultural operations and lacked a bureaucracy capable of supervising sizable numbers of workers on widely dispersed plantations; those tasks were more efficiently performed by independent, property-owning planters. Thus, when it became plain in the mid-1620s that the Company would neither profit from tobacco nor produce any return on its old investments, it lost the ability to raise further funds. Change then became essential. The revocation of the Company's charter and the institution of royal government accordingly is best understood as an analogue to a modern chapter eleven bankruptcy reorganization that facilitated future investment from other sources, namely, independent planters on the ground and the merchants and other individuals in England who were willing to invest in them.

Once Virginia had been reorganized, its law changed rapidly to induce the planters and those with whom they dealt to stake their lives and fortunes on Virginia's future. This chapter will trace in detail how the law succeeded in creating new opportunities for profit and thereby rechanneling capital flows. First, it will discuss the privatization of the economy, including some steps taken to encourage that privatization. Second, it will analyze Virginia's adoption of the rule of law, which was essential to stabilize the private property system and enable entrepreneurs to plan their investments.

But privatization backed by the rule of law did not alone suffice to make Virginia's economy flourish. Two additional ingredients were still missing. One was a reliable labor force. Accordingly, the third section of this chapter will turn to the law of servitude to examine how it combined rule-of-law features intended to induce Europeans to immigrate with harsh mechanisms of coercion contrived to insure that, once present in Virginia, they would work. Finally, the chapter will address the law of debt, which was designed to encourage investors to advance money by promising them repayment.

A. LAW IN A PRIVATED ECONOMY

Privatization of Virginia's economy did not just result automatically from the decision by the Virginia Company, outlined in the previous chapter, to grant land to individuals; it also was necessary for courts to elaborate a considerable amount of legal doctrine to resolve the many kinds of disputes that would arise between private economic actors.

Land law was one of the first subjects on which doctrine had to be developed. By the late 1620s, land had become a valuable commodity, making protection of ownership important. Accordingly, the General Court promulgated rules to make land ownership easier and more secure; the rules provided, for example, for the surveying of land, the inventory of estates, and the recording of land transfers.[3] Land ownership also gave rise to litigation, such as title and boundary disputes.[4] Other cases raised more complex issues of law, such as the consequences of one person building on land that another had abandoned or the consequences of damage to property between the time of contract and the time of conveyance. Another case held that a man could give a full power of attorney to his wife "to enjoy all his goods and estate in Virginia" when he departed from the colony.[5]

The produce of the land—tobacco—and the commodities it would buy similarly gave rise to complex contractual transactions and commercial litigation. Some of these cases were "very intricate and full of difficulties."[6] Virginia's commercial activity also produced a shipbuilding industry, which, in turn, led to disputes over contracts to build ships.[7]

The buying and selling of indentured servants was another subject with which the law had to deal. On occasion, men failed to deliver the servants they had promised to provide.[8] Another issue that arose was whether a purchaser of a servant could recover damages from the seller if for some reason the servant died or had to be set free. Yet another case required a man supervising a servant who drowned to pay damages both to the servant's owner and to the man who had rented him from the owner.[9]

Finally, there were issues of admiralty law: the James River and the Lower Chesapeake Bay became a major international port—a fact giving rise to litigation. One issue that arose was whether a seaman who had lost a bill given to him by his captain in England could recover on that bill in Virginia. Another was whether a man had to pay for the passage from England of the woman he married. A third was whether a captain could resell tobacco consigned to his vessel for shipment to London or a servant consigned to a buyer in Virginia.[10] Of course, there were also suits about seamen's wages and terms of employment, the seaworthiness of vessels, and goods damaged in transit.[11]

B. THE RULE OF LAW

In order to encourage Englishmen to settle and invest in Virginia, the colony's rulers, as we have seen, had proclaimed in 1619 that hence-forth they would govern "by those free laws which his Majesty's subjects live under in England." It was a proclamation they kept repeating. Thus, when opponents of the Virginia Company complained five years later that the Governor was ruling on behalf of the company rather than the king, a sitting councillor responded "that he thought that the Governor always governed for the King, for in all things he governed according to the King's laws." Four decades later the policy remained, "as near as the capacity and constitution of this country would admit, to adhere to those excellent . . . laws of England."[12]

Having proclaimed that Virginia was bound by rule of law, the General Court also began acting as if it were. Thus, in the 1625 case of *Powell v. Matthews*, the court found "no such right invested in Captain Powell and his children in the land now in controversy whereby we can *by a legal order* put Captain Samuel Matthews who is presently seated thereon out of possession." Accordingly, it complied with the law and gave judgment for Matthews. Likewise, the General Court began to insist that judges and litigants follow proper rules of procedure. Thus, in *Taylor v. Wormley*, the General Court reversed a judgment of a local court which had "refus[ed] oath in the cause and . . . pass[ed] judgment without taking any deposition," while in *Geney v. Whittakers*, decided in late November 1624, it denied the plaintiff the provisional relief she sought because she "ha[d] not orderly proceeded, by way of petition preferred in Court of her wrongs." In the spring of 1625, the judges again displayed their growing sensitivity to the rules of orderly procedure when they held that "writings" in connection with a dispute over an estate were "so defaced and imperfect that they [could] not be recorded" or even, it appears, considered in evidence.[13]

The revocation of the Virginia Company's charter in late 1625 did not slow the emerging tendency of judges to rely on juridical concepts in the decision of cases. Only one month after the first royal governor had arrived and the General Court had been reconstituted,[14] the court freed an apprentice who had been bound "contrary to justice and equity." With "the price of tobacco falling" a year later, the court resolved that Virginians should pay their debts but that it would "proceed according to equity and justice & pass by the law when too rigorous." The next year, when the court confronted a case that "could not be well decided it being very intricate and full of difficulties," it did not rush to an arbitrary judgment; instead, it postponed the case in order to give it careful consideration under law. And a decade later a man found guilty of fornication was required to do public penance during divine service "according to the laws of England in that case provided."[15]

By 1640, the General Court of Virginia had committed the colony's legal order to governance under the rule of law, though the commitment remained fragile. The case of Anthony Panton, the minister of the parishes of York and Chiskayack, will illustrate. The General Court, it appears, had banished Panton from Virginia under pain of death if he returned, apparently because he had called Richard Kemp, the colony secretary, "unfit for his place." Panton accordingly had sailed to England, where he obtained orders from the Privy Council directing the General Court to reconsider his case. At that point, Kemp fled to England, taking the files of Panton's case with him.[16]

Kemp's appropriation of the colony's files, as well as the original sentence of Panton, violated the law. However, as the court noted, Kemp's theft of the files "disabled" it from conducting "any full review of the cause that might justly acquit or condemn the said Panton," even though "the secretary's flight" generated a "strong presumption of self guiltiness" on his part and "depositions taken on Mr. Panton's part and other pregnant circumstances" suggested quite strongly that the original proceedings against him were unjust. It appeared

> that he was denied a copy of the information against him to answer it in writing, his trial in a summary way began in an afternoon and sentence given that night and a copy of that sentence denied him which rigorous and illegal proceedings appear to rest mainly on Mr. Kemp, which contrary to all courts of law acted both the part of an advocate and a judge and in the penning of the sentence that clause of full power and authority for any one to execute him in case of his return for which we conceive he cannot show any precedent (and most dangerous one to make) appears to be added by him since Mr. John Harvey the then governor and the rest of the then council disclaim it.

Although the court could not properly adjudge his case, "things [spoke] so far on the said Panton's behalf as we conceived we should do no less than restore him" to half his tithes and to a half share of the ministerial duties in his parishes. This preliminary order was to stand until the Privy Council "upon hearing of the whole cause shall please to settle a further and final order herein."[17]

In sum, the General Court condemned its own prior unlawful behavior, bent the law to annul that behavior, and recognized the jurisdiction of the Privy Council to do ultimate justice. The court thereby pledged its adherence to the rule of law even while bending rules of procedure to achieve adherence.

As the years progressed, the judicial system's commitment to deciding cases under legal norms grew stronger. For example, in the 1643 case of *Coleman v. Robins*, the evidence showed that Coleman's original mistress, Mrs. Charltons, had told him that she planned to free him a year earlier than the time set in his indenture and that when she sold Coleman to Robins, she asked Robins to do the same, to which he agreed. Nonetheless, because a jury could "not find it done legally," it concluded that Coleman was required to serve his full term.[18] Similarly, another jury denied a plaintiff recovery on several matters at hand when it found that they had "no relation at all to common law, neither by petition nor evidence," while a third returned a verdict that a defendant had "acted legally" in concealing a chest of a decedent.[19]

Judges behaved similarly when, for example, they ruled that only "a physician...approved & qualified by the Custom of England" could give medicine, that giving a gun to a Native American leader was "conformable to all the laws & constitution of...[the] English nation," and that attachment of clothing for debt was "contrary to equity & right."[20] In another case, in which a bailee tried to pay his creditors with his bailor's goods, his attempt was said to be "condemned by law as unjust & improper" and against the "perfect justice & equity of the case," while in yet another a defendant was directed to prove how he came into possession of a boat "by legal course of law." Even arbitrators strove to decide cases according to "equity & justice" and to "give universal satisfaction of the reasons, motives, causes and...conclusion" of their decision.[21]

An important case was *Inhabitants v. Cololough*, in which residents of Northumberland County, including four members of the county bench, brought a proceeding against George Cololough, another member. That left only two members of the county court to take depositions. Anxious to adhere to the rule of law, those two members wrote, "In regard that we find no law extant for the taking of depositions before two Commissioners & being ambiguous whether or not the said interrogatories may be sworn unto in this case [and] finding no law to admit thereof or authorize us, we think not fit to take those depositions."[22] The two thereby used the law to avoid resolving a conflict between political antagonists that could not be decided legally.

By the early 1660s, the need to rule by law had become so pressing that even county judges found "it very necessary that a statute book be provided for the Court's use" and therefore issued an order "to send for and procure the statutes at large out of England the next shipping." The judiciary's commitment to the rule of law was also displayed in a case involving "a frenchman unacquainted with terms of the English laws...& thereby uncapable to plead his cause." Knowing that this Frenchman could not function in a court of English law, the court took charge of his case on his behalf.[23]

Intertwined with the judiciary's growing reliance on rule of law norms in civil litigation was a concern for proceeding fairly in criminal cases. Perhaps the earliest manifestation of this concern occurred when several drinking companions of Captain William Epps reported that, after they had gone to sleep in a single room, Mrs. Alice Boise "lay down upon the bed besides Capt. Epps" and that thereafter "there was a great stirring & motion in the bed" on several occasions during the night. There was testimony that on two occasions Mrs. Boise said, "Oh, my leg;" that on another she said, "I pray let it alone while the morning;" and that when she got out of bed, her clothes "were raised to a great height." But the witness who testified in greatest detail was "not able to say that Captain Epps was upon the said Mrs. Boise." On considering, weighing, and debating all the testimony, the court therefore concluded that it was "not proved or manifest... that Captain Epps and Mrs. Boise ha[d] offended the law."[24]

Similarly when the court considered "diverse examinations touching William Garret['s]... lewd behavior with Katherine Lemon, his fellow servant," it did "not find sufficient proof to punish the said... Garret." Likewise, the House of Burgesses, sitting as the colony's highest court, acquitted Edmund Scarborough of all charges against him and reversed a judgment of the General Court suspending him from office, "finding no positive proof to convict him." And, on the county level a blasphemy charge was dropped when the court found that "the testimony was not competent notwithstanding the charge being so high" and "no further evidence... appeared" after the court had directed that the case be adjourned "to see and find out better evidence."[25]

Courts would dismiss prosecutions on legal as well as factual grounds. When Colonel Guy Molesworthy was prosecuted for removing four people from the list of tithables in his family, the court "upon consideration of the matter" concluded that the issue did "not appear by the law to be triable" and "therefore dismiss[ed] and acquit[ted] the said Col. Molesworthy." Similarly, Stephen Charlton was acquitted of employing a Native American to hunt for his family when he showed that the "said Indian... had a gun (allowed him by authority) therefore (in this question he has not transgressed the law)." Even a fourteen-year-old defendant charged with homicide was able to use technical rules of the common law to his benefit—first, to obtain a jury that found him guilty of manslaughter rather than murder and then, to avoid capital punishment by pleading benefit of clergy: when asked after the jury verdict "what he had to say for himself that he ought not to die demanded his clergy; whereupon he was delivered to the ordinary, etc."[26]

The judiciary's tolerance of pro-defendant procedures in criminal cases necessarily reflected a judgment that society could function and order could be maintained even if some people accused and perhaps even guilty of crime went unpunished. A similar understanding manifested itself in a trend beginning as early as 1625 toward lower penalties in criminal cases, especially sedition cases.

Thus, when one defendant argued that the King of France and not the King of England was the sovereign of France, he received no harsh physical penalty; he was merely required to take the "oath of supremacy upon the holy Evangelists."[27] When another defendant told the Governor that he would not obey his commands and prayed for "an easterly wind to bring in a new Governor and then I shall have Justice for now I have none," he was merely degraded from his title of Lieutenant, fined 1,000 pounds of tobacco, and required to find sureties for good behavior. By 1640, a fine "for speaking contemptuous words" would be remitted if the speaker begged forgiveness, and "words of dangerous consequence concerning the king's most excellent majesty" would be punished only by a fine and two hours in the pillory. Even a fight between litigants in open court, which constituted a "contempt of the Court" taking "into consideration and noting the great indignity thereof, reflecting upon the authority from whom [the judges]...derive their power to negotiate the affairs committed to their care and trust," resulted only in a fine, which was further "moderate[d]" on the defendant's "humble petition & submission."[28]

The Virginia judiciary, in short, seemingly came to understand that what one case called "the power of justice" could be used as effectively as physical coercion to maintain social order. Always worried that justice's power might be "too much undervalued," the judges prosecuted all who challenged them and their power. But the goal of these prosecutions was not punishment; the goal was to induce anyone who challenged the judiciary's pronouncement that it governed Virginia justly and under law to "acknowledge[] his errors and show[] his submissiveness with promise of amendment." Even when a judge, in the midst of England's Civil War, "in a disturbing uncivil manner affronted" the other judges, "whereby his Majesty's business could not be performed in that peaceable manner as it ought to have been," the offending judge was merely suspended and required to give security for good behavior, while a written report of his conduct was transmitted to the Governor and Council.[29]

The courts prior to 1660 behaved similarly in dealing with the few challenges to religious norms that came to their attention. Thus, a minister was punished for marrying a couple without a license, and another man was held for the General Court, albeit with no final verdict, on grounds of being a heretic and "seducer of the people to faction" who "denied the manhood of Christ."[30] The efforts of the judiciary to wipe out the Society of Friends, on the other hand, were a total failure. When Quakers first appeared in Virginia in the late 1650s, they were whipped and fined and ordered into exile in Maryland, and a "general persecution of Quakers [was] directed." Judicial proceedings against Quakers continued for several more years but then in the early 1660s simply ceased, as the judiciary abandoned efforts to eradicate this group of free men and women, however much their antinomianism may have tended "to destroy religion, laws, communities and all bonds of civil society."[31]

Offenses against sexual morality—a form of offense against religion— were rarely prosecuted, and, when prosecutions were successful, punishments were minor. In one adultery case, for example, the convicted adulterer was required only to give a bond to avoid the company of the co-respondent, while a female servant who ran away from her married master after he had impregnated her was merely whipped.[32] Of course, women, mainly female servants, who gave birth to illegitimate children were routinely whipped, fined, made to serve additional time to compensate their masters for the costs of pregnancy, and sometimes forced to confess before their local church congregation. Similarly, men guilty of bastardy could be sued for child support and also might be required to do public penance during divine service.[33] But there were almost no prosecutions for clandestine sexual offenses, whether heterosexual or otherwise, however sinful they may have been, if they did not result in birth of a child, and more public cases of sexual misconduct typically resulted in verdicts of not guilty, as in the case of Captain Epps, who spent an apparently amorous evening in bed with Mrs. Boise, but was adjudged not to have violated the law. Even premarital intercourse resulting in a premature birth was rarely prosecuted, and the few prosecutions that did occur may have been brought for reasons other than the punishment of sin; in two early cases, for example, couples were prosecuted because the woman's pregnancy had forced masters to consent to marriage and thereby lose at least some of the value of their servants. Indeed, because "many great abuses and much detriment...to the service of many masters" had been "occasioned through secret marriages of servants" or by their "committing of fornication," the legislature had been prompted to take action. In short, the sinful nature of sex outside matrimony, considered by itself, simply did not prompt Virginia judges to undertake serious efforts to suppress it.[34]

The significance of Virginia's shift to the rule of law emerges with singular lucidity in the case of *Confession of Willmote*, a bastardy prosecution for which an unusually comprehensive record remains. The case was against a servant girl, Anne Willmote, who had accused Argoll Yardley, her former master and a longtime justice of the county court, of being the father of her expected child. One day, as he was walking past her lodgings, John Stringer, the county sheriff, heard Anne groaning and "immediately went in" and "demanded how she did." Willmote answered that "she was very ill," to which Stringer replied, "[T]hou has brought thyself to a fair pass. And all through thine own wickedness." On this cue, Willmote inquired what she should do, and Stringer, knowing that his high rank required Willmote to heed his advice, instructed her, "I would have thee to acknowledge thy offenses to God. And be sorry for thy bad course of life thou has hitherto run, and confess who is the true father of the child thou goes with (not wronging any man)."[35]

Willmote must have understood what Stringer expected of her, but she could not bring herself to do it. She promised to confess, but requested "leave" until she was "somewhat better," to which Stringer responded, "[T]hou will do well in so doing. And God will the sooner forgive thee, for the truth will shame the Devil." He then departed.[36]

He returned the next day and asked, "[W]hat sayest thou to that business that thou told me of yesterday?" "I will tell you," she answered, "it is Owen the Irishman that got me with child. He has lain with me several times. He lay with me that day my mistress was buried & several times since." That was all Willmote confessed that day, and accordingly Stringer departed.[37]

On the third day, Stringer returned again, this time with a witness named Lucas, and inquired, "[W]hether she were still in the opinion that it was Owen the Irishman his child?" Willmote responded, "[I]t was no man else, for he lay with me a month (or thereabouts before my mistress died). And that day she was buried... and several times since. Notwithstanding diverse fallings out,... we were sure together above a year & half." Then Lucas demanded in Stringer's presence, "Then why would thou wrong thy master so much and in his absence?" Fully appreciating what Stringer and Lucas wanted to hear, Willmote "replied that she was advised unto it by that base fellow Owen, who told me (after I had told him I was with child by him) I doubt whether it be mine or not (although I have had to do with thee). And I know the Esquire has lain with you wherefore put it upon him. And I will marry thee & free thee." Thereafter, Owen "had often lain with" Anne, but "now [that] he has done all the injury he can (thinking he is quite cleared) has cast me off."[38]

In the end, Owen Scott was not cleared; on the basis of Anne Willmote's ambiguous statement, he was prosecuted for fornication, convicted, and made to serve his and Anne's master for one additional year.[39] Willmote herself was never prosecuted, perhaps because the court was satisfied that by accusing Scott she had exonerated Yardley, even though she did not deny that Yardley had had intercourse with her and thus had not fully eliminated the possibility that Yardley was the father of her child. To have prosecuted her thus would have reopened the possibility that she would again accuse Yardley.

We should pause to take stock. We ought not think Whiggishly about Virginia's shift to the rule of law. Virginia did not change its law because its people were striving for some eighteenth-century Jeffersonian vision of liberty; seventeenth-century Virginians could not know what the next century would bring. Nor should we imagine that the advent of the rule of law put an end to coercion. Officials, such as Sheriff Stringer, remained quite capable of administering the rule of law coercively. The advent of the rule of law did not end coercion and manipulation, for law ends neither. It merely created mechanisms that could be used without bloodshed by those with the capacity to coerce and manipulate.

Anne Willmote, for one, succeeded in manipulating the law to achieve the result she wanted—no prosecution of herself. The minions of the law likewise used their powers of coercion to protect one of their own— Justice Argoll Yardley—from prosecution and punishment. But the rule of law often has its victims—the poor and powerless, as in this case, Owen the Irishman.

Such an understanding of law's malleability and power is especially important in connection with the rising commercial litigation discussed earlier in this chapter. In cases dealing with land rights, commerce, and the purchase and sale of servants, it did not matter what rule the courts adopted: what was important was only that law be present so that various commercial actors could try to take advantage of it. It is true that some rules, such as those providing for the inventory of estates and the recording of land transfers, were explicitly designed to promote the rise of a market economy by clarifying who owned what and thereby rendering ownership of property secure. Thus, when the General Court issued a proclamation in 1640 requiring "that every person who shall take up any land shall set up their bounds at the monthly court," it stated that its "intent" in promulgating this rule was "that no after claims may be made thereto."[40] But, on the whole, the doctrines adopted by the General Court simply laid down background norms around which parties could, if they wished, negotiate as long as the norms were transparent.

Virginia officials themselves understood this need for transparency; thus, Governor Francis Wyatt issued a proclamation concerning the meaning and "intent" of a 1639 tobacco marketing act "for avoiding of such questions as might arise by misinterpretation of the act" and thereby promoting "due execution of the act."[41] By the 1640s, the judges had come to understand that entrepreneurs, which is what the free men of Virginia had become, need to know the law in order to maneuver against each other, enter into contracts, and thereby make profits and accumulate wealth.

Indeed, by the 1640s, the hallmark doctrine of market capitalism— "[t]hat free trade be allowed to all the inhabitants of the colony to buy and sell at their best advantage," however unjust and detrimental to the weak, the poor, or the witless free trade might be—had been enacted by statute. Consider, for example, the 1643 case of a seaman on a Dutch vessel who sold his goods at an agreed price, later learned that his shipmates had sold similar goods at a higher price, and then tried to get out of his contract. The court responded austerely: it "ordered" that the seaman "shall perform his bargain or else execution, etc."[42]

Regulatory laws also collapsed in the face of the emergence of freedom of contract and free market dealing. Thus, in the midst of England's Civil War, King Charles issued a proclamation prohibiting Virginians from shipping tobacco to London, the center of Parliament's domain, even if a shipment were in repayment of a debt. Virginians, on the whole, favored the king over Parliament, but by the 1640s loyalty to the crown had become less important than repaying debts in order to insure that loans and investments would continue in the future. Given this balance of priorities, the presiding judge of the Northampton County Court not surprisingly directed one planter to ship to London, "saying God forbid we should refuse to pay [even] Turks or Jew for what we have received." A week later, in response to "doubts" expressed by Londoners, the House of Burgesses "pledg[ed] the faith of the colony for a continuance of a free and peaceable trade to them."[43]

As they embraced the idea that they should rule by law, Virginia lawmakers turned to their English legal heritage, and especially to the common law, for their rules. The General Assembly directed judges to decide cases "as near as may be according to the laws of the realm of England," and later the House of Burgesses pointed with pride to the "near approach" the colony had "made to the laws and customs of England in proceedings of the court and trials of causes." Indictments, for example, followed a common-law format as early as 1623.[44] Common-law words of art similarly made an early appearance, and their use persisted.[45]

Doctrines that are recognizably common-law rules of law also were adopted in Virginia. Thus, Virginia courts held that a legacy to a widow did not diminish her dower and that "one of the half blood cannot inherit."[46] Likewise, the most important institution of the common law—the jury—became central to Virginia's legal order. The first jury trial in a criminal case occurred in 1623, and in a civil case in 1624. The first inquest by a jury was in the same year.[47] It was soon clear that any case would be tried by a jury if any party thereto so demanded, and thousands of jury trials occurred during the next several decades. Juries were impaneled by the sheriff summoning "the most able men of the county," who did not necessarily need to be property owners to serve, although most undoubtedly were.[48] Most litigants did not demand jury trial, however, and thus most cases were tried only to the court.

Finally, shadows of the common-law writs and of the forms of action surfaced in the Virginia records. As early as 1627, a defendant in a suit on a bond confessed in the language of common-law pleading that the instrument at issue was "his own deed and act," and in 1643, the county court of Accomack-Northampton made reference in the language of the common law to "an action of debt." A decade later "an action of the case" appeared in the same county.[49]

But Virginia did not adopt the common law slavishly. Thus, as Warren Billings has shown, Virginia litigants typically did not commence suit by writ; rather, they used bill procedure as that method had been developed in Chancery and the Court of Requests. Bill procedure was far less technical than procedure by writ, and thus, following the directive of the House of Burgesses, cases were not dismissed in mid-seventeenth-century Virginia on technicalities.[50]

The Virginia legal order also departed from the common law's institutional design. A main engine of departure was statute: the legislature always was ready to enact statutes to further the achievement of goals that its constituents wanted their law to achieve. Indeed, by the late 1650s "the acts" of the House of Burgesses had "through multiplicity of alterations and repeals … become so difficult, that the course of justice [was] thereby obstructed" and those charged with administering the law were by "their uncertainty be[ing] drawn to commit unwilled errors." The legislature therefore repealed all former laws and enacted a code of 130 sections, which it published and sent to various localities.[51]

Much legislation regulated the jurisdiction and procedure of the courts[52] or authorized judges to engage in actions that did not conform to common-law practice; particular crimes, for example, were sometimes created by statute.[53] Two significant departures from English legal practice involved the assumption of ecclesiastical jurisdiction by secular courts and the blending of chancery jurisdiction with that of the common law in a single hierarchy of courts.[54] Another was in the design of local courts and their relationship to the General Court.

Initially, the settlers of Virginia all lived in Jamestown and a few satellite locations. But the spread of tobacco cultivation altered this pattern of settlement. For some years, in an effort to keep up with world demand, Virginians planted more and more tobacco each year, for which they needed more and more land. Unfortunately, tobacco is a crop that quickly exhausts its soil, especially when planters do nothing to replenish the soil, and thus Virginians every year needed not only more land but new land. To find it they spread far out from Jamestown.

The original plan had been for the Governor and Council to constitute a General Court, which would meet frequently in Jamestown to address all disputes and breaches of law. Indeed, in 1624 the court announced that it would meet "every Monday... to hear causes and that men that have any business shall attend that day."[55] But Jamestown was too far away for some to come to court there, and within a year other jurisdictional provisions began to emerge.

The plantation at Accomack was the first to require special arrangements. Its location on the Eastern shore meant that parties and witnesses would have to cross the Chesapeake Bay and sail up the James River to attend to litigation at Jamestown—a trip that with favorable winds took a day. "[T]he charge and trouble of sending up of witnessses" in "small cause[s]," especially those that ended "by way of compromise" once the litigants appeared in court, seemed especially counterproductive. Accordingly, the General Court granted Captain William Epps, the ranking officer at Accomack, "full power & authority to administer an oath to any person or persons there inhabiting for the better deciding of any small cause... [or] the ending of any suit or suits that are to be tried at this Court depending between any [of] the inhabitants of Accomack."[56]

From the outset, it was understood that this grant to Epps of jurisdiction merely to examine witnesses was only a temporary expedient "until there be some order taken for a commission for determining petty differences at Accomack." No documentary evidence exists, but it nonetheless appears that some sort of local court began sitting in Accomack within the year. Such a court must have been sitting by August, 1626, when the new royal governor, Sir George Yeardley, pursuant to earlier legislation by the General Assembly, issued commissions for the establishment of courts at Elizabeth City, Charles Hundred, and the Upper Parts—locales less in need of their own court than Accomack "in regard of the great distance of Accomack from James City." The new courts were to sit "for the determining of petty controversies not exceeding the value of 200 pounds of tobacco and for the punishing of petty offenses." Appeal lay in all cases to the General Court.[57]

These early orders established the basic pattern of jurisdiction for the rest of the colonial era; there was to be one central court and a series of local courts, each, unlike most courts in England, with jurisdiction over both civil and criminal cases. Ultimately, local courts also would have "liberty to make laws for themselves...to be binding upon them as fully as any other law" and to nominate the men whom the governor would then appoint to the bench.[58] The central court was to hear appeals from the local courts. But the early orders were vague as to details. In particular, the orders failed to define the concept of "petty controversies" in any rigorous fashion that courts could follow consistently, and they failed to specify how the courts were to proceed with their work. They also were vague about the scope of the central court's appellate jurisdiction, with the result that in one early case an "erroneous judgment" of a local court was not merely reversed, but the judges also fined.[59]

Over the course of the late 1620s and the early 1630s, the details were elaborated. Not surprisingly, the General Court and the Assembly did not spend hours of time in committees specifying the details one by one. The men who governed Virginia had something better to do with their time—to earn profits and accumulate wealth by growing tobacco. Thus, as early as 1629, they took the easy way out, when they defined petty criminal jurisdiction to encompass "the conservation of the peace so far as is belonging to the Quarter Sessions of the Justices in England, life only excepted." Three years later, the Governor gave the local monthly courts "the same power as Justices of the Peace" in criminal cases, and in civil cases required the courts "to proceed according to the laws of England [in] all causes under £5" sterling. Then, in 1634, Virginia was divided into eight counties, and each of the local monthly courts became county courts. Again there was reference to the counties functioning "the same as in England"; in particular, the General Court provided that "as in England sheriffs" were to be chosen in each county and "to have the same power as there."[60]

The decision to define the powers of local institutions by reference to English law is pivotal to the analysis presented here. Those institutions could be directed to depart from English rules; as we have seen, they often were so directed when, for example, they combined civil and criminal jurisdiction in one court, assumed the jurisdiction of ecclesiastical courts, and blended chancery with the common law. But English legal practice remained the baseline, and for three reasons that baseline proved enormously valuable to those who were crafting Virginia's law.

First, English law was what they remembered. It was within the scope of their experience. They did not need to study alternatives about which they knew nothing in order to get their legal system off the ground.

Second, English law—in particular, the common law—provided a rich body of rules and doctrines that could serve definitional functions without anyone's having to sit down and write a legal dictionary. No one had to think about issues that might arise in the future, but also might not arise. It was necessary to resolve only those legal issues that, in fact, had arisen, and then only by finding existing law, which is often an easier task than making new law. Of course, if existing law proved unsatisfactory, new law could then be made. Recourse to the law colonists remembered from England thus was comparable to bargaining in the shadow of the law; it fostered efficiency by making it unnecessary to address issues that did not require immediate resolution.

Third, by the early seventeenth century, England had developed a cheap means of governing peripheral localities distant from the center. The crown had no army or bureaucracy to dispatch to the counties; thus, it had to govern England by relying on local courts composed of unpaid, high-status volunteers who, in turn, worked closely with other subjects in the locality, mainly through the jury system, to ensure that crime was punished, disputes resolved, and the peace kept. By conferring power and honor on local leaders, the crown co-opted them, and they, in turn, co-opted the people around them by doing justice and preserving order.

Perhaps the Virginia Company could have employed a military model indefinitely to govern a small settlement at Jamestown. A coercive system often will produce obedience as long as someone is prepared to pay the salaries of those who administer it. But, with the revocation of the Company's charter, there was no one who could continue to pay. King Charles, who soon was striving to rule without Parliament, was always strapped for funds, and, with tobacco prices falling throughout the 1620s and 1630s, so were Virginia's planters. Moreover, the dispersion of population into the eight regions that became counties in 1634 would have necessitated at least eight times as much expenditure as would have been required to govern Jamestown alone.

Short of finding resources they did not have or inventing a model of governance that was totally new, those who were crafting Virginia's government did what was easiest as they searched in the mid-1620s for a means to maintain the social order. They turned to what they knew from experience back home. They created a system of local courts and directed them to rule by law—by a combination of English law and local practice and legislation—law that everyone knew, that most people would obey, and that many free men would help enforce. In the process, the free population of Virginia progressed from a government of men to a government under law—from a command and control regime to a consociational polity.[61]

C. THE LAW OF SERVITUDE

Indentured servants did not benefit nearly as much as free people did from Virginia's move toward the rule of law. Harsh treatment of servants, as a means of compelling them to work, remained the norm throughout the mid-seventeenth century. But the same forces that pushed Virginia as a whole toward the rule of law—the need for certain and predictable rules that would induce people to invest their wealth in the colony—also operated to a lesser extent in connection with the law of servitude. People willing to migrate voluntarily from England to Virginia needed reassurance that the promises made to them when they departed England would be honored when they subsequently lived and worked in Virginia. Thus, the law of servitude needed to protect the expectations of volunteer servants while retaining enough harshness to frighten them into working.

Much harshness did remain. Judges dealt sternly, for example, with runaway servants. The standard penalty on a runaway's return was to extend his period of service by twice the amount of time he had been absent. This extension would be increased further if a master could prove that he had spent large sums of money in getting his servant returned. On occasion, runaways also would be whipped.[62] And, to keep servants under their masters' watchful gaze the law made it criminal for one free man to trade with or entertain the servants of another or to use "mutinous and seditious words tending to the tumultous and dangerous behavior of several servants."[63]

The law was especially harsh on servants who spread scandalous statements or behaved violently toward their masters, as well as on servants who, after claiming that their masters abused them, failed to prove their claims.[64] Thus, a woman who charged her master with "abus[ing] her by very unlawful & causeless beatings" had to remain with him, potentially subject to further abuse, while her case was pending.[65] Even a servant who proved a claim of abuse would not be freed, but merely protected against retaliatory abuse or, at best, transferred to a new master.[66] It also should be noted that juries summoned to determine whether servants who met violent deaths had died from abuse typically were unwilling to indict masters for homicide.[67] In sum, servants who were abused were between a rock and a hard place: if they failed to bring a claim, their abuse might continue and even worsen, while if they brought the claim they would remain under their master's control while suit was pending and ultimately, at best, be sold to a new master.

The same was true for at least some servants who claimed freedom but failed to establish it. Thus, when John Holden sued for and won his wife's freedom because "no indenture" was found, the wife's master requested time to obtain an indenture from England; when he produced it four months later, the wife was put back in servitude and required to compensate her master for her period of freedom between her two court hearings.[68]

On the other hand, the courts did deal fairly and honor the expectations of servants who proved they had completed their term of service; courts would order such servants to be freed.[69] Legislation also prohibited "harsh or unchristianlike usage," such as imposing sexual demands on unwilling servants or assigning apprentices to tasks other than those for which they had been apprenticed.[70] Courts also required masters to provide needed medical attention and food, clothing, and "other necessities" "as a servant ought to be provided for."[71] Finally, masters were required to give corn and clothes to former servants upon the expiration of their terms.[72]

Goffe v. Buck[73] provides an apt illustration of the manner in which courts dealt with servants. The issue in the case was whether Goffe was bound for four or seven years. When Goffe first brought his suit for freedom after serving four years, his master responded with the bill of sale through which he had acquired Goffe—it showed a seven-year term. Although the court ordered Goffe to remain in Buck's service while suit was pending, it did not find the bill of sale dispositive and ordered Buck to produce Goffe's original indenture at the next term of court. When Buck failed, Goffe was freed, given his corn and clothes, and paid 100 pounds tobacco for his labor during the intervening month. Buck, however, obtained a rehearing, at which the court demanded that Goffe swear whether his term was for four years or seven. When Goffe refused to take an oath, he was put back into servitude.

Thus, for all its harshness, the law regulating the treatment of servants strove to enforce the bargains that servants had made upon entering into servitude. Of course, the law tilted in favor of the master class. Thus, in *Lockolur v. Diggs*, where the issue was whether a man should serve for seven years, which was the customary period at the time he arrived in Virginia, or only for four years, which was a new period enacted for English servants by the House of Burgesses, the court's "unanimous opinion [was] that the said Lockolur ought to serve...according to the Act in force at his arrival."[74] Why? Partly because the master class that sat on the bench would, between two tenable rules, predictably choose the one that favored its interests. For the same reason, the master class construed the law to require Irish servants to serve to age 24, although English servants were freed at 21.[75] But there was also another factor—English servants, at least, needed to know that they would be held to service under the terms to which they had agreed. Otherwise, they might stop migrating.

Thus, the law left servants with some rights—above all, the right to institute a judicial proceeding in which a magistrate obliged to enforce rules would hear servants' evidence and examine their claims about the bargains they had made. Servants might lose most cases they brought and might suffer harsh penalties when they did. But sometimes they would win because the judiciary's need to honor the law and the evidence dictated that they should.

D. THE COLLECTION OF DEBTS

Virginia's adoption of rules protecting property and controlling the discipline of servants, along with its adherence to the rule of law, went a long way toward encouraging immigration, toward inducing free immigrants to devote their energies to profit making, and toward continuing to coerce labor from the unfree. They were economically rational rules that helped relieve the colony of its old dependence on the Virginia Company. But the rules did not bring sufficient cash capital into the colony. Attracting that capital became the main task of Virginia's legal system in the decades after 1625.

Once English investors had ceased giving money to the Virginia Company, which, in turn, had used it to buy goods needed to sustain the colony, a new way had to be found to induce those investors to give the money directly to Virginia planters, who, in turn, could use it to buy the goods they needed. Investors were not prepared to advance money against promises to pay uncertain profits in the future; they had advanced money to the Company on such terms, and profits had never materialized. Surely, individual planters presented a greater risk than the company. Vague resolutions on the part of the General Court that "the people shall pay their debts this year"[76] might help, but investors needed more—namely, enforceable promises to repay sums lent, with interest, at certain times in the future.

A key reason, perhaps, why Virginia's lawmakers turned to the common law to give specific content to the rule of law is that the common-law writ system provided mechanisms, particularly the writs of debt and assumpsit, to facilitate debt collection. But Virginia quickly moved beyond the common law. In addition to adopting common law remedies, Virginia enacted legislation to facilitate debt collection. In particular, statutes provided procedures for recording mortgages, for controlling debtors who sought to depart from Virginia while indebted, for payment of debts due in England,[77] and for regulating imprisonment for debt, including the terms of release from imprisonment.[78]

Judges also provided sympathetic forums for creditors. In two cases, for example, the General Court had to make sense out of and enforce perplexing patterns of indebtedness involving multiple parties. On another occasion, the Court was called upon to enforce an order from the Privy

Council directing a Virginian to ship tobacco to England, as per his agreement with English investors. And on a fourth, a Virginian who was indebted to an Englishman claimed to have delivered tobacco to a third party for shipment to England.[79]

Most significantly, however, the central concern of courts changed after 1625. Judges began to spend proportionately less time coercing labor and controlling deviance. After 1625, the judiciary and its subordinate officials spent most of their time assisting creditors in the collection of debts. The incompleteness and sloppiness of surviving court records make precise statistical analysis impossible, and any effort to engage in the most rigorous possible analysis would not be worth the trivial knowledge that the effort would produce. What is clear, however, is that any historian who examines Virginia court records from the 1640s and later decades will find what all historians have observed about eighteenth-century American records—namely, that entries about debt collection vastly exceed entries for every other category of case combined. Debt collection became a routinized process, with all the efficiencies that routinization brings.[80]

Routinization of the debt collection process was not an unmixed blessing for creditors, however. Routine, relatively inexpensive processes became available for creditors, but the same processes that were available to creditors became due to debtors. And, as debtors learned to manipulate those processes, due process became slow process. The assumption of the 1610s that courts would function with speed disappeared, and many terms of court typically might pass between the time a creditor filed suit and the time he or she received payment for the debt. Court records, as a result, began to contain language such as "procrastination," "unnecessary delays," and prayers "for expedition of justice."[81]

Warren M. Billings has described the best outcome that a creditor could obtain in debt collection litigation. As Billings notes, many debtors never contested suits lodged against them; some—actually a goodly number—showed up in court to confess judgment. Indeed, by the 1650s, it was not even necessary for the debtor to appear, provided he sent a written avowal of his debt to court. Parties also could avoid appearance by having attorneys enter and confess the debt on their behalf; some of them, perhaps, even agreed to such a procedure at the time they took out a loan. With any of these processes, the court would simply enter judgment.[82]

But entry of judgment did not guarantee payment of the debt. Some creditors were required to bring writs of *scire facias* to get their judgments enforced, and other entries in extant court records reflect informal equivalents of *scire facias*—entries in which the court notes that a judgment or other order had been obtained but remained unpaid and that further action by court and creditor was required. Indeed, we know of one case in which it took more than thirteen years to collect a judgment.[83]

Most debtors, moreover, were not so cooperative as to confess judgment; they simply ignored the suits brought against them. The most common way to commence a suit for debt was for the creditor to direct the sheriff to arrest the debtor. In theory, keeping the debtor in jail would compel him to respond to the suit, but in fact few debtors were imprisoned.[84] In labor-starved Virginia, where a man might have "nothing but his labor to pay ... [his] debts," both debtor and creditor were better off if the debtor could earn some money by working, and thus debtors were released as soon as someone put up security for them to appear in court on the date the case against them was calendared. The presence of security, however, did not force many debtors actually to show up, and when they did not, the creditor had to enforce the debt against the person who gave security, who, in turn, had to enforce whatever promise the debtor had made to induce the security to step forward.[85]

Even worse, debtors typically were released from debtors' prison even when no one put up security on their behalf. If no one offered bail, the sheriff simply let the debtor go free rather than face the alternative of guarding and feeding a prisoner with possible reimbursement only from the prisoner himself.[86] Of course, freeing the prisoner made the sheriff liable for the debt; in return for being thrust under that liability, the sheriff received an attachment against any property in the debtor's possession.[87] What remains unclear is whether this process produced rapid payment of debts. Since the men who served as sheriffs most likely did not lose money in office,[88] a reasonable speculation is that creditors were paid only as quickly as sheriffs could find goods to attach and that, when sheriffs could find no goods, they made no payments on judgments.

The maturation of the law of debtor and creditor and the commitment of Virginia's legal system to its administration put into place all but one of the main elements that for the next two centuries would be central to

Virginia law, and indeed the law of much of America. That one element, of course, was the law of slavery.

Soon after the arrival of the first Africans in Virginia in 1619, small steps were taken in the direction of slavery. Black servants were denied the right to bear arms and were punished more severely than white servants who ran away. Illicit interracial sex was punished with special severity. Most significantly, blacks were presumed to be servants for life rather than for a term of years. But some blacks, especially those who were Christian, could obtain their freedom and even acquire freehold property and hold other slaves. Slavery did not blossom fully until after 1660, and therefore it will be discussed mainly in subsequent volumes.[89]

With the development of private property, the institutionalization of the rule of law, and the protection of creditors' rights, the legal order no longer functioned to advance company, crown, or other public policies. Instead, courts and sheriffs lent public power to investors and moneylenders in the form of cumbersome mechanisms for identifying and marshaling assets that could be used to repay debts. The law, that is, no longer provided central direction to society; rather it had become a system that individuals could commandeer to advance their own interests and pursue their own profits. At the same time, the legal system recognized the necessity of allowing people it hurt to remain on the sidelines, delay compliance, and even to resist passively its commands.

Virginia always had been a society committed to profit, and with the demise of the Virginia Company, the commitment became one to private profit. Law merely reflected that commitment with its extensive protection of investors and its grant to laborers only of the bare minimum of rights needed to induce them to sign up for work. With the law of God and nature largely absent from their legal calculus, Virginia lawmakers had little incentive to do justice. And when they found a means of obtaining large numbers of workers by violent capture rather than bargained inducement, slavery, with its total denial both of rights and of justice, naturally fell into place.

3

PURITAN LAW IN THE BAY COLONY

It is impossible to understand the law and legal system of seventeenth-century Massachusetts Bay without understanding the utopian character of the colonial enterprise. The founders of Massachusetts were striving to build the best possible society on earth—a society that could serve as a model polity, if not for the entire world, at least for the English-speaking parts of it. But Massachusetts was not utopia as either Thomas More or we today would understand the concept. It was a Puritan utopia, and thus it is necessary to begin this chapter by outlining the essential beliefs of those Puritans who settled in Massachusetts.[1] Only then can we turn to the Bay Colony's substantive law.[2]

A. THE STRUCTURE OF A PURITAN UTOPIA

Puritanism was both a theology and a political theory. Puritans strove to comprehend the relationship between divine sovereignty and human free will as well as to structure a government that balanced hierarchical authority with liberty. Their goal was to avoid what they viewed as two evil extremes. The one extreme was Roman papacy and European monarchy, in which a small upper class, itself controlled through a hierarchy led by one man, either king or pope, dominated the masses by keeping them in ignorance. The other evil was radical antinomian Protestantism, in which every person blessed with faith (and who does not ultimately think she is so blessed) could receive divine revelation of the truth and rely on that revelation as the basis for disobeying the commands of those in authority. Puritanism represented a balanced and complex effort, both in the search for divine truth and in the structuring of human government, to reconcile liberty with hierarchy through ordered community.[3]

The conceptual basis for this reconciliation was self-restraint. The Puritans knew, as John Winthrop had told them on launching their 1630 trans-Atlantic voyage, that God had created a world in which "some [were] high and eminent in power and dignity; others mean and in submission." But God had not given any man power "out of any particular and singular respect to him..., but for the...common good of the creature, man." In Winthrop's view, "every man" had "need of others" so that they could be "knit together" in community "as one man." Accordingly, Winthrop urged both the strong and the weak to act by "moderating and restraining them[selves], so that the rich and mighty should not eat up the poor nor the poor and despised rise up against and shake off their yoke."[4]

In the words of John Cotton, the leading Boston minister, "all power that is on earth" had to "be limited." "[L]et there be due bounds set," he proclaimed, whether in the state, the church, or even the family. Although some might think it "a matter of danger to the state to limit prerogatives..., it is a further danger, not to have them limited: They will be like a tempest, if they be not limited."[5] The powerful had to restrain themselves through "love, mercy, gentleness, [and] temperance &c.," while at the same time, "the poor and inferior sort" were expected to behave circumspectly with "faith, patience, obedience &c."[6]

Unlike Virginia, the Massachusetts Bay Colony was not founded to generate profits either for investors who remained home in England or for colonial leaders who crossed the Atlantic to America. Although the profit motive was not absent, the founders' foremost goal was to establish orderly communities within a well-ordered polity grounded on Puritan values. For most Puritans, "the search for secure livelihoods never overrode the search for spiritual fulfillment"; indeed, the profit motive was "inseparable" from the goal of living within "the communion" and within a community "of saints."[7]

As a result, the pattern of settlement in Massachusetts differed radically from the pattern of settlement in Virginia. In Virginia, as we have seen, the need was for subsistence workers to cut down the trees, grub the soil, and cultivate the tobacco that individual planters could market at a profit. If profits were to be maximized, wages had to be kept as low as possible; there was no place, in general, for immigrant workers with families to support. Low wages, combined with a high death rate among newly arrived immigrants, also offered little inducement to self-disciplined, upwardly mobile youths to settle in Virginia if they did not possess sufficient capital to buy land. Thus, until the slave trade became the main source of labor in the late seventeenth century, Virginia received a stream of young, single, undisciplined, largely male immigrants who had inhabited the lowest rungs of British society.

Virginia's demographics were precisely the opposite of what the Puritan leadership of Massachusetts understood it needed to build its well-ordered society. Immigrants typically came to Massachusetts as families, and they were promptly given sufficient land to support themselves as families.[8] Once in Massachusetts, the law required them to live as families. A husband who did not live with his wife would be ordered to return to her[9] and "live together according to the ordinance of God as man & wife;"[10] even if his wife was in England and he had to return to England to be with her.[11] He was not excused from returning because "his business was not yet done and so he could not go home."[12] Wives living apart from their husbands would receive public assistance in rejoining them,[13] and a man (or woman) without a spouse would be directed to "settle himself in some orderly family" since Puritan judges understood that a person who lived "by himself contrary to the law of the country" was "subject to much sin and iniquity, which ordinarily are the companions and consequences of a solitary life."[14] Magistrates were worried even about an apparent homeless man who was living in Cambridge but had "no settled abode," and they found him guilty "of disorderly living & keeping company with the scholars [at Harvard] at night & by day, not only to the loss of their time but debauching their manners."[15]

Massachusetts differed demographically from Virginia in one other important respect. Tobacco drove the Virginia economy, and tobacco is a crop that quickly exhausts its soil. As a result, Virginia planters needed new land every few years, and they spread far out from Jamestown and from one another's plantations to obtain it. Moreover, because they were constantly on the move, the planters built few permanent buildings in Virginia's early years. In contrast, the Bay Colony required families to set-tle in towns, with fields typically fanning out from a town center in which residents lived within walking distance of their church.[16] Indeed, when one man raised objections about the "impossibility of subsistence" when "towns [were] so thick set together &...intended so to remain," he was hauled before the Court of Assistants and made to acknowledge his error. As a result of the policy, Massachusetts towns had a permanence about them that Virginia's plantations lacked, and they quickly became centers of culture and control for which there were no Virginia equivalents.[17]

The preservation of the religious establishment, about which more will be said later, was the most important town function. A close second was the duty to educate the town's children. The Puritans believed that the capacity to read and extract truth from the word of God was the only way to avoid the Scylla of papist autocracy and the Charybdis of antinomian chaos. As a result, literacy was high on their agenda.[18]

By the end of the 1630s, in sum, the landscape of Massachusetts dif-fered strikingly from the landscapes of either England or Virginia. Above all, Massachusetts lacked the vast differences in wealth that character-ized England and early Virginia. Although some men in Massachusetts were richer and better educated and enjoyed more leisure than others, they did not use their position to get richer; leaders of the Bay Colony such as John Winthrop were invested principally in making their uto-pian enterprise succeed. At the other end of the social ladder, there were few landless men barely eking out subsistence through labor for others; land was plentiful, and any family head willing to work could gain access to it. Unlike the inhabitants of Virginia, those of Massachusetts resided in compact, permanent towns where they could participate in public life free from the sorts of domination that great magnates exercised in most rural communities of England.[19] In their small, ordered communities, the people of Massachusetts thus possessed power that the common person lacked almost everywhere else in the world. And, to the extent the towns of Massachusetts succeeded in teaching the people to read and write, they created a society that was probably unique in its time—a society in which the governing class could not monopolize control over the flow of written information between localities as it could in most of the world. Ordinary people in Massachusetts, by gaining the ability to communicate with each other just as effectively as elites could, were empowered in all colonial institutions, not merely in their own towns.

B. THE LAW OF A PURITAN UTOPIA

Church and state were intimately conjoined in the Massachusetts Bay Colony: religious values were instinct in the law, and the colony's government exerted considerable effort in support of religion. Much of what its leaders did was commonplace throughout the English-speaking world and is familiar to historians. But other governmental activities were more unusual, and, in some cases, unknown. Moreover, these activities persisted throughout the period that the Massachusetts Bay Company's charter was in force.

In performing their familiar as well as their more unfamiliar activities, the leaders of Massachusetts generally adhered to the Puritan precept of restraint, especially self-restraint. Many of their efforts at proclaiming substantive law entailed the restraint of sin and sinners. Other efforts focused on encouraging powerful members of society to act with self-restraint in dealing with those under their control. Finally, even in restraining others, the leaders of the Bay Colony usually acted with considerable self-restraint.

1. Law and Religion.

Throughout the charter period the law of God was part of the law of Massachusetts. Major issues arose as early as 1641, when three servants of John Humfry had non-forcible intercourse with Humfry's three daughters, all under the age of ten. Many people demanded the death penalty. Intercourse with such minors was a capital offense at common law, but the 1641 Body of Liberties had provided that no one could be prosecuted criminally except under some "express law...established by a General Court..., or in case of the defect of a law in any particular case by the

word of God." The General Court concluded that the law of God prohibited both forcible rape and intercourse with a female under the age
of consent but did not make either offense capital, nor did any express
law of Massachusetts. Accordingly, the court sentenced the defendants to
corporal punishment, but not death.[20]

The legislature promptly enacted a law making the conduct of Humfry's servants a capital offense, and that law remained on the books until
1648, when it was dropped from the codification of that year, apparently
because the law of God did not justify capital punishment in such a case.
Thus, when Patrick Jeanison had intercourse with an eight-year-old girl
some two decades later, there was no statute prohibiting his act: rape had
been made a crime only when a female was at least ten years of age. In
the absence of applicable legislation, however, the General Court still
remained empowered to determine cases "by the word of God," which
it now interpreted to find Jeanison guilty of rape and to sentence him to
death.[21]

The law of God played a similarly dispositive role in a suit that Richard
Gardiner brought against Richard Nevard "for deflowering his daughter."
The jury returned a special verdict finding Nevard liable in damages if
"the word of God...be a sufficient ground for a jury to act upon...where
there wants an express law," and a county court gave judgment for the
plaintiff on the verdict. Finally, in a criminal case for carelessly fitting the
tackling of a ship, which resulted in the death of a seaman and injury to
others, the successful defense rested on citations to Mosaic law.[22]

Judicial efforts to protect the dominion of religion were ongoing. Thus,
people received corporal punishment and were banished for speaking
against the church's rule or for disputing its religious teachings. Anne
Hutchinson and Roger Williams were merely the most notorious.[23] Many
other people were regularly punished for missing church or otherwise
profaning the Sabbath.[24]

Perhaps, the most infamous case after the 1630s involved William
Ledra, a Quaker who on pain of death was banished from Massachusetts
Bay in 1660. He returned in 1661, called the colony's ministers "deluders" and its magistrates, "murderers," and declared "he owed no subjection to the wicked laws of this jurisdiction." He was promptly put to
death by hanging. Three other Friends—Mary Dyer, William Robinson,

and Marmaduke Stephenson—likewise were banished and, when they returned, executed.[25] Still other Quakers were banished, whipped, jailed, and fined.[26] And, one group of Friends, "for persisting still in their course as Quakers, were committed to the house of correction, there to be kept until they gave security to renounce their opinions or remove themselves from the jurisdiction."[27]

In contrast to Virginia, the Bay Colony's actions against the Society of Friends were harsh indeed. But, they were not totally unrestrained. The Quakers, who carried antinomianism to its limits, threatened to bring social disorder and religious chaos to Massachusetts. They disrupted Puritan worship services, for example, by interrupting sermons and strolling naked down the aisles. Nor did the magistrates proceed initially with corporal punishment. First they tried to persuade Quakers to alter their ways. When persuasion failed, Puritan leaders turned to other punishments like jail and banishment. Death was the final punishment, used only when a Quaker like William Leydra returned and denied the authority of the Bay Colony's government. Indeed, Mary Dyer, who had first been banished in the 1630s as a follower of Anne Hutchinson, returned as a Quaker in 1659, was banished again, returned a second time and was sentenced to death, was reprieved and banished a third time, and finally executed only after she returned yet again.[28]

In any event, these Quaker cases are unsurprising. The founders of the Massachusetts Bay Colony never intended to tolerate religious dissent, and their successors never deviated from their initial policy. Not only was Puritanism the established religion; to the extent the leaders of the colony could control events, they strove to make it the only religion.

The leaders also sought to make their church a united and harmonious one by giving "the civil authority...power and liberty to see the peace, ordinances and rules of Christ be observed in every church according to his word." That was a far more difficult task. Puritanism contained strong centrifugal forces within it: the congregational system of church governance insured that, if factions developed within a congregation, no superior entity within the church's governing structure could impose one faction's will upon another's. A council of neighboring clergy could be called to mediate a dispute, but such councils had no binding authority[29] and thus often proved ineffective. Only the state, with its control over the fisc and its system of appeals from individual magistrates to the county courts, then to the Court of Assistants, and ultimately to the General Court, contained mechanisms for bringing cases up to central authorities and sending back down orders backed by coercive sanctions.

Judicial intervention in religious affairs, even if only of a gentle sort, simply was inevitable if a united church was to receive public support. Consider, for example, *Giddings v. Brown*, in which a taxpayer brought trespass against a tax collector who seized his pewter dishes when he refused to contribute to giving the town minister a fee simple, at public expense, rather than a life estate in his residence, as authorized by statute. As David Konig has noted, the suit was especially interesting because the judge who initially decided it wrote an opinion relying on common-law rules of precedent and statutory construction and holding the tax void. In the end, it became a run-of-the mill statutory interpretation case in which the General Court ultimately decided that the statute authorized the tax in question.[30] But, because it involved taxation, it clearly was a case that only the courts and not the church could resolve.

Similar interplay between civil and church authorities had occurred during the 1630s, and the power of the General Court and Court of Assistants had proved essential in dealing with the key schismatics of that decade—Roger Williams, John Wheelwright, and Anne Hutchinson. Similarly, in the 1640s a Salem Quarterly Court had admonished a minister for his "rash act" in seizing a writ a parishioner had obtained "and throwing it in the fire...to stop proceedings and have the matter healed privately."[31] Throughout the charter period, the courts of the Bay Colony worked with the colony's churches and gave them their support, but they insisted on the judiciary's supremacy.

2. Law and Morality.

The Puritans gave their name to an attitude toward sex outside of marriage and toward various other trivial pleasures that remains with us today. The naming is appropriate. Throughout the mid-seventeenth century, the government of the Massachusetts Bay Colony worked continuously to restrain sexual sin and other sinful pleasures. But even here, magistrates typically acted with self-restraint.

The most common offense for which people were prosecuted in the Bay Colony probably was fornication. It must be emphasized, however, that the gravamen of the offense was not the birth of an illegitimate child that might require public support, but sex outside the bounds of matrimony. Fornication constituted "uncleanness or defilement" and "a sin which besmirched the soul."[32] Accordingly hundreds, if not thousands, of young couples were punished for having a child less than nine months after they were married.[33] Similarly, a young man was whipped for bragging of his conquests, even though no pregnancies resulted,[34] and two men, who were acquitted of raping "two young girls," were ordered to be whipped twice and the girls, once, when "the girls…upon search [were] found to have been deflowered."[35]

Adultery, for which the penalty was death, was another commonly prosecuted crime, although few adulterers were, in fact, executed.[36] Death was also the penalty for bestiality, although here, too, execution often was avoided as judges and juries showed self-restraint. One defendant, for instance, was found innocent, and another found guilty only of "a foul & devilish attempt to bugger a cow."[37] Homosexual behavior also was punished: thus, a woman was whipped for "unseemly practices betwixt her and another maid," and two men were punished in the stocks for their "uncleanness."[38] Finally, a husband and wife were fined "for defiling the marriage bed." Even masturbation was a crime, for which one man received six lashes.[39]

Finally, there were minor offenses against morality dealing with alcoholic beverages, cards and dice, singing, fiddling, and dancing, smoking tobacco, and violating the sumptuary laws.[40] And there were the odd cases—of a man whipped "for spying into the chamber of his master and mistress, and for reporting what he saw," and of a man charged with "singing a lascivious song and using unseemly gestures therewith."[41]

3. Morality and the Regulation of the Economy.

Moral values not only denied pleasures to the people of Massachusetts Bay; their values also affected the way they worked and did business. Puritans took seriously the notion of just price; unlike Virginia, Massachusetts did not quickly embrace in its law the idea that all its inhabitants should be allowed to trade freely and to buy and sell to their best advantage. While just price was a complex concept not completely unrelated to the concept of market price, its very complexity legitimated the regulation of market price. Thus, the Bay Colony's legislators felt comfortable enacting numerous wage and price controls throughout the 1630s, including one provision specifying that imported commodities could not be sold at more than 33 percent of their market price in England, while other commodities had to be sold "at a cheap rate." In addition, the Court of Assistants warned all merchants to "keep...a good conscience, assuring them that if any man shall exceed the bounds of moderation we shall punish them severely," and in a famous case, the prominent merchant Robert Keayne was censored for making excessive profits on the sale of goods.[42]

Even the price of corn was fixed for the winter of 1633–1634, but then deregulated when spring came and supplies became more plentiful.[43] Price regulations were enforced, at least periodically, throughout the charter period. Thus, a miller was fined in 1639 for overcharging, and two years later another man was fined for oppressive practices and extortion. In later years, county courts continued to convict sellers for overcharging.[44]

The legal system also regulated the quality of goods and services. In March of 1630/31, for example, the Court of Assistants fined a man who had taken "upon him to cure the scurvy by a water of no worth nor value, which he sold at a very dear rate" and also made him "liable to any man's action of whom he had received money for the said water." Later a tanner was prosecuted for selling leather that was insufficiently tanned and a miller fined for not having scales ready to weigh people's grists.[45]

Finally, there was wage and labor regulation. Following up on earlier legislation, the Laws and Liberties of 1648 authorized town meetings to set "the prices and rates of all workmen's labors and servants' wages" and to prosecute those who took excessive wages.[46] Moreover, all adults, both men and women, were required to work—when Mary Boutwell lived idly and took "away others' victuals pretending community of all things," she was sentenced to be whipped, although after receiving clemency she was merely admonished.[47] Legislation prohibiting idleness was adopted as early as 1633, and countless people were prosecuted for violating the law.[48]

4. Morality as a Restraint on Power.

The legal culture of the Puritan Bay Colony demanded throughout the charter period that servants, women, and others who lacked power be treated "as humanity & religion require[d]." Indeed, concern for those in positions of deprivation was so great that one defendant was sentenced to time in the stocks for "being uncharitable to a poor man in distress."[49] More significantly, servants and laborers, strangers, and women received special solicitude from the law.

In return for being compelled to work at wages fixed by law, laborers received a variety of protections. Before we turn to them, however, we must examine some of the standard rules of labor control that Massachusetts applied in common with other seventeenth-century, common-law jurisdictions.[50]

Runaway servants, for instance, were routinely whipped and made to serve extra time to compensate for their absence, often double the amount of time the servant had missed.[51] In addition, servants were whipped or made to serve extra time for assaulting, resisting, or speaking against their masters, and those who tried to assist servants in escaping were whipped or fined.[52] Theft by servants was punished in a variety of ways,[53] and they were prohibited by statute from engaging in trade without license from their master.[54]

More serious offenses were punished even more severely. One servant who conspired against his master's life was sentenced to slavery, while another who burned his master's barn received 21 extra years of service. A couple who testified that "they were in danger of their lives and fearful of their children in point of [the] lust" of their servant induced the court to put a shackle on his leg.[55] In all of these respects, it should be noted, the law of Massachusetts merely mirrored that of Virginia and other English-oriented jurisdictions.

But the law of Massachusetts, unlike that of Virginia, did not regard servants as property that masters could dispose of freely in whatever fashion they wished. Legislation regulated the master-servant relationship—sometimes to the benefit of masters and sometimes to that of servants. Thus, the law required labor for "the whole day," but with "convenient time for food and rest." Masters also were not permitted to sell or assign servants to work for another for more than a year; servants were thereby assured stability in their work and living arrangements. In return, the Court of Assistants prohibited masters from manumitting servants before the expiration of their term; masters, that is, were freed from pressures for early release of workers and thereby insured stability of their work force.[56]

Massachusetts law also required masters to exercise considerable self-restraint in dealing with those who served them, at least in comparison with the treatment servants received in Virginia. The most important Massachusetts rule made masters liable for abuse of servants.[57] One servant, for example, obtained a jury verdict in his favor after complaining to a magistrate that his master had "used him ill, unreasonably beat him, and threatened to beat out his brains"; another saw his master punished for cursing or swearing at him. In one egregious case, a grand jury indicted a master for cruel treatment of a servant that led to the servant's death, and, when the petit jury returned a verdict of not guilty, the Court of Assistants refused to accept the verdict. The case was then referred to the General Court, which found the master not guilty of murder, but guilty of "inhumane cruelties" and sentenced him to a whipping plus an hour on the gallows with a rope around his neck.[58]

The Bay Colony was especially solicitous of children who were servants. Thus, a female apprentice who was neglected was returned to her mother, while another child who had been "used...very well," but "left...alone in bed some evenings" was ordered returned to its father. An apprentice could also obtain release from his indentures if a master failed to teach a trade and was compensated for his costs.[59]

From the time of initial settlement, Massachusetts servants were different from Virginia servants. The Virginians were overwhelmingly lower class immigrants who arrived in the Chesapeake with no protection from kin or other ties. They were at the mercy of their masters and of the legal system their masters controlled; their only hope was freedom at the end of their period of service. In contrast, few servants in Massachusetts were immigrants: the law discouraged immigrant servants by imposing on them a presumptive nine-year term,[60] substantially longer than the customary four-to-seven-year term in Virginia. Instead, Massachusetts servants tended to be children of nearby townsmen who were in the vicinity and ready to protect their kin through the legal system they controlled, as by requiring, for example, that servants had to be hired for one-year terms even though they were needed in an agrarian economy only for a few months at a time and that servants could not be sold "beyond [the] seas."[61] In Virginia, in short, servants were at the margins of power until they became free; in Massachusetts, on the other hand, Puritan ideology and the presence of kin and friends required that laborers be treated with restraint.

Strangers were another group that received special solicitude from the courts. Judges played a major role in protecting from local prejudice minorities and outsiders who had received permission to reside in the colony; strangers were thereby assured fair treatment within the fabric of Massachusetts society.[62] For example, strangers who could not conveniently await the next session of the regular courts were allowed to request special Strangers' Courts that had jurisdiction over any sort of case.[63] Special efforts also were made to treat Native Americans fairly, at first to preserve the peace, but later out of apparent fairness.[64]

Finally, came women. Women were not legally equal to men in the Massachusetts Bay Colony. Only eldest sons, not eldest daughters, inherited a double portion from intestate parents.[65] Although, as the century progressed, some females received some education in town schools, they received less than males, and, of course, they could not attend Harvard College.[66] Finally, the rules of coverture remained in effect for married women, and children remained firmly under their father's control.[67]

Nonetheless, the Puritan concern for self-restraint required husbands and fathers to act with moderation, and the law accordingly generated some important rules protecting women and children. One allowed women readily to obtain divorces. One ground for divorce was that their husbands had deserted them and were living with other women. Impotence was another recognized ground. In at least one case, a wife received custody of the couple's children following their divorce.[68] Another rule protective of women, a result of legislation in 1641 and 1650, made it a crime for their husbands to beat them. Similarly, if a woman could establish that her husband had abused her, she would not be punished for refusing to live with him.[69]

C. LAW IN A LAND OF YEOMAN FARMERS

What made the law of Massachusetts Bay distinctive was its emphasis on protecting the religious institutions and moral values of Puritanism. That was not all, however, that the Colony's judicial system did. It also had to perform most of the usual functions of courts and government in the English-speaking world, although Puritan ideology impinged even on the performance of these.

First and foremost, the judges had to preserve their authority, which they did by punishing all contempt of authority. Much of what they punished was the speech of either disappointed litigants[70] or political opponents who proclaimed, among other things, that "this captious government will bring all to naught adding that the best of them was but an attorney"; that the government "ma[de] laws to pick men's purses"; and that an order about swine was "against God's law, and he [the defendant] would not obey it."[71] More mundane cases involved men who failed to serve on juries or grand juries.[72] Preserving judicial authority also required courts to maintain the appearance of fairness. Thus, the magistrates refused to give "counsel concerning cases propounded to them in matter of law, they being to be judges often times when actions or crimes (grounded upon their answers) are brought before them to be heard & determined."[73]

The leaders of Massachusetts Bay had a unique concern—that their authority would be undermined with royal officials in England, and thus they punished anyone who threatened to appeal a case to England or wrote "into England falsely & maliciously against the government & execution of justice here." Another man was whipped "for saying if ministers which come will but rail against England some would receive them."[74]

With their authority secure, the judiciary was able to prosecute standard crimes of the era, such as homicide, assault, burglary, theft, and perjury.[75] Surviving records suggest that little serious crime existed except in the more urban setting of Boston, where prosecutions for theft were more frequent than elsewhere.[76]

Defamation was another matter commanding judicial attention. Almost all the defamation cases were of two sorts. In the first, someone made abusive statements about a public official.[77] In the second, accusations were made about sexual misconduct, as by calling another's wife "a light woman and that he could have a leap on her when he pleased."[78] Occasionally, suits were filed involving business slanders—for example, "defaming the plaintiff to his principals in England by writing, rigorous handling, vexing, prosecuting, unjustly molesting and imprisoning him."[79]

The law of defamation collided, however, with the Puritan concept of "'holy watching,'" by which the faithful bound themselves to watch over each other's souls in order to promote their spiritual and moral welfare.[80] It also collided with the need to preserve civic harmony by encouraging open but restrained discussion of community issues. These collisions produced the interesting case of *Elmer v. Holton*, where the plaintiff sued for defamation when the defendants accused him of causing a breach in the peace of the town.

In considering the case, the court began by observing that "the speaking of a man's failings and infirmities may be disorderly and yet not a defamation." It then continued:

> [I]t appears that the ill management of matters on both sides had been the occasion of the breaches in the town. But it does not appear that Edward Elmer was the cause of them, and therefore to charge him for making the breach we find to be some degree of defaming him. Though in regard of some blame worthy carriage found in Goodman Elmer about those matters we lay no damage upon the defendants to pay to the plaintiff.[81]

This result strove to balance, as Puritanism demanded, all the competing concerns of protecting reputation, restoring community harmony, and improving everyone's awareness of their faults and moral imperfections.

Puritanism and its related ideal of harmonious community also affected the law of the Bay Colony in a final respect. Together they kept seventeenth-century Massachusetts from becoming the debt-ridden outpost of British colonialism that Virginia became.

As we have seen, the central concern of Virginia courts by 1660 was assisting creditors in the collection of debts. By that time, Virginia had become part of a transatlantic credit economy in which colonial planters, in an effort to market ever greater quantities of their tobacco staple in Europe, kept borrowing money against anticipated profits that never materialized. As a result, they were constantly being sued for debts they could not pay.

Like Virginia, Boston became part of the transatlantic commercial economy, although the court records do not suggest that Boston's merchants were deeply in debt. The rest of seventeenth-century Massachusetts, consisting of small towns of self-sufficient yeoman farmers, never became dependent on the transatlantic economy, however, and debt-collection litigation never became the dominant concern of seventeenth-century Massachusetts courts that it was in Virginia's.[82] Indeed, legislation discouraged such litigation by prohibiting arrest and imprisonment for debt unless a plaintiff could show that his debtor was secreting assets; indeed, by making debt collection difficult, the legislation probably discouraged lending and cheap credit, which, as we have seen, was the mainstay of Virginia's economy.[83]

The Bay Colony's leadership took steps as early as 1631, which were later codified in the Laws and Liberties of 1648, to facilitate transatlantic commerce when it made bills assignable and otherwise easily circulated.[84] And court records show that Boston and its surrounding waters quickly became a thriving commercial center. There were suits by seamen for wages, suits involving London merchants, and suits for recovery of profits from international trade.[85] Cases such as these forced judges to confront sophisticated issues of commercial law, such as whether a buyer's acknowledgement of receipt of goods constituted full evidence of receipt.[86]

But cases such as these, and even debt collection cases, were not the main stuff of adjudication in the seventeenth-century Bay Colony as a whole.[87] More important was building the infrastructure of the interior towns that would enable them to prosper over time. Hundreds of cases dealt with recording land titles, building roads, opening schools, erecting mill dams,[88] and otherwise maintaining pounds, stocks, weights and measures, and other public goods.[89] No wonder one taxpayer accused the Court of Assistants of "making laws to pick men's purses"[90]—building infrastructure costs money. Unlike Virginia, however, Massachusetts had the infrastructure for civilized community living in place within a few years of its settlement. And, if the court records reveal what the people of the Bay Colony cared most about, it appears that the farming communities of Massachusetts thrived, as people brought suits over title to land, title to animals, and damage to both.[91]

We must not think anachronistically of the seventeenth-century Massachusetts Bay Colony as an agrarian paradise; it was not one. Developers busily bought up land, and entrepreneurs sought profit.[92] Nonetheless, the law did point the Bay Colony in a different direction from Virginia, its Chesapeake neighbor to the south. The law pointed Massachusetts away from unbridled entrepreneurial capitalism and from the exercise of political power unconstrained by anything but the forces of the marketplace and the formalistic black-letter rules that the marketplace demanded. It prevented those wielding political, economic, or social power from pressing their advantage and exploiting those under their control to whatever limits the market would permit.

On the contrary, Puritan concepts of law, which aimed not at profit but at community righteousness, compelled leaders to act with self-restraint and in pursuit of public-regarding principle. The law also pushed the people, who led self-sufficient, religiously based, agrarian lives, to internalize Puritan religious norms; the law made the citizens of Massachusetts "concerned, considerate, and cooperative" and facilitated "[c]onsensus and [a] common sense" approach toward governance that encouraged people to be compassionate toward and to compromise with each other.[93] Puritanism, in short, created a legal and social culture which, although far from perfect, strove to shine forth as a model for others to emulate. And, at least until Charles II was restored to his throne in England, the Puritan leaders of the Bay Colony were able to keep their utopian legal culture largely on course.

4

POPULAR POWER AND THE RULE OF LAW
IN MASSACHUSETTS

Because of the high level of literacy of its people, popular power anchored
in local communities enjoyed a degree of strength in Massachusetts in the
1630s that was unusual in the seventeenth-century world. But this popular power was not unchecked. The royal charter of the Massachusetts Bay
Company, which everyone largely assumed to be the Bay Colony's governing document,[1] had important aristocratic characteristics, at least on
its arrival in Massachusetts in 1630.

There was nothing inherently aristocratic in the charter, which created two governing bodies—a General Court consisting of all members
of the company, who were known as freemen, and a Court of Assistants, a
group of magistrates elected by the freemen to run the company's affairs
on a day-to-day basis. The charter became aristocratic when the General
Court in the summer of 1629 voted to terminate the company's affairs
in England and transfer the headquarters of the company, charter and
all, to New England. The purpose of transfer, it appears, was to reduce
the capacity of authorities and others in England to interfere in the pro-
jected colony's affairs. In any event, in the spring of 1630 twelve of the
magistrates, with the charter in hand, set sail and by the time they arrived
in Massachusetts Bay in the summer, they were the Bay Company. All
the other assistants had resigned, and practically none of the freemen
who were not magistrates came with them. The twelve magistrates thus

constituted both the Court of Assistants and the General Court, and for four years they alone governed the new colony by conferring on the Court of Assistants plenary legislative power.[2]

In the spring of 1631, however, the Court of Assistants decided to create a new body of freemen, consisting eventually of adult men who were full members of one of the colony's local churches. We do not know why the Assistants took this step: perhaps they simply believed, as John Cotton would proclaim a few years later, that all power on earth, including their own, had to be limited. In any event, the renewed existence of freemen put the General Court back into existence.

The General Court was not a democratic body by modern standards; membership was highly restricted by a religious test and in no way represented a fair cross-section of the Bay Colony's population. But it was more representative of ordinary people in the towns than the aristocratic Court of Assistants. It promptly began exercising prerogatives on behalf of the townspeople, and with every prerogative it exercised, it demanded additional ones.

First, in 1631, the General Court began electing the assistants and in 1632, the governor and deputy-governor as well. It also protested a tax levy by the Court of Assistants. Two years later, a group of freemen demanded to see the charter; upon seeing it, they learned that the General Court possessed plenary legislative power, which they then insisted on exercising. The assistants caved in, reconstituted the General Court for most purposes as a representative rather than plenary body of freemen, and conceded its role as a major organ of government with full legislative and adjudicative power.[3]

But, although the assistants were willing to concede a major role to the representatives of the freemen, they were unwilling to concede unlimited control or anything approaching democratic self-rule. The magistrates' goal was a polity that balanced local, popular liberty, on the one hand, and aristocratic authority, on the other, through the restraint of both. Relying on language in the charter, the assistants accordingly claimed power to cast a negative vote to block any legislation pending in the General Court. On the whole, their claim met with success especially when a law of 1644 provided that, unless the deputies and assistants agreed otherwise, henceforth they would meet as separate bodies and that the concurrence of both would be required for the enactment of legislation. The magistrates also claimed a negative in matters of adjudication, but here, as we shall see, the outcome was murkier.[4]

With the organization of the General Court settled, the leaders of the Bay Colony turned to the creation of other institutions—in particular, institutions for the adjudication of disputes. Of course, the Court of Assistants remained—it possessed original jurisdiction in major cases and appellate jurisdiction in all others. Immediately below it were the Quarterly Courts, which later evolved into the County Courts, composed of designated magistrates and additional associates or commissioners. Magistrates and commissioners, sitting mainly individually but occasionally in pairs, constituted the lowest level of the judiciary. In addition, town selectmen possessed some minor judicial powers.[5]

Jurisdictional bounds were not as clear, however, as this summary suggests. On the contrary, they were unsteady and flexible, as the General Court used available manpower to deal as best as it could with pressing needs, often on an ad hoc basis.[6] For example, when a minister complained to the Court of Assistants about lack of pay, the court noted that "proper congnisance of this matter belongs" to the county court. Then, it urged the town selectmen to act in the temperate fashion expected of all Puritan leaders:

> [Y]et because of the address made unto us & that we might prevent further trouble, we have thought good to recommend this matter unto your speedy consideration to do what in equity you are bound therein.... However we determine not in a case unheard from each party, but only move you to do of yourselves what is right.[7]

Similarly, appeals, which usually were taken to the next highest court with territorial jurisdiction over the county where an action had originated, at times were taken laterally—that is, from one county court to another[8]— or directly to the Court of Assistants or the General Court,[9] even from the lowest of courts.

Assistants, also known as magistrates, were elected annually by the General Court, although once elected they tended to serve for lengthy terms. Associates and commissioners were chosen by the General Court, the Court of Assistants, or the county courts on the recommendation of the localities in which they would serve.[10] But, on one occasion, a local community would produce a judge. In February 1638/39, for example,

> the inhabitants of Agwam upon Connecticut [i.e., Springfield,] taking into consideration the manifold inconveniences that may fall upon us for want of some fit magistracy among us, being now by God's providence fallen into the line of the Massachusetts jurisdiction, and it being far … to repair thither in such cases of justice as may often fall out among us[,] do therefore think it meet by a general consent and vote to ordain (till we receive further directions from the General Court in the Massachusetts Bay) Mr. William Pynchon to execute the office of a magistrate.[11]

Pynchon served for some three years on this basis until the General Court formalized his status.[12]

The key point about institutional arrangements in seventeenth-century Massachusetts, in both the General Court and the lower courts, is their suppleness and adaptability. Massachusetts adopted jurisdictional rules that, in the ordinary run of affairs, made sense, and they departed from them immediately whenever they ceased to make sense. For the leaders of the Bay Colony, procedure had no purpose in and of itself, but served only to advance the Colony's substantive objective—the creation of a godly commonwealth in which self-restrained leaders restrained the sins of others.

Massachusetts was equally lax in its treatment of the common law. As in Virginia, the common law served as a handy background norm when lawmakers needed to adopt a rule but lacked time to fashion it carefully. Thus, one of the first acts of the Court of Assistants was to appoint several of its members as justices of the peace and grant them "like power that justices of peace have in England for reformation of abuses and punishing of offenders."[13] The colonists were equally ready to abandon the common law, however, when the needs of their enterprise dictated.

They abandoned much of it through their adoption of the provision, in the Body of Liberties of 1641 that " [n]o summons, pleading, judgment, or any kind of proceeding in court, or course of justice shall be abated, arrested, or reversed upon any kind of circumstantial errors or mistakes, if the person and cause be rightly understood and intended by the court" and through the further provision that while litigants could "employ...any man" to represent them in court, they could give him "no fee or reward for his pains."[14]

A legal profession was one victim of these provisions; without fees, it could not exist. The common-law writ system was another casualty. Massachusetts plaintiffs used writs, especially the writ of case, to institute civil actions, but the writs chosen by plaintiffs often were the wrong ones, at least if the measure of rightness is Frederic William Maitland's classic, *The Forms of Action at Common Law.*[15] Thus, there were numerous writs of case brought on bonds or for trespasses and assaults, as well as writs of debt brought on unsealed instruments.[16] There also were unusual suits such as "an action of the case for not doing a sufficient days work for the wages of a day," "an action of the case for unjustly stealing away the affections of...his [the plaintiff's] espoused wife," and "an action of the case for a replevin of two cattle."[17]

But no one cared whether wrong writs were used. As prior scholars have observed, the English legal heritage that the Puritans brought with them to Massachusetts embraced not only the common law but a vast body of local law and custom as well—local law and custom that varied significantly from place to place in England. In some of those places, litigants used writs with the same sort of informality that later would occur in the Bay Colony.[18] Perhaps Massachusetts litigants simply were following some body of local practice correctly rather than trying to emulate the common-law courts in London in the way they used writs.

Along with their failure to adhere to common-law forms, the Massachusetts courts exercised considerable powers in equity.[19] From the outset, they chancered bonds.[20] But their powers were much broader. In one case in the 1670s, for example, a county court considered "the equity of his [i.e., the defendant's] case, after the verdict of the jury against him," when he showed that goods delivered to him did not meet up to contract specifications. In at least two others from the same decade, juries ordered specific performance of contracts for the sale of land. Then there was a complex case of mortgage indebtedness, in which the Court of Assistants directed the debtor to remain in possession of the premises while the plaintiff gathered his proof and promised that after trial it would "set down a final order in the premises, as shall be agreeable to equity."[21]

The courts also ignored technical objections and achieved substantial justice in other sorts of cases. In a contested election case from Woburn, for example, the Court of Assistants refused to examine objections against the two slates of candidates, but merely urged the town to "study & pursue the ways of peace & love" and to hold a new election. In a Hampshire county case in which the parties "found" themselves "very insufficiently provided either to prosecute or defend having no testimonies at hand," the court offered to remit all costs if the parties would "let the matter wholly rest and trouble each other no further," while in Essex the parties agreed to commit a case to referees upon "[t]he jury finding it very dark."[22]

There is much that is praiseworthy in a legal system flexibly committed to principles of equity and justice. But such a system also raises problems. In the case of Massachusetts, where the ultimate standard of justice was the law of God, ordinary people feared that the magistrates might not interpret God's word consistently. Indeed, as the previous chapter showed, the General Court did not interpret the Mosaic law of rape consistently from case to case, and, as anyone at the time observing the course of the Thirty Years' War in Germany and the Civil War in England knew, fundamental disagreement existed over the meaning of divine law. Moreover, even if the magistrates had acted consistently, those who had to know the law in order to obey it would have had trouble predicting what the courts would do. "[I]t was very unsafe & injurious to the body of the people to put them to learn their duty and libertie from general rules" such as those in the Bible; it was necessary "to have principles or fundamentalls...drawn out into so many of their deductions as the time and condition of the people may have use of."[23]

As early as 1635, the townspeople of Massachusetts accordingly demanded that their law be reduced to a detailed written code that would be accessible to them. This movement for codification resulted from two separate though overlapping urges—first, the colonists' "distrust of discretionary justice" as administered by their betters, and second, the "importance" they "attached to stable and written laws" that they could readily ascertain and obey. As George Haskins has shown in eloquent detail, they waged their battle over the rule of law for thirteen years until they achieved first, a partial code in the Body of Liberties of 1641 and finally, a fuller code in the Laws and Liberties of 1648.[24]

The subjects that the 1648 code addressed, as well as those it left untouched, suggest, however, that the impetus for moving toward the rule of law in Massachusetts was different from that in Virginia. The Massachusetts code comprehensively reenacted all prior legislation intended to remain in force and also codified for the first time much public law, criminal law, inheritance law, and domestic relations law. These were critical matters for farmers concerned with providing for their families and worried that central authorities would intrude on their lives. The code, in contrast, did not deal with subjects that lawyers today would place in the categories of contract and tort, matters of special concern to mercantile and entrepreneurial types planning investment strategies.[25] The inference to be drawn is that the impetus for the rule of law did not come, as it had in Virginia, from merchants and commercial farmers eager to attract investment; the catalyst was a more popular form of pressure emerging from peripheral farming communities anxious to preserve an independent way of life.

But the 1648 code did not give popular forces all that they had wanted. Many of its provisions stated general principles that required interpretation in future cases and thus left people under a duty to deduce their specific obligations from general rules. Other provisions specifically conferred discretion on future adjudicators: for example, the section on fornication directed the sentencing of convicted defendants with fines, corporal punishment, an order that they marry, or any combination of those penalties, in whatever fashion was "most agreeable to the word of God."[26]

Thus, the 1648 code did not put an end to contention between magistrates seeking to preserve discretion in applying the law of God and townspeople intent on circumscribing the assistants' freedom. It merely transposed that contention to another locus where the people could rely on a method other than fixed and certain rules to control the magistrates—namely, the jury box. From the earliest days of the Bay Colony, everyone had understood that powerful juries could reign in judges, and hence the right to trial by jury received statutory protection both in the 1641 Body of Liberties and in the Laws and Liberties of 1648[27] in cases "betwixt party and party"[28] and in "criminal cases,"[29] especially those involving "life or banishment."[30]

The courts almost invariably granted a jury when a litigant requested one.[31] Courts also protected the integrity of the jury trial system when, for example, they prohibited Thomas Lechford "from pleading any man's cause" because he had gone "to the jury & plead[ed] with them out of court." But Massachusetts was prepared to depart from common-law rules when exigencies required, as when in 1638 the settlers of the Connecticut Valley agreed, "seeing a jury of 12 fit persons cannot be had at present among us, that six persons shall be esteemed and held a sufficient jury"[32] or when a Quarterly Court "committed" a case "to eight jurymen," the others "being taken off as parties in the case."[33]

On the other hand, courts sometimes denied defendants trial by jury and dealt with them severely when it suited their perception of the Colony's needs. Before the right to trial by jury was codified in the 1641 and 1648 laws, a number of famous individuals—Thomas Morton, Phillip Ratliffe, Roger Williams, and John Wheelwright—were banished by the Court of Assistants using procedures reminiscent of those used by Star Chamber in England,[34] as were several other men described "as persons unmeete to inhabit here." The Assistants' denial of juries persisted even after codification. As late as 1676, two Native Americans, "having been open & murderous enemies," were sentenced to death without the intervention of a jury,[35] while a few years later two Frenchmen were banished without jury trial—the one, who also stood two hours in the pillory and had his ears cut off after protesting his innocence of coin clipping but then admitting, when presented with the evidence, that he possessed instruments for clipping coins, and the other, who was "a dancing master & a person very insolent & of ill fame that raves & scoffs at religion [and] of a turbulent spirit no way fit to be tolerated to live in this place."[36] In ordinary criminal cases, one man was convicted by a court alone of theft on the disputed testimony of a co-defendant and sentenced to twenty lashes and the payment of treble damages, while another man, acquitted of rape by a jury, was nonetheless banished by the court. A third man who had confessed to witchcraft but then demanded a trial by a jury, which acquitted him, received a fine and a further penalty of thirty lashes for "his wicked & pernicious willful lying," which "put[]the Country to so great a charge" in bringing him to trial.[37]

Lower courts also heard cases without juries. Hundreds of petty offenses were disposed of without jury trials. William Pynchon, the chief magistrate of the Connecticut Valley, was involved in two noteworthy nonjury cases. In one highly contested case, he convicted Mary Parsons, who later would herself be accused of witchcraft, of criminal defamation for falsely accusing another of being a witch.[38] And, in another case, two Sabbath wardens

> saw Samuel Terry standing with his face to the meeting house wall...chafing his yard [i.e., his penis] to provoke lust, even in sermon time; and because they said they had kept it private I gave him private correction with a rod on his bare back 6 lashes well set on.[39]

Terry, like thousands of embarrassed sexual offenders thereafter, simply waived his right to trial and accepted the state's punishment rather than permit public revelation of his behavior.

In the cases above that came to public attention, judicial proceedings without juries led to popular disapproval[40] and to the codification in the Body of Liberties and the Code of 1648 of the right to trial by jury. They also led to an ongoing conflict about the power of juries in cases in which juries did participate—a conflict related, in turn, to the claim of the magistrates to a negative voice in matters of adjudication before the General Court and ultimately to the movement for codification. At a deeper level, the conflict was about the proper balance between communitarian populism and aristocratic hierarchy in the Puritan colony.

We must begin with the provision in the 1641 Body of Liberties that, "[i]f the Bench and Jurors shall so suffer [i.e., differ] at any time about their verdict that either of them cannot proceed with peace of conscience the case shall be referred to the General Court."[41] The Laws and Liberties of 1648 contained a like provision, as well as a further one authorizing juries to request advice in open court from sources other than the judges—presumably the clergy.[42]

In the two decades following the 1640s codes, numerous bench-jury disagreements occurred,[43] many of them political or religious in character. In one case, for example, a defendant was accused of blasphemy for saying, "Jehovah is the Devil, & he knew no God but his sword." When the jury found him not guilty of a capital offense, the magistrates rejected the verdict, but before the General Court could decide the case the defendant escaped. In another criminal case, in which a defendant was accused of gaming with dice, the jury found him not guilty of playing for money; when the Assistants rejected the verdict, the General Court upheld them, finding the defendant guilty by his own confession and "a very ill example to the youth of the place." Similarly, when an Essex County jury sympathized with a defendant who had harbored a runaway servant who was "his countryman," a "Scotchman," the magistrates applied the law and rejected the verdict. And, when the Governor sued on behalf of the Colony to recover land legally forfeited by the defendant, the magistrates set aside a verdict for defendant.[44]

What happened to the cases, often sensitive in nature, when they arrived at the General Court? There too, communitarianism and aristocracy at times were in tension. The first conflict between the deputies, chosen as representatives of the freemen, and the assistants occurred in 1636 over Thomas Hooker's emigration to Connecticut. As a result of the conflict, the General Court adopted a statute providing that the Court could not issue any order without the approval of both the majority of the deputies and the majority of the magistrates and that in cases of disagreement between them a committee consisting of equal numbers of deputies and of magistrates and of an umpire chosen by the committee would " 'hear and determine the cause in question.' "[45]

Together with the magistrates' jurisdiction to reject jury verdicts, the 1636 settlement evenly balanced the power of local communities and hierarchical aristocracy. Both the freemen, represented on the jury and by the deputies, and the magistrates, who presided over the county courts, constituted the Court of Assistants, and sat as assistants in the General Court, were required to agree to all judgments. If they failed to agree, the case went up to a next level and ultimately to an equally staffed committee, which chose a mutually acceptable umpire to cast the decisive vote.

But the 1636 settlement quickly proved unstable. In 1644, a new statute provided that the General Court henceforth would meet in two separate chambers—the Deputies and the Court of Assistants. It is not completely clear whether the umpireal committee survived this establishment of full bicameralism.[46] What is clear is that the General Court could not act effectively as the highest court of the Bay Colony, at least in cases that came before it as a result of bench-jury disagreements, if no procedure existed for reaching judgments when the deputies and magistrates were at odds. Giving both the aristocracy and the representatives of local communities a negative or veto could work in the context of legislation, but in matters of adjudication it was no way to run an efficient judicial system capable of resolving the disputes presented to it. Either the deputies or the assistants had to have the final say, or else appeals to the General Court would lie unresolved.

It was in the context of this need for finality, as well as the failure of the 1648 code to fully cabin the magistrates' discretion, that the General Court in 1649 again revisited the issue of the assistants' negative. It provided that in cases of disagreement between the deputies and the assistants, "'the General Court should hear the case together, & determine the case by the major vote.'"[47] Further legislation in 1652 made it clear that the 1649 settlement applied only to judicial and not to legislative matters, where both bicameralism and the magistrates' negative survived throughout the colonial period. Nonetheless, the 1649 act meant that the deputies would have the controlling voice in adjudicatory matters since they outnumbered the magistrates by about three to one.[48]

Thus, the 1649 act made the local communities dominant over the central hierarchy. Under that act, bench-jury disputes at the county level would go to the Court of Assistants and, if the bench and jury still disagreed there, to the General Court.[49] In the General Court, the assistants would lose if the deputies, who were the analog of jurors, still wished to press the local community's point of view. The 1649 act thus had the effect of significantly reducing the discretion that magistrates had retained pursuant to the Laws and Liberties of 1648: magistrates could exercise discretion when they found it necessary, but jurors could disagree with them, and when they did, discretion ultimately would fall to the representatives of the towns sitting in the General Court.

During the rest of the colonial period, this triumph of local community power never would be effectively challenged. The presence of ultimate power in local communities does not mean, however, that juries used that power with any frequency in a fashion adverse to the wishes of the bench. Most of the time juries acted with self-restraint and cooperated with the judges. One jury in the Court of Assistants, for example, expressed a common viewpoint when dealing on appeal with a verdict in the court below, "the legality of which we do not understand; not finding any evidence to guide us therein and therefore we leave it unto the bench to determine the case." In numerous cases in which juries had no clear view on the law, they merely found the facts in a special verdict and left application of the law to the court.[50]

In short, the Massachusetts Bay Colony developed a remarkable body of procedural law during the half century of its existence. Although Massachusetts procedure was influenced by the common law, it was not, in essence, a common-law system. Nor, in essence, was it a religious system. The codes of 1641 and 1648 and the law of judge and jury and of the magistrates' negative, in particular, were indigenous growths that balanced popular communitarian concerns for the rule of law and aristocratic concerns for government by the law of God in an always changing mixture as political realities on the ground changed. Initially, it balanced them equally, but in the end, it gave superior power to representatives of the localities. But, even when community forces had the edge, they acted with restraint and typically did not choose to exercise their power.

Like Virginia, Massachusetts thus moved in the direction of government by the rule of law in the decades preceding 1660. But the rule of law had a different meaning and the law itself retained a different substantive content in the two colonies. In Virginia, the turn to the rule of law entailed the importation of English common-law concepts in order to establish fixed and certain black-letter rules that would facilitate entrepreneurial planning and thereby encourage investment in Virginia's economy. In Massachusetts, the purpose of the rule of law, which was advanced through legislation and the empowerment of local townspeople sitting on juries and in a mixed popular-aristocratic legislature, was to control the discretion of the governing elite and thereby prevent it from interfering unpredictably in the lives of ordinary people in the local towns. Different societal interests propagated the rule of law in the two colonies, and its adoption accordingly served two very different purposes. Indeed, those purposes were so different that we should understand the concept of rule of law as being quite different in Massachusetts and Virginia.

Moreover, even after the turn to the rule of law, the substantive law of the two colonies remained dissimilar. The reason is that their law was built on different foundations—that of Virginia, on the underpinning of a Spartan labor system, and that of Massachusetts, on the law of God. The foundations remained present after the rule of law was built atop them, since the core purposes of the two colonies—the maximization of investor profits and the creation of a Puritan utopia—did not change. The rule of law was designed only to provide a check on ruling elites to ensure that they did not treat socioeconomic groups essential to each colony's success arbitrarily.

5

THE NEW ENGLAND SATELLITES

In addition to Massachusetts Bay, four colonies existed in New England in 1660—Connecticut, New Haven, Plymouth, and Rhode Island. All four were geographically small entities that were about the size of the current state of Rhode Island, with large segments of their territory unsettled. Connecticut was established as a sort of outpost of Massachusetts, and New Haven, by settlers from England politically tied to the Puritan cause; both were in the Massachusetts orbit. Although Plymouth was founded a decade before Massachusetts, and Rhode Island was settled by men and women who were dissenters from the Massachusetts religious establishment and had been driven into exile as a result, they, too, were strongly influenced by the Bay Colony.

The religious values of the five New England colonies also were similar. Although the churches of Plymouth and Rhode Island had governance structures differing from those of Massachusetts, Connecticut, and New Haven, they remained, in their theological beliefs, within the Puritan fold. The churches of all five colonies were nonhierarchical, Protestant ones dedicated to purification of their own people and to providing a prototype for the salvation of Christians elsewhere in the world. The exiles who moved to Rhode Island directed their lives toward the same ends as their persecutors in Massachusetts, but disagreed about how best to attain those ends. They were far closer in their worldview to the ministers and magistrates of Massachusetts than to the planters striving to make money out of tobacco in Virginia.

But the chief reason for thinking of Connecticut, New Haven, Plymouth, and Rhode Island as legal satellites of Massachusetts is that they all possessed, albeit some more than others, "a distinctively Puritan legal regime."[1] The law of the four colonies, in the main, copied that of the Bay Colony and gave New England, in most significant respects, a single, nearly uniform legal system. After focusing on the uniformity, this chapter turns to the ways in which the legal systems of the four ancillary New England jurisdictions sometimes differed in detail from that of Massachusetts.

A. UNIFORM CHARACTERISTICS OF NEW ENGLAND LAW

The law of God constituted the foundation for the legal system of every New England colony. The founders of New Haven provided, for example, "that the words of God shall be the only rule to be attended unto in ordering the affairs of government." The Connecticut General Court agreed that the duty of all New England judges was to do "justice according to our laws and the rule of righteousness" and "to settle" matters "as in equity and justice they shall see fit, that peace and truth may be continued."[2] It followed "that the judicial laws of God, as they were delivered by Moses," were to be "a rule to all the courts" and that all judges had a "duty to do the best they [could] that the law of God may be strictly observed."[3]

New Englanders who disagreed about the bearing of divine law were punished. Thus, one man in New Haven was fined for declaring that "the laws of the jurisdiction... [were] the wills of men," while another was chastised for "reproach[ing] those that walk in the ways of God." Similarly, a Connecticut man who announced that "he hoped to meet some of the members of the Church in hell ere long, and he did not question but he should" was whipped, and one from Plymouth fined for speaking against the church's rule. Another Plymouth man was required to acknowledge his offense of blasphemy for saying "he neither feared God, nor the devil."[4]

Except in Rhode Island, people were prosecuted for disagreeing publicly with official theological dogmas. Thus, the Plymouth Colony made it a crime to "deny the scriptures to be a rule of life." Pursuant to this and other legislation, one man was indicted in Plymouth for objecting that the churches in Massachusetts and Plymouth did not baptize infants and for criticizing the magistrates for failing to take the oath of supremacy, while a decade later a group was prosecuted for "continuing of a meeting upon the Lord's Day from house to house." Likewise, a woman guilty of "faulty" speeches during public worship had her whipping respited in the hope that she would "be warned by the present sentence and admonition to offend no more," but when she committed the same offense a second time, the whipping was administered.[5]

Pursuant to statute, innumerable individuals were fined for failing to fulfill religious duties, such as not attending church on Sunday, otherwise violating the sabbath, or using profane language.[6] A New Haven man was whipped for "a rash & sinful oath." Perhaps, the most infamous example after the 1630s of judicial activism to protect dominant religious beliefs was that of William Ledra, a Quaker who on pain of death was banished from Massachusetts Bay in 1660 after being banished earlier from Plymouth.[7] Except in Rhode Island, Quakers were banished for "divers horrid errors,"[8] whipped, or fined.[9] Viewing them as "subversi[ve] of the fundamentals of Christian religion, church, order, and the civil peace," the Plymouth Colony banished them, and the General Court set aside a day of fasting and humiliation to seek God's blessing in saving the colony from the "infection and disturbance" of those "fretting gangrenelike doctrines and persons commonly called Quakers."[10]

Judges also strove to help religious authorities eradicate sin. A sin prosecuted with great frequency was fornication—a sin that, in the words of New Haven magistrates, "shuts out of the kingdom of heaven, without repentence."[11] Vast numbers of single women were punished for getting pregnant, and many more young couples prosecuted for having a child less than nine months after they were married.[12] In New Haven, a defendant and his wife were whipped "for their filthy dalliance together"; two servants were prosecuted "for diverse unclean filthy dalliances"; and a third servant whipped "for defiling himself by diverse unclean passages with one of his master's children." Similarly, in Plymouth a young couple was whipped "for unclean practices each with other." On the other hand, when Jane Powell explained that she had committed fornication with an Irish servant out of "hope...to have married him" and thereby escape her "sad and miserable condition by hard service," the Plymouth court ordered her "cleared for the present" and sent her home to see if she was pregnant.[13]

Single men also were prosecuted for fornication, and a man would be required to support a child he was accused of fathering "if it shall appear to be his." But many prosecutions encountered difficulties. If a woman failed to prosecute a man, he would be "cleared."[14] An accused father also was entitled to a trial by jury if he demanded it, and the courts treated men accused of fornication fairly and were careful not to convict the innocent.[15] The judiciary's sympathy for men emerged with special clarity in the weird case of John Uffoote, who, after being divorced from his wife for "insufficiency," managed to get Martha Nettleton pregnant. Although "he was sorry for his sin," he was now convinced that he would not have suffered from impotence "if his wife had carried it toward him as she ought"; "finding the need of that help" from Martha, he "was by the power of temptation and corruption in his own heart overcome" and accordingly sought the court's permission to marry Martha. Although the court found "it is a strange thing that after all this he should miscarry in this manner," it allowed John and Martha to marry after fining both of them.[16] Judges were much less sympathetic to women, as, for example, when Martha Richardson testified that a man unknown to her impregnated her after she had passed out in a fainting fit and the court ruled that it "could not but judge her guilty, both of known fornication and continued impudent lying, believing that no woman can be gotten with child without some knowledge, consent and delight in the acting thereof."[17]

Another sexual sin prosecuted with some frequency was adultery. Death was the official penalty for adultery only in New Haven;[18] elsewhere adulterers received lesser punishments. For example, a married woman in Plymouth who committed "uncleanness" with an Indian was only whipped at a cart's tail and required to wear a badge, while there is no record of the outcome of two other Plymouth cases—the first, in which a man was accused of "lascivious carriage" in grabbing a married woman's clothes and "enticing her by words, as also by taking out his instrument of nature that he might prevail to lie with her in her own house," and the second, in which a woman was presented for the "sin of fornication with her father in law."[19]

Death was also the penalty for bestiality, and some defendants were executed. Thus, one man was put to death for "buggery with a mare, a cow, two goats, divers sheep, two calves, and a turkey." Similarly, when a fifteen-year-old boy committed the crime with a dog, "his sin [was] such as by the law of God ... he ought to die, and therefore the court dare do no other but pronounce the same.[20] But here too execution often was avoided as judges and juries showed self-restraint. One defendant, for instance, was found guilty only of an unsuccessful attempt at bestiality and another only of "penetration but not ... effusion of seed"; a third man was let off with a whipping because only one witness testified to the completed act.[21]

The same pattern was true of sodomy, for which there were few actual prosecutions.[22] More numerous prosecutions occurred for lesser offenses committed between persons of the same sex. Plymouth, for example, administered a whipping for "lewd & sodomitical practices tending to sodomy," while Connecticut instituted proceedings against two men for the "sin" of "uncleanness." Other Plymouth prosecutions were brought against two men, both of whom were whipped and one banished, for "lewd behavior and unclean carriage with one another, by often spending their seed upon one another," and against a woman who was forced to acknowledge her "unchaste behavior" with another woman "upon a bed, with divers lascivious speeches."[23]

Sexual offenses could be of such a great variety that Connecticut did not even try to codify them; it merely authorized the judges to proceed by fine, imprisonment, or corporal punishment, "according to their discretion," against the "several ... ways of uncleanness and lascivious carriages practiced among us." The judges used their discretion to "correct" several defendants "for ... self pollution" and to punish another man, perhaps a servant, for "his running away" with a man "and his wife, and drawing them into sinful ways and practices."[24] Finally, there were miscellaneous cases—of a woman prosecuted for nudity, of a father whipped for attempting incest, of a man charged with lewd behavior and uncivil carriage toward a woman, and of a youth convicted of "lascivious carriages ... in attempting the chastity of his father's maid servant, to satisfy his fleshy, beastly lust."[25]

The smaller New England colonies also joined Massachusetts in the criminalization of minor offenses against morality dealing with such

matters as the "brutish" "sin of drunkenness" and other misuses of alcoholic beverages,[26] singing, fiddling, and dancing, smoking tobacco, and
idleness.[27] As in Massachusetts, moral values also affected the way people worked and did business. Thus, price regulations set by legislation
were enforced, at least periodically, throughout mid-century. Connecticut and New Haven copied the provision of the Massachusetts code of
1648 against "oppression," which they defined as "taking excessive wages
for work, or unreasonable prices for commodities." In Plymouth, retailers
were fined for overcharging, a baker punished for his efforts to market
underweight bread, and other millers fined for not having scales ready to
weigh people's grists.[28] New Haven allowed only a 25 percent markup of
goods or such other markup "that neither buyer nor seller shall suffer in
the rates," and in Connecticut a man was fined in 1642 for "encouraging
others to take excessive rates for work and wares."[29] Even the price of corn
was fixed, and when William Pynchon, the chief magistrate of Springfield, Massachusetts, "was not so careful to promote the public good in
the trade of corn as he was bound to do," he was fined by the Connecticut General Court. Although people in Connecticut after 1650 were "left
at liberty to make their bargains for corn," the traditional just price also
remained in place as a background norm—the law provided that "where
no price is agreed betwixt persons, corn shall be payable" at the old prices
that had been set by statute.[30]

Finally, there was wage and labor regulation. Idleness was prohibited, specific wage rates set, and workers guilty of "breach of the law of
oppression" in the form of taking excessive wages prosecuted.[31] On the
other hand, judges understood "that poor men should be paid for their
labor," and thus, in one of the earliest entries in Connecticut's records, a
man who was watching over another man's grain was granted "so many
bushels as . . . [were] reasonable for his pains and labor."[32]

Religious values also led New Englanders to treat their servants more
gently than Virginians treated theirs.

Like Massachusetts, the lesser New England colonies applied basic
common law rules of servant discipline. Runaway servants, for instance,
were routinely whipped and made to serve extra time to compensate for
their absence.[33] In addition, servants were whipped or made to serve extra
time for resisting or speaking against their masters;[34] in Connecticut,

incorrigible or rebellious servants were even subject to hard labor in prison.[35] For the same reason, men who sought to marry female servants were subject to punishment or, at least, required to compensate the servants' masters.[36] Legislative regulations also impinged negatively on servants. For example, it was a crime to "entertain" other men's servants "in the night, or at other unreasonable times."[37] Theft by servants was, of course, punished, while drunkenness led to public or "family correction." As in Massachusetts, legislation in Plymouth prohibited the manumission of servants.[38]

Despite following these commonplace rules that were unfavorable to servants, New England magistrates demanded that masters exercise considerable self-restraint in dealing with those who served them, at least in comparison with the treatment servants received in Virginia. All servants were entitled to adequate food, clothing, and shelter, and one even had his term reduced when he showed that his master "had disbursed little for him."[39] Servants were entitled to release at the end of their term and could sue to have a court determine the proper length of the term; likewise, one who had been made a servant without proper consent would be freed.[40]

A more important rule made masters liable for abuse of servants.[41] In egregious cases, the courts imposed stern penalties. Thus, in one Plymouth case, a jury convicted a master of manslaughter in the death of his servant and sentenced him to branding with a hot iron, while in Rhode Island, a master was criminally prosecuted "for oppression in the way of his servant." A New Haven master was required to free his servant two months early "for undue correcting him, striking him upon the head with a hammer." Another rule prohibited selling servants "beyond [the] seas."[42]

As in Massachusetts, children who were servants enjoyed special protection. It was clear that apprentices at their own suit or suit of a kinsman could obtain either damages or release from their indentures if a master failed to teach a trade. More generally, it appears that parents were able to monitor the well-being of children whom they had placed in servitude and even to take their children back, at least if they were willing to compensate a master for his costs in caring for a child.[43] And, when a fourteen-year-old boy was convicted of burning down his master's house out of revenge for a whipping, a New Haven court showed its solicitude by "seriously consider[ing] what God called for in this case, and...agreed to spare his life," "considering he [was] young...and somewhat childish in his way."[44]

The judges of Connecticut, New Haven, Plymouth, and Rhode Island, like those of Massachusetts, offered special protection to other under-classes. New Haven, for example, granted "strangers," who took precautions on the Sabbath to protect their ships from harm, an exemption from the ordinary rules of not working on the Sabbath, while Connecticut prom-ised that all persons, "whether they be inhabitants or foreigners," would "enjoy the same justice and law that is general for this colony."[45] Similarly, in the Connecticut case of *Goodhart v. VarLeet*, the court granted a con-tinuance to allow the defendant to send a "Dutch writing" to Manhattan to have it translated into English. And, special efforts were made to treat Native Americans fairly. Thus, three Plymouth men were convicted in 1639 by a jury and executed for murdering and robbing an Indian. There were also convictions for thefts from Native Americans. On the other hand, Connecticut was not welcoming to a Jewish merchant whom it fined for trading provisions with children when family heads were absent.[46]

Women were not legally equal to men in New England—they had a distinctly second-class status. As one Connecticut court declared, for example, in construing an ambiguous will, money was left so "that the sons shall have learning to write plainly and read distinctly in the Bible and the daughters so to read and sew sufficiently for the making of their own ordinary linen." In a like vein, a New Haven court "reproved" a woman "for her forward disposition, remembering her that meekness is a choice ornament for a woman."[47]

Nonetheless, religious precepts about self-restraint required husbands and fathers to act with moderation, and the law accordingly generated some important rules protecting women and children. One required men to support their wives and take responsibility for their debts.[48] Another protected women from spousal abuse—a concept that was extended in Connecticut even to a husband who was fined "for bequeathing his wife to a young man."[49] A third allowed women readily to obtain divorces on grounds that a husband was impotent or that he had deserted his wife and was living with another woman.[50] Of course, a man with a wife in England would not be permitted to marry a new wife in New England.[51]

Acceptance of these religious precepts created societies in the satellite New England colonies similar to the society of Massachusetts. As in Massachusetts, people were not permitted to "withdraw from all public ordinances and Christian society." They were expected to live with families,[52] and even a man who "lived with his family remotely in the woods from neighbors" would be ordered to move "near some neighborhood." Land was plentiful, and any family head willing to work could gain access to it. Indeed, on one occasion in Plymouth, the General Court invited "such young men or others as wanted land" to apply for it.[53]

The availability of land made the southern New England colonies, like Massachusetts, into agrarian communities inhabited mainly by yeoman farmers even though their legal systems took some steps to facilitate commerce. Legislation, for instance, did make bills and other evidences of debt assignable, and courts did hear maritime cases in seaport towns like Saybrook and New Haven, in which they were forced to confront issues of commercial law, such as whether a creditor of a vessel or sailors seeking wages had priority.[54] Even most commercial cases, however, involved straightforward issues of law. In one, for example, a defendant who owed a specified amount of beaver but pleaded he could not obtain any beaver was ordered to "pay the debt in some other pay so as it may equal beaver." In another, a tanner provided leather to a shoemaker, who agreed, in return for a specified payment, to make fourteen dozen shoes that the tanner then sold to the public. The shoes proved defective and, when worn, would "fall in pieces." After hearing witnesses, the court "call[ed] in some workmen, both shoemakers and tanners, that they might see it and judge whose fault it was." The workmen found "the leather...very bad, not tanned," and the shoemaker's "workmanship bad also." The court accordingly found both men "faulty," but placed "the greater fault and guilt" on the tanner. Both were fined and awarded no damages, and the shoes that remained were ordered sold only to customers given notice of their defects.[55]

The law of the satellite New England colonies, however, was not centrally about commercial litigation or even debt collection. Indeed, one colony, Connecticut, tried like Massachusetts to discourage debt litigation and, perhaps, lending and borrowing as well by prohibiting arrest and imprisonment for debt.[56] More important was building the infrastructure of the interior towns that would enable them to prosper over time. Thus, the Plymouth Colony decided that "the rawness of the country" made it necessary to give widows and children of bankrupt or insolvent decedents priority over creditors and enacted legislation to do so,[57] while hundreds of entries in New England legislative and court records dealt with recording land titles,[58] building roads, erecting mill dams, starting up ferries, and otherwise maintaining pounds, stocks, and weights and measures.[59] And, if the court records reveal what the people of New England cared most about, agriculture appears to be the answer. People brought innumerable suits claiming title or damages to land and animals[60] or damages caused, for example, by a defendant's "negligence" in not being "as careful as he might" in cutting down trees.[61] They also fought over such matters as rent, and "the wintering of a cow."[62]

Like the judges of Massachusetts and Virginia, those of the smaller New England colonies had to preserve their authority, induce people "to live submissively to this government," and "reform... such as are in legal sort reformable."[63] Many cases dealt with contemptuous speech: thus, one man in Plymouth was presented for "stirring up the people to mutiny" and another "for disgraceful speeches, tending to the contempt of the government." A third, found guilty of "speeches tending to sedition & mutiny," was banished.[64] Rhode Island prosecuted three men who were "ringleader[s] in new divisions in the colony"; a man who proclaimed, among other things, that "the magistrates here were disorderly men"; another who said that a defendant "cared not a fart [or] a turd for all their warrants"; and a final man who called the judges "just asses" and said that "he looked at the magistrates as lawyers." New Haven had considerable difficulty when a man whose liquors had been seized brought a civil action in Connecticut against New Haven's governor; the New Haven General Court fined him for his effort "to sow discord among brother colonies... a high provocation of God, as being a sowing discord among thousands of brethren."[65] Other contempt cases involved the speech of disappointed litigants and men who failed to serve on juries or grand juries.[66] At issue in another case was an alteration in a writ of execution.[67]

Preserving judicial authority also required courts to maintain the appearance of fairness. Thus, a magistrate might recuse himself if challenged. Fairness also required that courts obtain truthful testimony, and thus there were prosecutions for perjury and suborning perjury.[68] But the concern went further, as one man was fined for "pretending great damage" when he "could prove but little."[69]

With their authority secure, the judiciary was able to prosecute standard crimes of the era, such as homicide, assault, burglary, theft, arson, and witchcraft.[70] Defamation was another matter commanding judicial attention. Almost all the defamation cases involved either abusive statements about a public official or accusations about sexual misconduct,[71] as by slandering a woman by "saying he would go home & lay with her." Occasionally, suits were filed involving business slanders—for example, accusing the plaintiff of seizing excessive property in payment of money owed. Other occasional cases involved claims that the defendant had falsely called someone a witch.[72]

B. IN THEIR OWN WAY

In most respects, the law of the smaller New England colonies thus replicated that of Massachusetts. But there were some differences. One was that the magistrates of the smaller colonies possessed more discretionary leeway and, at least on a few occasions, acted more assertively than those in Massachusetts. Recall, for example, the Connecticut legislation authorizing judges to proceed "according to their discretion" against the "several...ways of uncleanness...practiced among us." They also were more willing to use their authority against local, popular forces. In one Plymouth case, for example, the General Court set aside an election and ordered a new one since it found the electoral victors "unmeete persons for such a place" and chosen "in contempt of the government." Similarly, in a Connecticut case in which the residents of Saybrook objected to being forced to work on building a courthouse at wages set by the magistrates, the General Court took note of their argument about "[c]ourts passing sentence in their own case." But it found the "unreasonableness" of the argument "easily obvious" because its acceptance would have made "all Courts incapable in many cases of determining by themselves what may concern their peace and comforts." The Connecticut court also protected the integrity of its deliberations when it announced that any "member of the General Court" who "reveal[ed] any secret" or made "known to any person what any one member of the Court speaks concerning any person or business that may come into agitation in the Court" would be fined.[73]

As we saw earlier, the townspeople of Massachusetts labored over decades to empower juries and thereby limit the discretion of judges. In contrast, the legal systems of Connecticut, Plymouth, and Rhode Island left the judiciary's power over juries largely intact, and New Haven dispensed with juries altogether.[74] The four colonies used other methods to cabin the freedom and authority of magistrates.

Like Massachusetts Bay but unlike Virginia, the satellite New England jurisdictions did not have recourse to black-letter reception of the common law to control discretion. They did use common-law writs to institute civil litigation, but, as in Massachusetts, plaintiffs did not follow classic rules in selecting their writs and, when they chose the wrong ones, no one cared. Thus, there were writs of case brought for trespasses, as well as writs of debt brought on unsealed instruments or to balance accounts.[75] There were a few clearly repugnant actions, such as a writ of "debt upon the case" and "an action of the case of equity."[76] Then there were unusual suits such as an action of case "concerning a deed…conceived to be fraudulent," an action of case "for setting of traps and catching of swine," an action of case for unjustly stealing away the affections of the plaintiff's wife," "an action of debt…about mowing of grass," and an action of case for replevin.[77] There was even an instance of an "action of manne." Occasionally, though, one would see odd forms of common-law sophistication, as in a Connecticut writ of "case for *indirect* taking away a mare" and in a Plymouth writ of case brought by plaintiffs "for *burning* their house accidentally."[78] New Haven went even further than its sister colonies and for nearly two decades did not use writs at all, although they began to appear in the mid-1650s. Of course, when writs did appear, plaintiffs often did not follow strict common-law rules.[79]

Courts also ignored other sorts of technical objections. Rhode Island, for example, adhered to the philosophy that "a verbal oversight" in a pleading could "be rectified" as long as the other party "clearly understood & answer[ed] according to the scope of it." In another case, the Connecticut Particular Court did not force a jury to submit a verdict, but permitted it to return a case to the court when "they could not find evidence to determine" it.[80] Similarly, when faced with a schism in the church of Hartford, the Connecticut General Court did not force itself to judgment, but "withheld their votes" since the "way of peace according to God...for the healing of those sad differences in the Church" had not yet material-ized. And, total informality reigned in *Smith v. Notts*, a defamation suit in which the court ruled that Smith's actions "presume[d] too far," but that Notts's words "were too high and far above and beyond the nature of the thing and therein to be blamed." It accordingly directed both parties to exhibit "a loving carriage each to the other and to forbear exasperating expressions or straining of neighbor's actions."[81]

So far, the courts of the satellite colonies were following the lead of Massachusetts. But they did not follow the lead to its conclusion. Unlike Massachusetts, they did not systematically use juries to rein in judges. Although the right to trial by jury was protected everywhere but New Haven "according to the precedents of the laws of England as near as may be,"[82] courts throughout the smaller New England colonies imposed lim-its on jury freedom. Plymouth, for example, appears to have developed a procedure allowing judges to set aside verdicts on the basis of newly discovered evidence, while the Rhode Island courts set aside verdicts that were "contrary to law."[83]

The record is clearest in Connecticut, where the General Court weakened the jury system by authorizing the use of six-man juries and directing juries to give verdicts first by majority vote, and then later by a two-thirds vote, when they could not agree unanimously; the assump-tion is that smaller juries and non-unanimous ones are less able to resist judicial pressure than twelve-member juries requiring a unanimous ver-dict. Connecticut legislation also provided that, if a jury did "not in the judgment of the Court attend the evidence given in Court, it shall be in the power of the Court to impanel another jury and commit the consid-eration of the case to them" or to "alter the damages given in by the Jury," subject, however, to the right of either party to appeal the case to the Gen-eral Court. Once a case came to the General Court, both the magistrates and the deputies had to concur in the judgment, although it is unclear what would happen if they did not.[84]

In the ensuing decades, many bench–jury disagreements occurred.[85] In one Connecticut case, for example, a defendant appealed three verdicts to the General Court, which could "see no just cause to vary from or alter" two of the three, although it did significantly reduce the jury's damage award in the third.[86] In another case, the General Court saw "no[] reason to confirm the full verdict of the Jury," but it did award the plaintiff some of the damages he had obtained below, since "the law allow[ed] liberty to the court to alter & vary damages as they see cause according to the rules of righteousness." In a third case, the Court reversed a plaintiff's verdict on a bill of exchange when it concluded "that it was not an authentic bill." And, in a case where a jury could not agree, the court recommended that the parties either settle it or submit to decision by the court.[87] There were also cases where juries returned special verdicts, finding only the facts and leaving determination of the law to the court.[88]

Nonetheless, it is important not to exaggerate the authority and free-dom of New England magistrates outside Massachusetts. Sometimes they were constrained by popular demands for codification and the sheer need to make their laws publicly accessible and known, as, for example, in Con-necticut, which even before Massachusetts, published its penal laws in 1639 and its capital laws in 1642. Rhode Island similarly published a first, partial code in 1647; New Haven did the same in 1656; and Plymouth enacted a lengthy code in 1658.[89] In addition, Rhode Island limited the discretion of its magistrates by agreeing to "be governed by the laws of England, together with the way of administration of them" and by prohib-iting anyone to be "molested or destroyed, but by . . . some known law, and according to the letter of it"; thus, when a man was accused of "matters of very pernicious nature against the peace of the place: yet no particular law being found that is of force in the colony, which takes hold of the said offense," the Rhode Island court declined to proceed against him.[90]

Judges also constrained themselves by adhering to basic principles of due process of law. New Haven, for example, accepted a defendant's claim that "he was not bound to accuse himself," while in the case of a young girl accused of aiding and abetting arson, the court "wanting due proof [could] not proceed to censure," even though the defendant's sister had testified against her and "by all circumstances duly weighed she seems to this court to be guilty." Similarly, when a woman was accused of witchcraft, the court found "the evidence [was] not sufficient as yet to take away her life," although "the grounds of suspicion remain[ed] . . . as strong as before and she [was] found full of lying."[91] And, in a civil case, *Jessup v. Crabb*, the court awarded a conditional judgment in Jessup's favor, but "because it is but one witness that speaks punctually to it, and...there is possibility of mistake," it promised to reopen the judgment if Crabb came forward with more evidence within a year, while in a breach of contract suit against a defendant who was "dead," another court postponed rendering judgment because "none present...can clearly answer for him." Finally, in Rhode Island, juries refused to give verdicts in the absence of an "indictment according to law" returned by a properly constituted grand jury.[92]

In short, when faced with the issue of controlling their rulers' discretion, Connecticut, New Haven, Plymouth, and Rhode Island behaved more like Massachusetts than Virginia. Like Massachusetts, the townspeople of the smaller New England colonies did not seek to control the law out of a need to promote the certainty and predictability needed for entrepreneurial investment. The impetus for control emerged mainly in matters of criminal law, where people feared interference in their daily lives. But the mechanisms of control were different: Connecticut, New Haven, Plymouth, and Rhode Island relied less on juries and more on codification of the law and on judicial adherence to norms of due process.

C. IN THEIR SEPARATE WAYS

We have so far seen how, to a significant extent, the law of the satellite New England colonies mirrored that of the Bay Colony. Even when the smaller colonies did not copy Massachusetts, they developed legal norms similar to one another's. But on one important set of issues—the relationship between church and state—they diverged from Massachusetts and from each other, although even here, convergence in the direction of uniform practice occurred.

As we saw earlier, the churches of Massachusetts received full support from and ultimately were under the full control of the state. When the centrifugal forces of Congregationalism produced schisms in local parishes, Bay Colony magistrates ultimately became involved, pushed parishioners into harmony, and used the coercive mechanisms of the law to enforce their will. Connecticut followed the same pattern as Massachusetts, even more rigorously. But Plymouth and Rhode Island, which were founded by people who believed in separation of church and state, strove with differing levels of success to preserve a church/state boundary.

1. Connecticut and New Haven.

At the heart of government control of religion lies taxation. Although Connecticut hoped that its people would support their ministers voluntarily, it was prepared from the outset to impose taxes. Thus, the General Court provided in 1644 that the residents of each town should be called together annually to provide for the ministry,

> that every man voluntarily set down what he is willing to allow to that end & use, and if any man refuse to pay a meet proportion, that he may be rated by authority in some just & equal way; and if after this any man withhold or delay due payment the civil power to be exercised as in other just debts.

A similar procedure was imposed to support scholars from Connecticut who were studying for the ministry at Harvard College.[93]

Townspeople who supported a church, of course, could come to court if the church mistreated them. In one case, for example, a man petitioned "for relief against the Church of Hartford, in regard of his censure of excommunication, wherein he affirms he has been wronged by the said Church." At least some excommunication cases appear to have involved religious differences, as in one in which the excommunicants were seeking a "way for the composing [of] their differences," and the court directed the church to find "some way that may effect the issuing [of] their sad differences."[94]

Needless to say, the judges did not always support dissidents. Thus, in one case in which some members who had left a church "ha[d] taken occasion unjustly to question the station and being of the said Church," the court held "that the said Church is the true and undoubted Church of Wethersfield," and it ordered the dissidents to accept that fact. At other times, judges might discipline both sides to a dispute; in a case involving schismatics in Middletown, for example, "there appearing such unsuitableness in their spirits," the court ordered both sides to obtain "another able, orthodox, and pious minister" who could bring them back together. In return for financial support, the clergy accepted its subordination. As one New Haven minister declared, "he did not judge it unlawful for a minister of the word to present his case to the judgment of the magistrate, for the determination of such civil controversies as may arise between themselves & others." Were it otherwise, the clergy would "be in worse case in that respect than other men,"[95] and for the Connecticut and New Haven clergy, power and standing in the community were more important than independence.

2. *Rhode Island and Plymouth.*

The liberty of individuals to work out their own relationship to God had led Anne Hutchinson, Roger Williams, and others to settle Rhode Island, and accordingly, they kept their churches entirely distinct from their government. Likewise, the leaders of the Plymouth colony strove to set up churches independent of government. Even more than the founders of Rhode Island, the Pilgrim fathers fit within a broad separatist tradition that directed true believers to keep themselves and their churches apart from the state and from state-supported churches, which by their inclusion of all subjects necessarily comprehended nonbelievers and other sinners.[96]

Rhode Island succeeded over time in maintaining the separation of church and state. Religious taxes were never imposed, and the judicial records of the colony contain none of the cases of enforced contribution, excommunication, schism, and subordination of the clergy that occurred in Connecticut and Massachusetts. Probably the ministers possessed less wealth.

Perhaps because Plymouth never progressed beyond being a poor, agrarian outpost, its religious institutions proved unable to maintain themselves without the aid of the state. The inhabitants of Rehoboth, for example, found it necessary to petition the General Court "to assist them in a way according to the orders of other colonies about them" in raising money for a minister. The signers of the petition alleged that the nonsigners contributed nothing to the church. Initially, the matter was resolved on a voluntaristic basis, when the town's magistrate promised that, if petitioners would pay their share of the church's cost on the basis of value of their estates, the nonsigners would pay theirs or he would personally make up the difference.[97]

But elsewhere, the magistrates had to turn to more coercive approaches. When the town of Marshfield petitioned for help in supporting the ministry, the General Court sent Miles Standish and John Alden to call a town meeting and "signify unto them the Court's desire is, that the inhabitants of the said town would take notice of their duties so as to contribute according to their abilities freely to the maintenance of the minister." Two years later, in 1657, the General Court by statute declared that every town was "engaged" to "the public worship and service of God" and authorized the levy of taxes for that purpose. And, two years after that, outright coercion was applied to the town of Yarmouth, when the General Court directed the calling of a town meeting so that "each particular man will freely engage towards" support of the minister. This time, however, the court was explicit when it provided that, if everyone did not "freely engage," four men would be chosen to levy on those who refused to contribute, and the constable directed to distrain their goods.[98] With this 1657 act and its subsequent enforcement, Plymouth was well on the path toward a religious polity nearly identical to that of its neighbor, Massachusetts Bay.

In sum, the law of the smaller New England colonies displayed a striking tendency to converge in the direction of the law of Massachusetts Bay. By 1660, Rhode Island continued to differ from the rest of New England in a significant respect: churches remained separate from the state and were not tax-supported. The five colonies also used different approaches to constrain the power of magistrates. Connecticut and Rhode Island, at least in criminal cases, required magistrates to proceed under legislative guidance and not to act outside the bounds of their legislative mandates. New Haven, Plymouth, and Rhode Island relied on rules of procedural due process to keep judges in check. Massachusetts Bay used codes, but more important, empowered juries to control the bench, and it backed up jury power by authorizing appeals to the General Court, which was structured to give dominance to the lower, popular house. More important than these differences in means, however, was the constitutional end that all five New England colonies shared in common—the use of some form of law to rein in judicial discretion.

In all other important respects, the five New England colonies shared the same law. Ultimately, that law was shaped by Puritan aspirations, which dominated society throughout New England, that families live together in godly communities where the faithful could watch over each other to promote the spiritual and moral welfare of all. Throughout New England, these aspirations pushed the law toward punishing those who behaved sinfully or rejected community norms. Unlike Virginia, early New England was not an individualistic, highly mobile society of single, young men geared toward doing whatever was needed to make money. Virginia, not New England, was the first place in America where market forces took root. New England's law, in contrast, provided early nurture to religious and moral values that still remain alive in America today.

6

THE BATTLE FOR MARYLAND

The first quarter century of Maryland's history uniquely reflects the main theme of this volume—that those who possessed political and economic control of a colony routinely used their power to steer that colony's law in directions that would further their ends and goals. Maryland was founded as a refuge for upper-class Roman Catholics, and its early law served their needs. Later, Puritans settled in Maryland, took control of its government, and attempted to impose New England law on the province. Then, Lord Baltimore, the Catholic proprietor, induced the government of Oliver Cromwell to return Maryland to his dominion. But Maryland had grown beyond the point at which Baltimore could exercise detailed control, and economic forces similar to those in Virginia pushed its planters to emulate the legal system of its southerly neighbor.

Early in the spring of 1634, as England was drifting toward high church Anglicanism under the leadership of Archbishop William Laud, sixteen Roman Catholic gentlemen, accompanied by their families and by two Jesuit priests, established a new colony in Maryland as a haven for the persecuted members of their faith. From the beginning, though, they were outnumbered by the Protestant laborers and servants who also accompanied them and, as a result, Catholicism's hold on Maryland was always tenuous.

At the outset, the Maryland colony was governed by Leonard Calvert, the younger brother of the proprietor, Cecilius Calvert, Lord Baltimore, whose title rested on a charter from Charles I. Governor Calvert immediately encountered opposition from William Claiborne, the occupant of Kent Island, which was located within Maryland's territorial boundaries, but which Claiborne sought to keep as part of Virginia, where he enjoyed significant political influence. Nonetheless, in 1637 Calvert took possession of the island, and the Maryland legislature attainted Claiborne for his crimes against the colony.

The onset of the Civil War in England emboldened Maryland's Protestants, and Claiborne, burning with revenge, retook Kent Island in 1644, at the same time that another Protestant rebel, Richard Ingle, angered at his arrest for treasonable words against the king, took control over St. Mary's, the colony's capital. But Governor Calvert regained full control over his brother's colony by 1648, after his brother had staved off an effort in England to revoke his charter. Leonard Calvert then went to England, and, in an effort to reach out to Protestants, Lord Baltimore replaced him with William Stone, Maryland's first Protestant governor.

Until Stone's appointment, Maryland's Catholic rulers had had to struggle with indigenous Protestants, Protestants from Virginia, and Protestants in England to retain their control. Stone further complicated matters when in 1649 he invited a group of some 500 Puritans to settle what is now Annapolis. As the proprietor's representative, he soon found himself on the defensive when the Commonwealth government in England appointed Maryland's old enemy Claiborne, the Puritan leader at Annapolis, and two Protestant sea captains to obtain the submission of the Chesapeake colonies. Claiborne and the Puritan leader went to St. Mary's in 1652, ejected Stone from the governorship, and sought to establish a new administration under their control. When Stone, under orders from Lord Baltimore, resisted, they appointed William Fuller as governor, and in 1655 civil strife broke out. The Puritan faction quickly won a decisive victory.

But resistance to Puritanism continued, and meanwhile, back in England, Lord Baltimore petitioned the Cromwell government for help. The regime directed the Maryland adversaries to come to an agreement, and they did. Baltimore regained full control of his province, and in 1657 he appointed Josias Fendell as the new governor, with instructions to forgive the past deeds of all parties and to treat them fairly and equally in the future. Fendell, however, proved disloyal when early in 1660 he resigned his commission as governor and accepted a new commission from the assembly; Baltimore, with the support of Charles II and assistance from the governor of Virginia, promptly replaced Fendell with his younger brother, Philip Calvert.[1]

The law of early Maryland reflected the colony's Roman Catholic origins, the chaos resulting from Puritan efforts to subvert Catholic rule, and the proximity of its huge neighbor, Virginia. The central question in Maryland's seventeenth-century legal history was whether Maryland would develop in some distinctively Catholic fashion, pattern itself on Puritan New England, or copy Virginia's law.

A. RELIGIOUS TOLERANCE—AND INTOLERANCE

From the outset, Lord Baltimore had understood that, if he wanted the Roman Catholic minority to be tolerated in Maryland, he would need to tolerate Protestants. Accordingly, he aspired to create a colony where Catholics and Protestants could live side by side together in peace. The principal foundation of his program was the Act Concerning Religion, personally drafted by Baltimore and ultimately promulgated in 1648. It provided "that no person whatsoever professing to believe in Jesus Christ [should] be molested for or in respect of his or her religion or the free exercise thereof."[2]

The act remained an important one. In one key case, *Proprietary v. Fitzherbert*, where the defendant was prosecuted for treason, sedition, and rebellious speeches, in that he "endeavor[ed] to seduce & draw from their religion the inhabitants assembled" at a militia muster, threatened to force a council member and his family to attend his church, and, as a result of his speeches, "caused several inhabitants of this province to refuse to appear at musters," the Maryland Provincial Court upheld a demurrer to the indictment based on the 1648 act. It agreed that "preaching & teaching is the free exercise of every churchman's religion" and that it constituted "neither rebellion [nor] mutiny to utter such words as is alleged." Similarly, when Protestant servants complained that their Catholic master had called Protestant ministers and Protestant books "the instruments of the devil," the court fined the Catholic master and required him to enter into a peace bond not to "offend the peace of this colony or of the inhabitants thereof by injurious & unnecessary arguments or disputations in matter of religion." And, when a Protestant man charged with bigamy and a Protestant minister who had performed the allegedly bigamous marriage requested "that a Protestant jury might pass on" the matters at issue, the court granted their request.[3]

But there were limits to the policy of toleration. Jews were one group outside those limits. Thus, when Jacob Lumbrozo, referred to in Maryland records as "the Jew Doctor," was asked about Christ's resurrection and answered, "That his Disciples stole him away," he was prosecuted for blasphemy. But since Lumbrozo was "by profession a Jew" and did not say "any thing scoffingly or in derogation of him Christians acknowledge for their Messiah," the prosecution ultimately was dropped. Likewise, when Quakers first appeared in Maryland in the late 1650s, they were whipped and fined and ordered into exile, and a general persecution of Quakers was directed. Judicial proceedings against Quakers, who "delud[ed] the people with visions & such like fancies very prejudicial to...peace & government,"[4] lasted only briefly and in the early 1660s simply ceased.

More important, Lord Baltimore's policy of toleration was not always followed during the periods of time when Baltimore himself was not in charge. In those occasional years when the Puritans ruled Maryland, they prosecuted people for religious offenses such as missing church or otherwise profaning the Sabbath. Similarly symptomatic of the religious conflict of the time was a prosecution for swearing.[5]

When they attained power, the Puritans also instituted the practice of prosecuting bastardy. For instance, in *Proprietary v. Palldin*, a woman received thirty lashes for giving birth to a bastard, while its father was required to give security "both for the keeping and bringing up of the said child." "[T]he usual custom" was that "the woman's oath would stand against" whomever she accused of fathering her child,[6] and thus when a female servant accused another servant of being the father of her child, the court issued an attachment against him, "forasmuch as he ha[d] been caught suspiciously and uncivilly with her and he obscure[d] himself from the sheriff." Likewise, a pregnant woman successfully sought support during pregnancy from the man she accused of fathering her child "according to the rank and quality she came into the Province."[7]

But men were not without remedies. Typically, they would suffer no penalty at all if they could prove they did not have intercourse,[8] and at least one court held there would be "no proof of a carnal copulation" without "sufficient evidence that had seen them Rem in Re." Even when intercourse was admitted, a man might go unpunished. Thus, there was a case in which Lucie Stratton came to Arthur Turner's "bed & put [her] hand under the cloths & took [him] by the private parts" and made a "faithful promise unto him to be his wife," which "made him act what he did." But then she refused to marry him because "she could not love him," saying "that he was a lustful man, a very lustful man, & that she never could be quiet for him." On these facts, the court ruled that she "ought to provide for & maintain the said child herself."[9]

Contrary to practice in New England, prosecutions against fornicators in Maryland were not truly about morality. For example, when Anne Williams accused Richard Smith of fathering her bastard, he called her an "impudent woman" and accused her of "scandalously cast[ing] aspersions upon" him. Nonetheless, he did "think it most mete for me to let her run on in her own perdition" and to "trust[] in the severe judgment of God against perjured persons." He therefore agreed "to take the child and maintain it" while denying paternity. Since Richard was willing to pay, the Maryland court, unlike New England courts, found it unnecessary to adjudicate his moral innocence or guilt and simply gave him the child, while giving Anne thirty lashes. Indeed, bastardy cases usually would be dismissed once it became clear that the public would not be chargeable with support of the bastard child. But in the mid-1650s, at the height of Puritanism's influence in Maryland, at least one couple was prosecuted for conceiving their child before marriage[10]—the fact that they would support their child did not erase their sin of premarital sex.

Once Puritanism entered Maryland's law, it remained, and the colony's courts periodically enforced Puritan values, though not too stringently. The law of adultery is illustrative. On the one hand, when Edward Hudson and the wife of Robert Holt were found guilty of having gone to bed together, they both were whipped for their "misdemeanors," while in a somewhat later case a grand jury indicted a defendant for "being a whore" for "bedding with a man" not her husband.[11] On the other hand, a member of the judiciary found guilty of "adultery, fornication, and ... [a] lewd and scandalous course of life" was only fined 5,000 lb. of tobacco, while another man who denied a charge of adultery was acquitted while his female accuser, who claimed she "yielded to his will" because he had "put [her] into a fear," was whipped.[12]

In other cases of sexual misconduct, the Maryland courts entertained defamation suits, as, for example, in *Hollis v. Boys*, where the defendant was charged with calling the plaintiff's wife a "whore." In another case in which a man reported to friends that "he had uncivil doings with" his girlfriend—"that he had layne with her," a jury returned a verdict for damages and also required the man to ask her forgiveness "in open court upon his knees."[13] Finally, when the Maryland courts enforced an agreement between a husband and wife to live apart,[14] they effectively applied Puritan law allowing unhappy couples to separate.

B. THE COMMON LAW AND THE RULE OF LAW

In Virginia and New England, as we have seen, common-law forms and common-law rules frequently were ignored in the early decades of settlement. According to one early historian, Maryland, in contrast, adopted the common law by statute perhaps as early as 1635—a mere year after the colony's initial settlement—and certainly no later than 1639.[15]

Pursuant to its adoption of the common law, Maryland established a complex and sophisticated judicial system modeled on that of England. In addition to the central provincial court and local county courts common to all the American colonies, Maryland even boasted manorial courts. Lawyers also were welcomed and given employment in Maryland, and a legal profession was quickly established; as early as the 1650s, a man could not act as an attorney unless he could demonstrate his qualifications if they were challenged, and in the 1660s, the provincial court began formally admitting lawyers to practice.[16]

Common-law vocabulary also appeared early in Maryland court records, and its use persisted thereafter. Among the words of art that appeared were "subpoena ad testificandum," "bill of exchange,"[17] "nuncupative" will, "non compos mentis," "dedimus potestatem," "estate of a felo de se," "executor," and "feoffees in trust." The Maryland Provincial Court even held that "an essoin may be granted upon a real action."[18]

Doctrines that are recognizably common-law rules of law also were adopted. Thus, the Maryland courts held that "a formal will" was "required for the passing of lands by testament,"[19] that a sheriff could not turn a chattel over to a plaintiff on a writ of replevin if the defendant claimed property therein, and that a writ of case could not be maintained on "a naked contract" without "consideration."[20] They also ruled that a husband could not alienate the property rights of his wife without her consent.[21] Meanwhile, the common-law doctrine of coverture manifested itself in rules that a woman could not act as attorney for her husband and that both husband and wife had to be joined in any suit to recover for her indebtedness.[22]

Likewise, the most important institution of the common law—the jury—became central to Maryland's legal order. Thus, a grand jury was summoned and returned indictments in the second month of Maryland's history for which there are extant court records,[23] and the first petit juries in civil and criminal cases appeared six years later.[24] A jury would be impaneled, except in proceedings in chancery or admiralty, at the request of either party.[25] Juries also could be impaneled on the motion of the court, as on one occasion, when a required quorum of judges was absent from court and "the Governor ordered that all causes should be tried by a jury of 12 men." Juries of twelve were required to render their verdicts unanimously.[26]

When litigants chose to try a case by jury, the court and the jury typically functioned harmoniously. There were some special verdicts in early Maryland,[27] as there were in England. There also were cases in which the "defendant…pleaded the general issue" and then "g[a]ve the special matter in evidence."[28] But, in most cases, juries simply returned general verdicts after hearing evidence and receiving a barebones charge to "give in a just and true verdict to the best of their knowledge upon the evidence…produced."[29] Juries could ask judges to deliver more detailed instructions on the law,[30] and counsel could also request the court to state the law "for the better satisfaction of the jury." In one case, a jury returned a plaintiff's verdict and left the issue of damages to the court.[31]

On rare occasions conflict between courts and juries did emerge. For example, one jury "not all agreeing" was sent out "to consider further" and then "returned their joint verdict," while in another case the court refused to permit a jury to consider a defense of untimeliness of a plaintiff's demand for payment when the demand was only one day late, and that, only because of "extremity of weather." The court "conceive[d] in equity no advantage ought to be taken thereupon." Similarly, when a jury declined to find that certain hogs belonged to a plaintiff, because the brands on the hogs did not perfectly match the plaintiff's brand, the court rejected the jury's verdict on the ground that "the plaintiff may have… relief in equity though the mark did not exactly appear to be his." And, in a homicide case, in which a jury found that the killer had acted "accidentally and unwittingly" and without "negligence or carelessness," the court nonetheless imposed a fine of 500 lb. tobacco. But in this instance the Lord Proprietor put any conflict between court and jury to rest by remitting the fine.[32]

Finally, the common-law writs and the forms of action emerged. As early as 1637/38 in Maryland, the language of a writ of assumpsit appeared in the records of the Provincial Court. Later in the same year, the court recorded "an action of debt" and "an action of detinue" and, four years later, "an action of trespass for hunting & killing…swine."[33] A plaintiff's failure to name the form of action would result "an abatement of the writ …according to the law of England." In other matters, a defendant sought judgment because the plaintiff had sued "him in a wrong action,"[34] and a writ was abated because "there can be no action of the case in any claim of dower," while an action of case to recover money due on an instrument "under…hand and seal," which instrument, however, the plaintiff had lost, was abated because "no such action can lie in this case, at the common law."[35] There is also a case involving a plaintiff's demurrer to a defendant's particular plea of the general issue on the ground that there was "no such plea to an action of trespass upon the case, the said plea being proper to an action of trespsss only." And, in one action of debt, the common law was followed closely, when a defendant proposed to defend by wager of law, to which the plaintiff took exception. At that point the court put the Commander of Kent to his oath, and he testified that the "defendant (according to the best of his judgment)" had "formerly taken a rash oath." The court then "received the plaintiff to prove his account by his own oath" and gave judgment for the plaintiff.[36]

Historians long have disagreed about the reasons for Maryland's early adoption of the common law. No one, however, doubts that the Lord Proprietor, Cecilius Calvert, favored its adoption, and one early historian, Bradley Johnson, argued that Lord Baltimore championed the common law, along with private property, religious toleration, and representative government, because it protected the rights of Englishmen. Observing that Lord Baltimore took sides with Oliver Cromwell during the English Civil War, Johnson inferred that Baltimore was disturbed by the efforts of Charles I in the 1630s to circumvent common-law rules, to promote the Anglican church, and to govern without calling Parliament. In short, Johnson portrayed Lord Baltimore as a precursor of eighteenth-century Whigs and Maryland's early adoption of the common law as an important step toward the creation of a nineteenth-century liberal state.[37]

But there is no need to be wedded to such a Whiggish interpretation. Perhaps the Maryland legislature adopted the common law not for grand political reasons, but only to make it clear that it was rejecting some alternative body of law. It might, for example, have wanted to reject martial rule of the sort that Dale's Laws had introduced into early Virginia. In fact, there was cause for concern that Maryland might turn to martial law. The Maryland charter gave its proprietor all the powers of a lord of an English palatinate, such as the bishop of Durham, to govern, if he chose, under martial law.[38] In an effort to attract investors and settlers, the leaders of the Virginia colony, it will be recalled, had repealed Dale's Laws and had promised in the late 1610s to govern by the king's law. Perhaps, the Maryland legislature's adoption of the common law in the 1630s reflected an analogous policy judgment—a judgment that may even have been patterned on the earlier judgment in Virginia.

The common law also faced a more immediate competitor in Maryland—namely, the law of the Roman Catholic Church. The Jesuits who came to Maryland quickly acquired a great deal of land for their order from the native inhabitants and thereby threatened to create an entity rivaling the proprietary government in wealth and power. They also claimed that they had a right to govern themselves under ecclesiastical law and that they were exempt from secular jurisdiction.[39]

For Lord Baltimore, many Catholic gentry, and the Protestant inhabitants of Maryland, a grant of such independence and power to the Jesuits
was unacceptable. For a half century prior to the settlement of Maryland, English Catholics had been divided into two groups. A reactionary
group, led by the Jesuits, had sought to undo the Reformation, restore the
Roman church to its old position in England, and return England fully
to the Roman fold. A more liberal group, to which Baltimore and most
upper-class Catholic gentlemen adhered, accepted the results of the Reformation, including its transfer of land from monastic to lay owners, and
asked for nothing more than toleration for their practice of their Catholic
faith.[40] It may well be that a legislative declaration that Maryland would
be governed by secular, common law was merely a way of indicating that
no place existed in the colony for ecclesiastical law or for the vast ecclesi-
atical power that the Jesuits wanted.

Whatever the reason for Maryland's quick adoption of the common
law, it did not adopt it in its entirety. Much of that law was inconvenient.
The people of Maryland did not need the full panoply of common-law
institutions and remedies, nor did they have the wealth to support them.
They did not, for example, need a separate chancery court. Accordingly,
until 1661, chancery jurisdiction was blended with that of the common
law in a single hierarchy of courts, which made the Provincial Court of
Maryland, for example, "a court of equity as well as law" and also gave
county courts jurisdiction to entertain "demands in Chancery," to regulate "hard conscience and extreme dealing... in point of equity," and to
invalidate contracts because of "negligence" of one of the parties.[41]

They also did not need fixed rules specifying the time and form of
appeals from local courts to the provincial court. Thus, a litigant did not
need to await a verdict or judgment in order to appeal, but could take an
appeal any time after suit had been filed, even after all the evidence had
been presented.[42] The effect of this practice was to give parties a form of
pretrial discovery of each other's evidence before a suit went to final trial.

Appeals to the provincial court were subject, in turn, to an ultimate
appeal to the upper house of the legislature, especially in suits "long
depending" with "many depositions... contradicting one the other." And
politically sensitive cases, such as those arising out of the civil strife of the
1640s, might be sent *ab initio* to the General Assembly or lower house.[43]

Other cases involved rejection of common-law procedures. Thus, in one early suit involving breach of an implied warranty of merchantability of a small quantity of tobacco, William Upton ignored common-law procedure and "complained by word of mouth" against Thomas Cornwallis, who "defended himself likewise by word of mouth." A decade after the Maryland legal system was up and running, plaintiffs could commence suit by "petition"[44] or could bring actions in equity even when a writ was available to cover the matter at hand. There were other instances in which writs either were not used at all or court clerks did not bother to record them.[45]

Still other cases turned on legislation modifying or rejecting substantive common-law rules. Maryland statutes required, for example, that debts due more than nine months be reduced to writing and that creditors not assign debts without their debtors' consent.[46] When Maryland law and English law were in conflict, as in a case concerning a rescue of a man charged with treason for supporting Parliament during the English Civil War, the province's attorney general delivered an opinion "that the court [was] bound to proceed according to the laws of this Province." Later judges agreed that Maryland was not bound by the law of England if "there be some law or precedent to the contrary in this Province."[47]

What mattered was not whether English jurisdictional, procedural, or substantive rules were followed. What mattered was judicial adherence to the rule of law—to the idea that fixed, certain rules applied by professional lawyers and impartial judges would govern relationships between political, economic, and religious competitors in Maryland.

Thus, Maryland lawyers and judges quickly developed the habit of raising and ruling on questions of law, recording their rulings for the future, and thereby creating a body of precedent from which indigenous law could develop. For example, when one defendant objected to the admission in evidence of a copy of a deed rather than the original "and thereupon cited the Lord Coke," the court "took time to consult," until the plaintiff produced the original. In another case involving nonpayment of customs duties, the defendant argued that, as an admiral of the province, he was not required to pay; the court voted, 4–3, that his defense was good.[48] In a contract action, the court ruled that a clause requiring performance to the plaintiff's personal satisfaction was invalid, while in a debt-collection case in which a defendant pleaded payment, "[t]he Court argued concerning the custom of the province...& found it to be...that the defendant in any case of debt might require to have the plaintiff's oath concerning the dueness of his debt demanded; & if the plaintiff should refuse to make oath that his debt were due, then the defendant might be received to discharge himself of his oath taken of the undueness of the debt." And, when the plaintiff refused to take an oath, the defendant was sworn, and the jury returned a verdict for the defendant.[49] Another case was postponed because the evidence was scanty and the court wanted the litigants to uncover better evidence.[50]

Courts would dismiss cases not only on factual but also on legal grounds, such as lack of jurisdiction or lack of legal responsibility. For example, a prosecution of one Mary Taylor, the wife of Robert Taylor, who was accused of incest with her brother, was dismissed because "the offense" was "done in Virginia under another government, and...the court or government here is conceived to have no cognizance." Likewise, Edward Prescott, accused of hanging a woman as a witch on a voyage from England, was acquitted when he proved that, although he owned the vessel on which she died, he was not in command and thus not involved in the hanging.[51]

Other cases arose out of the defense of the statute of limitations. Plaintiffs also were nonsuited when their writ gave defendants the wrong names, when they failed to serve their declarations at the time of service of their writs, and when they served process on only one of two joint administrators.[52] Likewise, actions were dismissed for "being wrong laid and stated," a writ was abated when it sought recovery of a debt in tobacco and the underlying bond was for a debt in sterling, and a bond issued by an administratrix was held void because she had "no lawful letters of administration."[53]

The need for recourse to law was urged by an attorney in a 1664 Maryland case, *Halfhead v. Nicculgutt.* The plaintiff was suing to force the defendant to perform as a servant and introduced an indenture in support of his claim. The defendant pleaded that a prior judgment had granted her freedom and that the plaintiff's oath that he had had no notice of the prior suit was "falsely and partially taken." The defendant then urged "that if orders of court be so weak and men's oaths so little available as thus upon every turn like to be brought to nothing, no man shall ever have either security for his debt or certainty of his cause whatsoever or howsoever ordered in so much that laws and courts to maintain the right of laws will seem excluded and totally overthrown."[54]

The Provincial Court agreed. It understood that the people of Maryland needed to be able to rely on its rulings both to ensure the security of their property and to guarantee their freedom from arbitrary political authorities. Hence, it made its rulings carefully. When faced, for example, with an issue about the scope of a sheriff's power to seize land in execution of a judgment, the Court, "being not desirous to ... make a precedent of this consequence without a full Council and the Lieutenant General be[ing] present," postponed a case to the next term.[55]

The Maryland courts consistently displayed sensitivity to following legal norms. Thus, when suit was brought against three partners, one of whom was a judge of the Provincial Court, the judge suggested "that he ought not to give any judgment in the cause, being himself a party in it," but the chief judge nonetheless demanded his view whether the province's legislation required the court to issue process for the plaintiff. The judge who thought he should recuse himself urged that the chief judge should issue process, and the court did so even though the third judge of the court dissented and thought otherwise. In yet another case, the court announced its adherence to the principle that a defendant ought "not to be forced to answer again to the same demand."[56] Finally, Maryland judges, understanding as did their counterparts in Virginia that "the power of justice" could be used as effectively as physical coercion to maintain the social order, used their contempt power with circumspection.[57]

C. LAW'S POLITICIZATION

In sum, Maryland took early steps to receive the common law and to abide by the rule of law. The reasons are not entirely clear. Certainly, one reason was to ensure that everyone would enjoy "security for his debt[s]"[58] and other property. But judges also adhered to the rule of law in nonproperty cases—criminal prosecutions, for example, in which the government was proceeding against individuals. Perhaps a Whiggish interpretation—that governing authorities in Maryland were striving to protect Catholic and other minorities from the political whims of a Protestant majority—is not far-fetched. As we shall soon see, however, politics could not be completely excluded from the legal process. When political-religious conflict developed in Maryland in conjunction with the Civil War in England, politics entered the courtroom.

The opening salvo took the form of a proceeding against Giles Brent, who was closely tied to Leonard Calvert, the colony's governor. Despite Brent's ties, an official of the colony filed a bill against him for failing to carry out a commission to lead an attack against some Native Americans. After informing the court that he intended to appeal to England and "seek my right at the hands of our sovereign the king," Brent interposed a legal defense—"that the said bill is uncertain & insufficient to require to be answered unto, in regard that by its form it appears not whether it be a prosecution civil or criminal, nor consequently will it permit him to make use (as proper for his answer) of such pleas & advantages as the law allows him severally according to the nature of the case."

The colony responded by bringing a civil action for damages, to which Brent entered a plea that his refusal to execute the commission was "made in all respects rightfully and warrantably" and that colony was not thereby damaged. Brent also challenged one of the jurors for "having expressed his inclination in the cause," but the court rejected the challenge. Nonetheless, the jury returned a verdict in Brent's favor, but judgment on the verdict was suspended on motion of the colony's attorney.

Next, the attorney filed a criminal bill, to which Brent pleaded that his "omission...[was] made...warrantably & upon good & just grounds" and put himself on the country. The attorney for the colony replied that Brent's answer was "not sufficieint in Law..., in regard it is a justification of the matter charged against him, by demurrer in point of law; which is not triable by the country, but to be determined by the court," and the court ordered Brent to put in a better answer. Brent finally pleaded "that his whole manage[ment] of the said business was guided by the best of his discretion for the honor & benefit of both his Lord [Baltimore] and the colony." The provincial court ultimately ruled in his favor in the criminal case and also accepted the jury verdict in his favor in the civil case.[59]

Soon after this case had ended, Leonard Calvert temporarily returned to England and left Giles Brent in his stead as acting governor. Under Brent's leadership, the provincial government then sought to institute a prosecution for treason against Richard Ingle, an ardent Protestant and ship captain who had spoken against the king and in favor of the parliamentary cause in the Civil War, but the grand jury refused to indict him. The Attorney General did succeed, however, in sequestering Ingle's goods for payment of royal customs duties, on the theory that the captain was preparing to sail for London where Parliament rather than the king would have collected the duties. Ingle's response was forcibly to seize control of St. Mary's, the colony's capital, while his Protestant ally, William Claiborne, recaptured Kent Island. When Leonard Calvert returned from England, he needed assistance from the governor of Virginia to regain control of his colony.[60]

Then, Leonard died, and Margaret Brent, Leonard Calvert's sister-in-law and Giles Brent's sister, was appointed his administratrix. She argued that her appointment gave her power not only to manage the Calvert estate but also to govern the colony. The provincial court, however, ruled otherwise. It responded "that the administrator ought to be looked upon as attorney both for recovering of rights into the estate, & paying of due debts out of the estate, & taking care for the estate's preservation; but not further." Only "his Lordship...[could] substitute some other as aforesaid."[61]

Meanwhile, Giles Brent remained politically active and active in the courts. In 1648, he brought suit against a defendant who had detained his cattle while the Protestant faction was in control of the colony. In that suit, the defendant answered "that he had the said cattle, by order of Justice, that then was upon the land, and detained them by virtue of that Justice." Brent replied "that those that pretended to have authority at that time [were] rebels & had no lawful authority to keep courts or exercise any other authority of judicature; & so consequently the said cattle [were] wrongfully taken & detained from him." The court, committed to using law to protect Catholic rights, agreed "that those that were then present upon the land, & that did hold courts, & exercise acts of judicature [were] rebels & their judgment [was] utterly illegal & unjust." A few months later Brent sought to increase his landholdings by seeking the "opinion of the [provincial] Court" whether forfeitures for rebellion went to the lord of the manor, of which he was one. The court responded affirmatively that "[t]he said rights usually belong[ed] to the Lord of Manor in England" and the words of Maryland's patent suggested the same ruling in the colony.[62]

But a few years later Brent was on the other side when the attorney general sued him about title to some cattle. By this time, it was clear, in the words of a man who had rescued prisoners from the sheriff's custody and declared that "he would obey no...order" from the sheriff, that "there was no law in the province & he would carry them away." In light of the lack of law, Brent did not try to interpose any legal defense but argued "that Captain William Clayborne a man now in power here claimed some interest in the wild cattle upon Kent and that the business did concern the whole Commonwealth and so [was] proper for an Assembly." The court agreed and referred the case to the General Assembly. Two years later, when Brent successfully brought suit for rent due for a boat "hired upon the Lord Proprietor's occasions," the attorney general moved that "(in respect the business did as he conceived relate to the Republic and therefore [it was] not proper that the charges thereof should be laid upon his Lordship)..., it might be given in with the other public charges the next Assembly to be allowed and cost into the public levy." The court agreed.[63]

Giles Brent and Richard Ingle were not the only residents of Maryland who found themselves involved with politicized courts. One John Price was fined 10,000 pounds of tobacco, for example, for armed rebellion against the province, as was Robert Clarke, whose plantation was seized in satisfaction of the fine. Five months later, however, Clarke was back in court seeking "relief in his exceeding deep distress not having any way of subsistence for himself and children." Rather than support his family out of public funds, the court returned his plantation to him, with a proviso that, if he should sell it, half of the proceeds should be paid toward his fine.[64] Other dissidents received lesser punishments, such as a whipping for striking a sheriff who was executing a judgment and fines for refusing to serve as jurors.[65] There was also an effort to suspend or disbar an attorney for his political activities.[66] Judges simply insisted that it was "the custom of England grounded upon the word of God that due respect be given to magistrates."[67]

Politics also intruded upon the adjudication of cases involving Dutch and other shipping at a time when England's Puritan government was embroiled in a war with the Netherlands. In one case involving a Dutch defendant who owned a vessel trading in the Chesapeake, before the captain

> could dispatch his business there, the State of England's ships came in and made prize of the said ships and goods. The defendant... suppose[d] it to be a casualty of the sea by which the said engagement [was] made void. The Court upon motion of the plaintiff [thought] fit to refer the business to a jury, twelve jurors were impaneled and their charge given as follows: viz., That they are to bring in a just and true verdict according to the evidences which shall be produced on either party whether the said ship being taken as she was in harbor be a casualty of the sea or no. The jury... [found] for the plaintiff the ship being in harbor was past the danger of the sea."[68]

With this verdict, local commercial interests and the Puritan government's war policies were vindicated, at the expense of the Dutch foreigners.

On the other hand, when a group of armed men seized a ship claiming it had unlawfully traded with the Dutch, the provincial court did not display anti-Dutch prejudices: it found that the armed men had acted without lawful authority, imposed fines, and ordered that the ship be returned to its owners. Similarly, when a grand jury refused to indict accused pirates, the court again opposed the local interests represented on the jury and banished the alleged pirates for being "dangerous & turbulent, & apt to raise mutiny & sedition."[69]

Cases involving Native Americans also produced political conflict in Maryland and resulted in judges standing in opposition to competing interest groups. The most important such case was *Colony v. Elkin*, which involved the murder of an Indian "at an Indian quarter in the woods."

> And the jury returned, not guilty. But explaining themselves that they delivered that verdict because they understood the last not to have been committed against his Lord's peace or the king's, because the party was a pagan, & because they had no precedent in the neighbor colony of Virginia, to make such facts murder &c. The Governor satisfied them that those Indians were in the peace of the king and his Lord & that they ought not to take notice of what other colonies did, but of the law of England &c. and therefore dismissed them to consider better of it.

> And then they returned, that they found him guilty of murder in his own defense, and being told that this implied a contradiction they returned to consider better of it; and then they returned for their verdict, that they found that he killed the Indian in his own defense.
>
> And the Governor willed that the verdict be not entered as a verdict, but that another jury be charged to enquire & try by the same evidence.[70]

In the second trial, "the Court importunately press[ed] & charg[ed] the jury...to proceed according to their evidence & conscience, & arguing & pleading the crime against the prisoner at the bar." And when one of the jurors "in an insolent manner upbraided & reproached the whole court...that [if an Englishman had been killed by the Indians there would not have been so much words made of it]," he was fined for his "great contempt & scandal." In the end, the second jury returned a verdict that the defendant was guilty of manslaughter.[71]

From 1642 to 1660, the period of the Civil War and Commonwealth in England, Maryland thus suffered significant civil strife, and that strife manifested itself in the courtroom. However, when Lord Baltimore was restored to full authority over his colony in the winter of 1657–1658, he took steps to restore harmony. Baltimore promised to pardon everyone's past political actions, to grant land to all applicants without discrimination, and to abide by the Act Concerning Religion, which granted toleration to all Christians. And, in *Proprietary v. Fitzherbert*,[72] which we already have examined, his agents in the colony abided by his promise and held that religious preaching constituted "neither rebellion [nor] mutiny." They thereby brought an end to Maryland's political and religious strife and enabled the colony's legal system to move forward in a more coherent direction.

D. BECOMING LIKE VIRGINIA

Ultimately, neither religion nor civil strife would dictate the direction of Maryland's legal development. After 1660, Roman Catholicism would be tolerated in Maryland, but the Catholic percentage of the population would decline, and the religion would become politically insignificant.

And, with Protestantism's ascendancy assured, the civil strife to which religious divisions had led would come to an end.

What determined the course of Maryland's legal development was the presence of the neighboring colony of Virginia. Maryland's neighbor to the south was much larger in area, population, and economic significance, and Maryland was dwarfed by Virginia in the same fashion that the smaller New England colonies were dwarfed by and became satellites to Massachusetts. Thus, one Maryland case, in which title depended on a "judgment in Virginia" that, one litigant claimed, had been obtained "unlawfully, and by the arbitrary power & favor of the then Governor," was remanded to the courts of the larger and more powerful colony in order to prevent "clashing or contradictory orders, or otherwise to engender any breach or just distaste between the two governments."[73]

Moreover, Maryland was a quarter-century younger than Virginia, and its early settlers could look to Virginia's experience for precedents with which to answer many problems that arose. In a major commercial case, for example, the provincial court took note of the "usual practice...in Virginia," while in *Colony v. Elkin*, which has already been discussed, a jury sought to acquit a man charged with murder of an Indian "because they had no precedent in the neighbor colony of Virginia, to make such facts murder &c."[74]

Most important, Maryland's economy took a direction virtually identical to Virginia's. With tobacco as its principal export crop, Maryland faced the same economic pressures that had determined the direction in which Virginia's law had evolved. Needless to say, Maryland's law evolved in much the same direction.

1. The Law of Servitude.

One subject on which similar economic conditions steered Maryland and Virginia in the same legal direction was the law of servitude. Harsh punishment of servants, especially runaway servants, was the norm. The standard penalty on a runaway's return was to to extend his period of service by twice the amount of time he had been absent. On occasion, runaways would also be whipped.[75] Servants who had defenses that might justify their release from service were returned to the jurisdiction from which they had escaped to assert them.[76]

The law was especially harsh on servants who spread false rumors and used scandalous or abusive language against their masters. Likewise, servants who stole property from their masters faced a broad range of penalties, including whipping and extra years of service. As was true in Virginia, a servant who charged her master with abuse and unlawful beatings had to remain with him, potentially subject to further abuse, while her case was pending.[77] Even a servant who proved a claim of abuse would not be freed, but would merely be transferred to a new master, at least for what courts considered relatively mild abuse—"three boxes on the ear" on one occasion and "a kick on the breech and a box on the ear and [a] threat…to knock her down with a chair" on another.[78] One servant, however, was freed when "the inveterate malice of her master" created an "eminent [sic] danger" that harm was "likely to ensue" if she remained in servitude, while another was freed after he had "been so ill treated…that the voice of the people crieth shame."[79]

It also should be noted that juries summoned to determine whether servants who met violent deaths had died from abuse typically were unwilling to convict masters of murder,[80] although one Maryland court imposed a fine for "unreasonable and unchristian-like punishment" on a master whose wife, after whipping a servant, "took water and salt, and salted her" while the servant, who later died, begged her "to use her like a Christian."[81]

In sum, servants who were abused either faced continuing, perhaps even worse abuse or, if they sued to remedy the abuse, they would remain under their master's control while suit was pending and, except in the most extraordinary of circumstances, would ultimately be sold to a new master.

On the other hand, the courts did deal fairly with servants who proved their claims. Thus, they recognized the freedom of servants who were manumitted by will or who had completed their term of service.[82] In such cases, judges even ordered the payment of wages for time worked following the end of the period of servitude. In cases of contracts to work for wages, courts ruled that masters had to pay for the time servants worked, even if they only worked for a portion of the time specified in the contract. In other cases, courts ruled that servants had been unlawfully bound and gave them their freedom, as in the case of a woman who had been brought from England to be a man's "Companion and bed fellow," not a servant.[83]

Judges also required masters to treat servants properly during the course of their servitude and to provide needed food, clothing, and medical attention, because, as the Maryland Provincial Court explained, "according to the law & custom of this Province no inhabitant thereof ought or may be deprived of all livelihood & subsistence."[84] In the early years of Maryland's settlement, masters also had to provide servants with corn, clothes, fifty acres of land, a hoe, and an axe at the end of their term. People entering into servitude also could bargain to receive a cash payment at the end of their term. But the provincial court would not permit servants to bargain with their masters once their term of service had begun; thus, it held that two servants who had agreed to produce a crop of tobacco in return for their freedom did not become free because "a bargain of that nature, between the master and his apprentice servants, was of no validity in law."[85]

McKane v. Gerrard[86] provides an apt illustration of the manner in which Maryland courts dealt with servants. McKean, an Irishman, alleged that he had been "taken by force out of his native country and brought here...and sold." He further claimed that he had served six years, was twenty-one years old, and had eight more years to serve, "which is contrary to the laws of God and man that a Christian subject should be made a slave." He then demanded a jury trial, but the jury returned a verdict that he was only nineteen years old and should serve until the age of twenty-one.

Like Virginia, Maryland extended the rule of law to servants. Servants had standing to bring lawsuits and received what on their face appear to have been fair, impartial adjudications from judges and juries. Nonetheless, servants remained under the domination of their masters. The jury's determination of McKane's age, for example, left him for the next two years at the mercy of a master who, if he wished, was free to obtain revenge for McKane's insolence in taking him to court. Unlike servants in Massachusetts, Maryland servants did not have the benefit of Puritan ideology or the presence of nearby kin and friends insisting that they be treated with restraint. The pressures of producing tobacco for the trans-Atlantic market steadily drove down the quality of their lives.

2. The Law of Debtor and Creditor.

The pressures of the marketplace also propelled Maryland's debtor-creditor law in the same directions as Virginia's. Like the planters of Virginia, those of Maryland needed capital to obtain new land, purchase additional servants, and obtain manufactured goods needed both to enhance tobacco production and to improve their standard of living. Thus, they had to borrow, and the prerequisite to borrowing was a legal system that facilitated creditors' collection of their debts.

Thus, in Maryland as in Virginia, the central concern of courts by the 1660s was assisting creditors in the collection of debts. Any historian who examines Maryland court records after 1660 will find that, as in Virginia, entries about debt collection vastly exceed entries for every other category of case combined. The judiciary and its subordinate officials had to assist creditors because, as the provincial court explained a few years after 1660, it was essential not to leave any creditor "remediless in the recovery of a just debt, which neither law nor equity can or will permit;" indeed, any "design of keeping" creditors "out of [their] debt[s]" would be "to the great discouragement of trade in this Province."[87]

One procedure that facilitated debt collection was confession of judgment, which existed in Maryland by the 1650s.[88] At times, the procedure simply involved a debtor's appearing in court and acknowledging his debt. At other times, it involved the appointment and empowerment of an attorney at the time of a loan to confess the debt on the part of the debtor on some specified date in the future. Of course, an even easier option for a debtor was not to appear when a creditor brought suit and to let a judgment by default be entered in the creditor's favor.

But entry of judgment did not guarantee payment of a debt. For one thing, in many cases "corn & other necessities" were "protected from executions," while in others creditors were required to bring writs of *scire facias* to get their judgments enforced. Most debtors, moreover, were not so cooperative as to confess judgment, but resisted in whatever ways they could. Often they simply ignored the suits against them. Even in cases begun by capias, the procedure for arrest and imprisonment for debt, debtors typically were released when no one put up security on their behalf and, in the words of one court, simply went "abroad at . . . liberty, and t[oo]k no course to satisfy the debt." Of course, freeing a prisoner or dissipating a prisoner's assets made a sheriff liable for the debt,[89] although that liability did not always translate into payment.

What remains unclear is whether this process produced rapid payment of debts. As procedures and processes for debt collection became routinized, debt collection became cheaper, but the rule of law's requirement that debtors receive the advantages of due and routine process also made collection slower. By the 1670s, it appears, "the way of proceedings" had become "so tedious that it ha[d] been to the ruin of many times both plaintiff and defendant and also [was] a great discouragement to any person to seek for his right at law."[90]

Nonetheless, by 1660, the main function of the legal order had come to be the conferral of public power on investors and moneylenders in the form of cumbersome mechanisms, such as requiring public notice from anyone planning to depart from the jurisdiction,[91] or identifying and marshaling assets that could be used to repay debts. Maryland law, that is, no longer had the main purpose that Lord Baltimore had perhaps intended it to have—creating a polity in which Catholics and Protestants could live side by side in harmony. After 1660, the rule of law took on a role, like the one it had in Virginia: the law became an instrument that individuals could commandeer to advance their own interests and through their interests, perhaps, the economic interest of the colony as a whole.

3. Law and the Emergence of a Commercial Economy.

The law, of course, played many roles in mid-seventeenth-century Maryland. First and foremost, judges had to maintain the law's supremacy. They had to deal, for example, with defendants who used profanity in open court or who refused to assist an officer such as a sheriff when called upon to provide aid. They also had to oversee the punishment of a broad spectrum of crimes, ranging from murder[92] and theft, especially of cattle and hogs,[93] through perjury to drunkenness, unlawful sale of liquor, and failure to plant the amount of corn specified by law.[94]

Like the courts of Virginia, the Maryland judiciary had to deal finally with matters of commerce that gave rise to a body of colonial commercial law. The buying, selling, and renting of servants was one such subject. On occasion, men failed to deliver the servants they had promised to provide or to return them in a timely fashion at the end of a lease.[95] Another issue that arose was whether a purchaser of a servant could recover damages from the seller if for some reason the servant had to be set free.[96] Finally, there was a case requiring a lessee of a servant to inform the lessor and defend the lessor's title if the servant sought freedom.[97]

Important issues of admiralty law also arose as the Chesapeake Bay developed into a major international port. One man, for example, sued a ship owner who failed to deliver his household goods and items from England necessary for his maintenance. Another issue was whether a seizure by an English warship of a Dutch merchant vessel anchored in the Chesapeake constituted a "casualty of the sea" that excused performance of a contract to sell the ship's goods. Maryland courts also had to deal with people who borrowed others' boats without making appropriate payments, and like Virginia, they dealt with them harshly. Indeed, in one such case decided only a decade and a half after Maryland's settlement, the provincial court reiterated a basic principle of property. The key fact in the case was that the boat owner had suffered no damages. Nonetheless, the court refused to dismiss the action because it "conceived that the said trespass could not be without some damage…, and likewise it would be a dangerous precedeynt…for that others might be thereby imboldened in actions of like nature."[98]

With cases such as these, the function of law in Maryland became clearer. Lord Baltimore, it will be recalled, may have counseled Maryland to protect property rights and abide by the rule of law to ensure that Roman Catholic and other minorities would be protected from the political whims of a Protestant majority. Maryland's law continued after 1660 to serve the function of protecting property, but it did so for a different reason—to provide investors and entrepreneurs with the clear, certain, and fixed rules they need to plan investments and commit resources to the colony's economy. With this new role, Maryland's law increasingly grew parallel to the law of Virginia, its giant neighbor to the south.

7

CONCLUSION

The Future of American Law

As early as 1660, some future directions that American law would take had begun to emerge. The laws of the various colonies had begun to converge, and regional and even continental uniformities had begun to appear. But, at the same time, important differences persisted, especially between the law of the Chesapeake region and the law of New England.

Consider, for example, Maryland and Virginia, which had completely different laws at the time of their founding. Virginia was governed under a sort of martial law that strove to empower a small governing class appointed by and working for the Virginia Company to exercise total control over the lives of settlers. The earliest Virginians enjoyed neither property rights nor the right to trial by jury, perhaps the two most important institutions of the common law. There was no place in early Virginia for any of the common law or for common lawyers.

Maryland, in contrast, adopted the common law by statute immediately after it was founded. The province thereupon established a complex and sophisticated judicial system modeled on that of England. It even boasted manorial courts. Lawyers were welcomed and given employment in Maryland, and a legal profession was quickly established; within three decades of the colony's founding, lawyers could not appear in court unless they had been formally admitted to practice by the provincial court. Private property and trial by jury were secure in Maryland, and the province's residents were guaranteed English freedom and even more—a freedom to practice their religious beliefs that was far greater than anything enjoyed in England.

There were twists and turns before 1660 in the legal history of the two colonies, especially in the history of Maryland, but the underlying similarities in their economies pointed their law in the same direction. Those who governed Virginia learned that they needed to adopt key elements of the common law, especially the law of private property, to induce settlers to immigrate and to provide hope, once they had arrived, that someday they would prosper. Virginia's rulers also found it necessary to turn to common-law institutions, such as the jury, so that local communities could govern themselves and thereby unburden central authorities, who could not afford the price of coercive military government once the colony had spread out into numerous plantations as far as one hundred miles from Jamestown.

The settlers of both Maryland and Virginia needed to encourage English investors to commit resources to America. After experimenting with other methods, the economic approach which they adopted was to buy the items they needed, especially capital items, from English merchants on credit and to pledge their future tobacco crops for payment. Both colonies adopted the common-law rules of debtor-creditor that were necessary to facilitate this borrowing. This common law was not especially favorable to creditors, but it did provide known and fixed rules that enabled creditors to calculate their chances of recovering money they lent and therefore the terms and conditions on which to lend it. Maryland and Virginia courts also spent considerable time on debt collection cases; indeed, they spent more time on them than anything else, regularly postponing them from term to term. Although the sense one obtains from the court records is that debt collection often was a process of a creditor's bargaining, postponing collection, or accepting less than the full amount due rather than standing effectively on her legal rights, it was centrally important that the judicial process facilitated this bargaining and through it the maintenance of a credit system that kept English capital flowing into the Chesapeake.

The tobacco economies of Maryland and Virginia shared another common need—the need for servile labor. Before 1660, most servants were young white men from the British Isles; the importation of large numbers of African slaves occurred later. Both jurisdictions accordingly developed a parallel law of servitude to accommodate their shared need. Their law was brutally harsh so as to compel servants to work, while at the same time remaining sufficiently fair so as not to discourage servants from immigrating.

Convergence also occurred among the legal systems of the five colonies established in New England prior to 1660. All five had strong religious roots, although those roots were somewhat different. Anne Hutchinson and Roger Williams, for instance, were forced out of Massachusetts and into Rhode Island because they would not accept all of the Bay Colony's particular Puritan beliefs; John Davenport, on the other hand, founded a separate colony in New Haven because Connecticut and Massachusetts were not sufficiently strict in their Puritanism. The legal orders of Connecticut, Massachusetts Bay, and New Haven all created tight links between towns and their churches, whereas those of Plymouth and Rhode Island initially strove to keep church and state separate, although Plymouth ultimately failed in its strivings.

The centrality of religion nonetheless produced much in common in the law of these five jurisdictions. People in all five colonies faced a common issue—how to control the discretion of magistrates. Everyone agreed that New England should be ruled by law, but they disagreed about what that law should be. The magistrates wanted to rule by the law of God. Most of the common people, on the other hand, found God's law ill-defined, ambiguous, and indefinite. Its vagueness, the people discerned, gave magistrates a broad discretion to resolve legal disputes and other issues however they wished. The common people wanted the law embodied in clearly written codes that everyone could interpret easily and uniformly and that left whatever discretionary power remained in the hands of local communities.

In 1648–1649, the people of Massachusetts won the battle in their jurisdiction. In 1648, after years of study and work, the Bay Colony's legislature adopted a code of laws that dealt with the main issues its legal system confronted. The code represented a compromise between proponents of the law of God and proponents of alternative rules, but to the extent the compromise left anyone with discretion, it was not the magistrates. By statute in 1649, the Massachusetts General Court provided that when a local jury sitting on a case disagreed with magistrates, the case would proceed on appeal to the General Court where the two houses sitting together would resolve it. Because the deputies in the elected lower house outnumbered the magistrates in the upper house by about three to one, the 1649 legislation insured that Massachusetts would be governed by clear, preexisting law unless the representatives of the local towns who controlled the General Court decided otherwise.

Like the people of Massachusetts, those of the smaller New England colonies—Connecticut, New Haven, Plymouth, and Rhode Island—strove to control their rulers' discretion, especially in matters of criminal law, where people feared interference in their daily lives. Connecticut, as we have seen, codified its penal laws even before Massachusetts did, whereas Rhode Island refused to prosecute people unless its legislature had enacted a statute declaring specific conduct criminal. New Haven and Plymouth used both codes and concepts of due process to constrain their magistrates. Constraining magistrates was a practice in which the people of all five New England colonies found it necessary to engage in some form.

The religious roots of New England produced an economy quite different from that of the Chesapeake and resulted in a different approach to debtor-creditor law and to the law governing servants and other underclasses. New England was settled by families, and the family farm rather than the plantation long remained the foundation of an essentially subsistence rather than cash-crop economy. Young male, immigrant servants were not the norm as they were in the Chesapeake; most servants were the children of people who lived in the neighborhood. Thus, the brutal laws of Maryland and Virginia were not required for the regulation of New England's servants, nor could they have been enacted given the tendency of parents to protect their children. Indeed, the law generally protected children in New England, whereas it did not in the Chesapeake. It also gave greater protection to women.

New England's subsistence farmers also appear not to have shouldered a level of debt comparable to that of Chesapeake planters. New Englanders paid for their imported goods largely through the region's ocean-going trade, which, in turn, was supported mainly by surplus foodstuffs from its subsistence farms. Farmers appear to have bartered for the imported goods they needed. They may have had no choice. Seventeenth-century New England court records are not filled with the debt collection cases that were so common in the Chesapeake, and there is no basis for inferring, as there is in the Chesapeake, that those who made the law of New England consciously strove to manage a debt-collection and credit-facilitating legal system, although they did aspire to advance mercantile interests in New England's port towns.

By 1660, in short, two regional bodies of law had begun to emerge in the continental English colonies—one in the North and one in the South. The North's law already was more egalitarian; the South's, more hierarchical. The South treated its underclasses brutally, with the economic interest of the master class as the sole restraint on that brutality. The men of the North may not always have treated their women, children, or servants kindly, but the law required them to display greater moderation. The Southern economy depended on the export of a cash crop, and the South's law reflected that economic reality. New England law promoted family farms, and those farms dominated the region, except in port towns like Boston, Providence, and New Haven, where the law was already facilitating the growth of mercantile capitalism.

Puritanism set the tone for much New England law, especially the law of crime. For the few years that Puritans wielded political power in Maryland, they likewise used their power to criminalize departures from their moralistic norms. Prior to 1660, they exercised no similar power in Virginia, although, as we shall see in a future volume, after 1660 they would.

The differences between the law of the Chesapeake and the law of New England, as of 1660, thus were real and substantial. But even these two diverse legal cultures shared a common commitment to govern under the rule of law and to extract governing law from their English legal heritage. By 1660, elements of English common law were in use everywhere in America. At a minimum, in New England, the common law constituted a familiar baseline that could serve definitional functions without anyone's having to sit down and write a legal dictionary. At a maximum, in Maryland, the common law had the force of statute behind it, and courts adhered to it rigidly.

We might think of colonial American law in 1660 as reflecting a sort of nascent federalism, with law being pushed toward uniformity, on the one hand, and toward diversity, on the other. But this nascent federalism differed from modern federalism in at least two profoundly important respects. First, no court or other formal institution with coerceive power, comparable to the Supreme Court of the United States, sat above the individual colonies and required their law to be uniform. Second, the mid-seventeenth-century North American colonies lacked nongovernmental institutions, such as an organized bar or a structured system of legal education, that generated a cadre of practicing attorneys with like-minded professional values.

Local legislatures had greater authority over the law than any other institution anywhere in British North America as of 1660. Every colony had established a formal legislative body by that date, and six out of seven of those bodies had enacted legislation, of greater or lesser extent, codifying their law. The seventh legislature, that of Maryland, had by statute declared the common law to be that province's governing rule insofar as local conditions warranted. In every one of the mainland colonies, in short, local legislatures had asserted a power to make law.

Such local legislative power obviously had vast centrifugal potential. But that potential went unrealized. Although economic and ideological differences among the colonies produced some important divergence in their laws, the common culture that all Englishmen shared began to set them on an essentially common course. No one came to North America seeking to abandon in their entirety their English ways; even the most radical Puritans were prepared to transport to New England most of the society and culture they had known in Old England. Moreover, those who governed had little leisure to ponder in detail and select carefully the precise rules by which to govern. It was easier simply to adopt common law rules and procedures with which they were familiar.

But they could not adopt the common law wholesale. The settlers of New England wished to create a different religious order than that of the mother country, while all the colonies, especially Virginia and Maryland, confronted different economic conditions than their people had known at home. They accordingly had to make some changes in the law. All the North American colonies, that is, faced a circumstance unknown in England—the need for legislation. In all the mid-seventeenth-century continental outposts, some entity had to identify what the society's governing rules would be.

At an early date, societal forces on the ground in all the British North American colonies thus gave legislation a preeminence in American law that it had lacked in England. This legislative foundation, which was shared by all American law, marked it as distinctively American rather than English. The legal systems of all the colonies also were similarly grounded in the common law. But those legal systems were not identical: the religious values that had motivated the early New England settlers and the economic conditions confronted by those in the Chesapeake gave the law of those regions distinctive characteristics that would persist for years to come.

Notes

Introduction

1. Willard Hurst was, of course, the leading student, but he did not write about the colonial period.
2. William N. Eskridge, Jr. and Philip P. Frickey, "An Historical and Critical Introduction to *The Legal Process*," in Henry M. Hart, Jr. and Albert M. Sacks, *The Legal Process: Basic Problems in the Making and Application of Law*, eds. William N. Eskridge, Jr. and Philip P. Frickey (Westbury, N.Y.: Foundation Press, 1994), li, liii.
3. Among the major works by the four authors on the colonial period were Julius Goebel, Jr. and T. Raymond Naughton, *Law Enforcement in Colonial New York: A Study in Criminal Procedure (1664–1776)* (New York: Columbia University Press, 1944); Julius Goebel, Jr., "King's Law and Local Custom in Seventeenth Century New England," *Columbia Law Review*, 31 (1931), 416; George L. Haskins, *Law and Authority in Early Massachusetts: A Study in Tradition and Design* (New York: Macmillan, 1960); Mark de Wolfe Howe ed., *Readings in American Legal History* (Cambridge, Mass.: Harvard University Press, 1949); Joseph H. Smith, *Appeals to the Privy Council from the American Plantations* (New York: Columbia University Press, 1950); Joseph H. Smith, ed., *Colonial Justice in Western Massachusetts (1639–1702): The Pynchon Court Record* (Cambridge, Mass.: Harvard University Press, 1961). Note should also be taken of the work of Richard B. Morris, *Studies in the History of American Law, with Special Reference to the Seventeenth and Eighteenth Centuries* (New York: Columbia University Press, 1930), and

Government and Labor in Early America (New York: Columbia University Press, 1946).

4. Elwin L. Page, *Judicial Beginnings in New Hampshire, 1640–1700* (Concord: New Hampshire Historical Society, 1959), xiv.

5. Even in a civil law system such as that of France, which purports to comprehend the entirety of its law in legislation, it is essential to apprehend the interpretive function of the judiciary. *See* Mitchel de S.-O.-L'E. Lasser, *Judicial Deliberations: A Comparative Analysis of Judicial Transparency and Legitimacy* (Oxford: Oxford University Press, 2004), 27–61.

6. *See* J.H. Baker ed., *The Reports of Sir John Spelman*, 2 vols. (London: Selden Society, vol. 93–94, 1976–1977), I: xvii; ibid., II: 5.

7. In 1987, the Oxford University Press committed itself to the publication of *The Oxford History of the Laws of England*. *See* Sir John Baker, *The Oxford History of the Laws of England: Volume VI, 1483–1558* (Oxford: University Press, 2003), v. So far, two volumes have appeared. See ibid.; R. H. Helmholz, *The Oxford History of the Laws of England: Volume I, The Canon Law and Ecclesiastical Jurisdiction from 597 to the 1640s* (Oxford: University Press, 2004).

8. Paul S. Reinsch, *English Common Law in the Early American Colonies* (Madison: University of Wisconsin Press, 1899), 6, 8.

9. *See, e.g.,* Cornelia H. Dayton, *Women Before the Bar: Gender, Law, and Society in Connecticut, 1639–1789* (Chapel Hill: University of North Carolina Press, 1995); Douglas Greenberg, *Crime and Law Enforcement in the Colony of New York* (Ithaca, N.Y.: Cornell University Press, 1976); David T. Konig, *Law and Society in Puritan Massachusetts: Essex County, 1629–1692* (Chapel Hill: University of North Carolina Press, 1979); Bruce H. Mann, *Neighbors and Strangers: Law and Community in Early Connecticut* (Chapel Hill: University of North Carolina Press, 1987); William M. Offutt Jr., *Of "Good Laws" and "Good Men": Law and Society in the Delaware Valley, 1680–1710* (Urbana: University of Illinois Press, 1995); A. G. Roeber, *Faithful Magistrates and Republican Lawyers: Creators of Virginia Legal Culture, 1680–1810* (Chapel Hill: University of North Carolina Press, 1981); Deborah A. Rosen, *Courts and Commerce: Gender, Law, and the Market Economy in Colonial New York* (Columbus: Ohio State University Press, 1997).

10. On slavery, for example, *see* John B. Boles, *Black Southerners, 1619–1869* (Lexington: University of Kentucky Press, 1983); Winthrop D. Jordan, *White over Black: American Attitudes Toward the Negro, 1550–1812* (Chapel Hill: University of North Carolina Press, 1968); Edmund S. Morgan, *American Slavery, American Freedom: The Ordeal of Colonial Virginia* (New York: W.W. Norton, 1975); Philip D. Morgan, *Slave Counterpoint: Black Culture in the Eighteenth-Century Chesapeake and Low Country* (Chapel Hill: University

of North Carolina Press, 1998); Thomas D. Morris, *Southern Slavery and the Law, 1619–1860* (Chapel Hill: University of North Carolina Press, 1996). On women, *see* Kathleen M. Brown, *Good Wives, Nasty Wenches, and Anxious Patriarchs: Gender, Race, and Power in Colonial Virginia* (Chapel Hill: University of North Carolina Press, 1996); Dayton, *Women Before the Bar*; Mary Beth Norton, *Founding Mothers and Fathers: Gendered Power and the Forming of American Society* (New York: Alfred A. Knopf, 1996); Marylynn Salmon, *Women and the Law of Property in Early America* (Chapel Hill: University of North Carolina Press, 1986). A classic work, dealing generally with law and labor, is Morris, *Government and Labor in Early America.* Another useful work of social history grounded in legal sources is David H. Flaherty, *Privacy in Colonial New England* (Charlottesville: University Press of Virginia, 1972).

11. One must begin with the corpus of Willard Hurst's work and then turn to such classics as Morton J. Horwitz, *The Transformation of American Law, 1780–1860* (Cambridge, Mass.: Harvard University Press, 1977). There is also my own *Americanization of the Common Law: The Impact of Legal Change on Massachusetts Society, 1760–1830* (Cambridge, Mass.: Harvard University Press, 1975). The scholarship on nineteenth-century American law is elegantly and comprehensively summarized in Lawrence M. Friedman, *A History of American Law* (New York: Simon & Schuster, 3rd ed. 2005).

12. The word "societal" is meant to incorporate political, economic, intellectual, and religious variables. Law not only reflects such variables but also affects them.

13. The best analysis of the primacy of religious values and their relation to profit in New England is Virginia DeJohn Anderson, *New England's Generation: The Great Migration and the Formation of Society and Culture in the Seventeenth Century* (Cambridge: Cambridge University Press, 1991). *See also* Stephen Innes, *Creating the Commonwealth: The Economic Culture of Puritan New England* (New York: W.W. Norton, 1995); Stephen Innes, *Labor in a New Land: Economy and Society in Seventeenth-Century Springfield* (Princeton: Princeton University Press, 1983); John Frederick Martin, *Profits in the Wilderness: Entrepreneurship and the Founding of New England Towns in the Seventeenth Century* (Chapel Hill: University of North Carolina Press, 1991). On the lesser prominence but nonetheless continuing significance of religion in Virginia, *see* James Horn, *Adapting to a New World: English Society in the Seventeenth-Century Chesapeake* (Chapel Hill: University of North Carolina Press, 1994), 381–418. *See also* Darrett B. Rutman and Anita H. Rutman, *A Place in Time: Middlesex County, Virginia, 1650–1750* (New York: W.W. Norton, 1984), 52–60.

14. *See* Bradley T. Johnson, *The Foundation of Maryland and the Origin of the Act Concerning Religion of April 21, 1649* (Baltimore: Maryland Historical Society, 1883).

15. *See* John Phillip Reid, *Rule of Law: The Jurisprudence of Liberty in the Seventeenth and Eighteenth Centuries* (DeKalb: Northern Illinois University Press, 2004).

Chapter 1

1. *See* James Horn, *A Land as God Made It: Jamestown and the Birth of America* (New York: Basic Books, 2005), 40–42, 236; Charles M. Andrews, *The Colonial Period of American History*, 4 vols. (New Haven: Yale University Press, 1934–1938), I: 124.
2. David H. Flaherty ed., *For the Colony in Virginea Brittania: Lawes Divine, Morall and Martiall, etc.* (Charlottesville: University of Virginia Press, 1969), 15, 17–19, 23–24. Spelling and punctuation have been modernized in all quotations.
3. *See* James Horn, *Adapting to a New World: English Society in the Seventeenth-Century Chesapeake* (Chapel Hill: University of North Carolina Press, 1994), 31–38, 139; Edmund S. Morgan, *American Slavery, American Freedom: The Ordeal of Colonial Virginia* (New York: W.W. Norton, 1975), 407–408.
4. *See* Horn, *Adapting to a New World*, 137–138; Morgan, *American Slavery, American Freedom* 158–159, 162.
5. Flaherty ed., *Lawes*, 9–10.
6. Ibid., 11, 13, 14.
7. Ibid., 19, 20.
8. David Thomas Konig, "'Dale's Laws' and the Non-Common Law Origins of Criminal Justice in Virginia," *American Journal of Legal History*, 26 (1982), 354, 364, 367, 375. *See* Horn, *A Land as God Made It*, 74–75.
9. Warren Billings, "The Transfer of English Law to Virginia, 1606–1650," in K. P. Andrews, N. P. Canny, and P. E. H. Hair eds., *The Westward Enterprise: English Activities in Ireland, the Atlantic, and America, 1480–1650* (Detroit: Wayne State University Press, 1979), 215. In a closely researched study, for example, Elizabeth Haight agrees that Virginians exhibited a "deeply ingrained reverence for law" that allowed judges to exercise an ethic of flexible paternalism, more intent on resolving conflict than coercing obedience. Instead of seeing a wide chasm between elite leaders and ordinary planters, Haight describes justices of the peace as conciliators whose effectiveness lay in their deep horizontal and vertical ties to the local population. Elizabeth Stanton Haight, "Heirs of Tradition/Creators of Change: Law and Stability on Virginia's Eastern Shore, 1633–1663" (Ph.D. diss.: University of Virginia, 1987). Terri Snyder's work shares Haight's social history methodology as well as her conclusions about law's stabilizing effect. In addition, her account of household violence also highlights local courts' effectiveness at restraining everyday

violence. Terri Lynne Snyder, "'Rich Widows are the Best Commodity this Country Affords': Gender Relations and the Rehabilitation of Patriarchy in Virginia, 1660–1700" (Ph.D. diss.: University of Iowa, 1992); Terri L. Snyder, "'As If There Was Not Master or Woman in the Land': Gender Dependency and Household Violence in Virginia, 1646–1720," in Christine Daniels and Michael V. Kennedy eds., *Over the Threshold: Intimate Violence in Early America* (New York: Routledge, 1999).

Much of the recent work done on the social history of Virginia law, such as that just cited, can be traced to Stanley Katz's call for just such work in his review essay, "The Problem of a Colonial Legal History," in Jack P. Greene and J. R. Pole eds., *Colonial British America: Essays in the New History of the Early Modern Era* (Baltimore: Johns Hopkins University Press, 1984). For a more recent review of the field, *see* Terri L. Snyder, "Legal History of the Colonial South: Assessment and Suggestions," *William and Mary Quarterly*, 50 (3d ser. 1993), 1, 18–27.

10. Christopher L. Tomlins, "Introduction: The Many Legalities of Colonization: A Manifesto of Destiny for Early American Legal History," in Christopher L. Tomlins and Bruce H. Mann eds., *The Many Legalities of Early America* (Chapel Hill: University of North Carolina Press, 2001), 6. Thus, David Konig's chief goal in his article on Dale's Laws is to link the harsh character of seventeenth-century criminal justice in Virginia with the martial practices of Tudor England instead of with English common law. Konig, "'Dale's Laws,'" 360. The same impulse animates those accounts that favor a more tolerant picture of Virginia's courts. Thus, Elizabeth Haight finds reverence for law to have been one of the cultural parcels brought with migrants to Virginia from county court culture in England, Haight, "Heirs of Tradition," 423, while Warren Billings investigates the links between the law of apprentices and the law of slavery in seventeenth-century Virginia in order to show their divergence from the common law's treatment of apprentices and its customary respect for property rights. Warren Billings, "The Law of Servants and Slaves in Seventeenth Century Virginia," *Virginia Magazine of History and Biography*, 99 (Jan. 1991), 45–62. Similarly, Bradley Chapin's investigation of whether criminal law was administered more by judgment of magistrates than by adherence to statute is grounded in questions of how perfectly the common law was "transported," "transplanted" or "received" by seventeenth-century Virginians, Bradley Chapin, *Criminal Justice in Colonial America, 1606–1660* (Athens: University of Georgia Press, 1983), 146–148. Thus, it is not so much the character of the administration of justice that is at issue, but its derivation from that of early seventeenth-century England. *See also* James Horn, *Adapting to a New World: English Society in the Seventeenth-Century Chesapeake* (Chapel Hill: University of North Carolina Press, 1994) (arguing that much in Virginia society was an attempt to recreate English culture on the frontier).

11. *See* Horn, *A Land as God Made It*, 210.

12. *See* Horn, *A Land as God Made It*, 238, 246, 280–284; Konig, "Dale's Laws," 354.

13. In discussing the origins of private property in Virginia, no one has improved on the classic work of Andrews, *Colonial Period*, I: 124–125, 128–133.

14. *A Briefe Declaration of the Plantation of Virginia*, in H. R. McIlwaine ed., *Journals of the House of Burgesses of Virginia, 1619–1658/59* (Richmond: Colonial Press, 1915), 28, 36.

15. *See* Order re Savage, Gen. Ct. 1624/25, in *Minutes of the Council and General Court of Colonial Virginia*, 2d ed., ed. R. B. McIlwaine (Richmond: Virginia State Library, 1979), 48 (prohibiting trade with Indians); Petition of Marshall, Gen. Ct. 1626, in *Minutes of General Court*, 99 (setting price of corn); Order re Prices, Gen. Ct. 1623, in *Minutes of General Court*, 5 (setting price of alcoholic beverages); Rex v. Yardley, Gen. Ct. 1623, in *Minutes of General Court*, 5 (condemnation of goods sold at excessive price); Order re Persons Remaining at Home, Gen. Ct. 1624, in *Minutes of General Court*, 18. *Cf.* Condemnation against Woodall, Gen. Ct. 1625, in *Minutes of General Court*, 71–72 (colony seizes badly needed medicines and promises to send owner in England "so much ready money as it cost with such reasonable profit as shall be to his content").

16. Petition of Tucker, Gen. Ct. 1626, in *Minutes of General Court*, 115; North v. Williams, Northampton County Ct. 1634, in *County Court Records of Accomack-Northampton, Virginia, 1632–1640*, ed. Susie M. Ames (Washington, D.C.: American Historical Association, 1954), 13. *See* Order re Weston, Gen. Ct. 1626, in *Minutes of General Court*, 109 (sale of fish at "reasonable rates"); Petition re Vessel Marmaduke, Gen. Ct. 1626, in *Minutes of General Court*, 127 (prohibition on "indirect bargains"); Order re Vessels at James City, Gen. Ct. 1626, in *Minutes of General Court*, 121 (order regulating resale of goods); Estate of Howe, Northampton County Ct. 1638, in *Records of Accomack-Northampton, 1632–1640*, at 118–119 (order re planting corn). *See also* Deposition against Richard Crocker, Gen. Ct. 1626/27, in *Minutes of General Court*, 132 (accuses Crocker of saying "that many great men went aboard ships and bought many goods & sold them at an unreasonable rate again").

17. *See, e.g.*, Laws of October 10, 1629, Act V, in *The Statutes at Large; Being a Collection of all the Laws of Virginia from the First Session of the Legislature in the Year 1619*, ed. William W. Hening (New York: R. & W. & G. Bartow, 1823), I: 141 (tobacco); Laws of August 21, 1633, Act I, in Hening, *Statutes*, I: 209–213 (tobacco); Laws of January 6, 1639/40, Act IX, in Hening, *Statutes*, I: 226 (tobacco); Laws of November 20, 1645, Act IV, in Hening, *Statutes*, I: 301 (millers); Laws of November 1647, Act IX, in Hening, *Statutes*, I: 347 (corn); Laws of August 21, 1633, Act IX, in Hening, *Statutes*, I: 218 (female cattle).

18. Order of Governor and Council, Gen. Ct. 1626, in *Minutes of General Court*, 104, 106–107; Order re Mountney, Northampton County Ct. 1641, in *County*

Court Records of Accomack-Northampton, Virginia, 1640–1645, ed. Susie Ames (Charlottesville: University Press of Virginia, 1973), 121. *See* Appointment of Menefrie, Gen. Ct. 1626, in *Minutes of General Court*, 109–110.

19. *See* Order re Mountney, Northampton County Ct. 1641, in *Records of Accomack-Northampton, 1640–1645*, at 121; Order re Hoskins, Northampton County Ct. 1641, in *Records of Accomack-Northampton, 1640–1645*, at 121.

20. Statement of Crowdicke, Gen. Ct. 1626, in *Minutes of General Court*, 113–114. *Accord*, Statement of Cawfey, Gen. Ct. 1626, in *Minutes of General Court*, 114.

21. Order of General Court, Gen. Ct. 1626, in *Minutes of General Court*, 114. *See* Order re Vessels at James City, Gen. Ct. 1626, in *Minutes of General Court*, 121; Laws of February 21, 1631/32, Act XLIII, in Hening, *Statutes*, I: 172; Laws of September 8, 1632, Act XXXI, in Hening, *Statutes*, I: 194.

22. Susan M. Kingsbury ed., *Records of the Virginia Company of London*, 4 vols. (Washington, D.C.: Government Printing Office, 1906–1935), III: 92. *See* Konig, "Dale's Laws," 354.

23. Lyon G. Tyler ed., *Narratives of Early Virginia, 1606–1625* (New York: Charles Scribner's Sons, 1907), 263; *Records of Virginia Company*, III: 479–480.

24. The following discussion is based on the report of Rex v. Sharpless, Gen. Ct. 1624–1625, in *Minutes of General Court*, 14, 21, 61, and on Konig, "Dale's Laws," 369–370.

25. Rex v. Sharpless, Gen. Ct. 1624, in *Minutes of General Court*, 14 (emphasis in original).

26. Five months later, at least, Sharpless's ears were gone, and questions about the proceeding were being asked. *See* Rex v. Sharpless, Gen. Ct. 1624–1625, in *Minutes of General Court*, 21, 61.

27. *See* Rex v. Barnes, Gen. Ct. 1624, in *Minutes of General Court*, 14; Rex v. Quaile, Gen. Ct. 1623/24, in *Minutes of General Court*, 12; Rex v. Nevell, Gen. Ct. 1625/26, in *Minutes of General Court*, 85; Rex v. Hatch, Gen. Ct. 1625/26, in *Minutes of General Court*, 93.

28. Rex v. Tyler, Gen. Ct. 1624, in *Minutes of General Court*, 19–20. Unfortunately, this case disappears from the records and the ultimate penalty imposed on the speaker is unknown.

29. Richard B. Morris, *Government and Labor in Early America* (New York: Columbia University Press, 1946), 1.

CHAPTER 2

1. A classic example of Whiggish writing on the history of early Virginia is Charles M. Andrews, *The Colonial Period of American History*, 4 vols. (New Haven: Yale University Press, 1934–1938), I: 98–213, which tells a teleological story of a society striving consciously to attain liberty. A more recent book in

a similar vein is Edmund S. Morgan, *American Slavery, American Freedom: The Ordeal of Colonial Virginia* (New York: W.W. Norton, 1975).

2. *See* James Horn, *A Land as God Made It: Jamestown and the Birth of America* (New York: Basic Books, 2005), 233–234; James Horn, *Adapting to a New World: English Society in the Seventeenth-Century Chesapeake* (Chapel Hill: University of North Carolina Press, 1994), 6, 136, 142–143.

3. *See* Laws of Feb. 21, 1631/32, Act XLIV, in *The Statutes at Large; Being a Collection of all the Laws of Virginia from the First Session of the Legislature in the Year 1619*, ed. William W. Hening (New York: R. & W. & G. Bartow, 1823), I: 173; Order re Inventory of Estates, Gen. Ct. 1626, in *Minutes of the Council and General Court of Colonial Virginia*, 2d ed., ed. R. B. McIlwaine (Richmond: Virginia State Library, 1979), 121; Order re Recording of Land Transfers, Gen. Ct. 1626, in *Minutes of General Court*, 121. *See also* Persey v. Kennells, Gen. Ct. 1627, in *Minutes of General Court*, 156 (holding new husband of widow who had failed to obtain letters of administration liable for deceased husband's debts, even though new husband received no money from deceased husband's estate). In one case in which the General Court divided, the majority of the court ruled that a man must swear to an inventory as entire and perfect, while the dissent required only that he swear it "to be true and perfect to the utmost of his knowledge." Peirce v. Gire, Gen. Ct. 1627, in *Minutes of General Court*, 156.

4. *See, e.g.*, Vincent v. Dodds, Gen. Ct. 1627/28, in *Minutes of General Court*, 166. (title); Hamer v. Baylie, Gen. Ct. 1624, in *Minutes of General Court*, 17 (title); Petition of Harman, Gen. Ct. 1628, in *Minutes of General Court*, 179 (boundary); Tailor v. Harris, Gen. Ct. 1626/27, in *Minutes of General Court*, 129 (boundary).

5. *See* Utie v. Jefferson, Gen. Ct. 1628, in *Minutes of General Court*, 173; Charde v. Michell, Gen. Ct. 1625, in *Minutes of General Court*, 79; Petition of Dowse, Gen. Ct. 1626, in *Minutes of General Court*, 113. The issue of one person building on land owned by another ultimately was regulated by statute. *See* Laws of March 2, 1642/43, Act XXXIII, in Hening, *Statutes*, I: 260.

6. Staffuerton v. Flint, Gen. Ct. 1628, in *Minutes of General Court*, 180. *See, e.g.*, Gunnery v. Jackson, Gen. Ct. 1627/28, in *Minutes of General Court*, 161 (delivery of tobacco to agent of English creditor); Adventurers of the Magazine v. Persey, Gen. Ct. 1626, in *Minutes of General Court*, 118 (enforcement of Privy Council order); Percy v. Waters, Gen. Ct. 1625/26, in *Minutes of General Court*, 87 (pattern of indebtedness involving five individuals).

7. *See* Pott v. Bennett, Gen. Ct. 1627, in *Minutes of General Court*, 158; Claybourne v. Wilcox, Gen. Ct., 1626, in *Minutes of General Court*, 124.

8. *See, e.g.*, Burland v. Bennett, Gen. Ct. 1628/29, in *Minutes of General Court*, 181; Bennet v. Preene, Gen. Ct. 1628, in *Minutes of General Court*, 170. *Cf.*

Copeland v. Burrows, Gen. Ct. 1625, in *Minutes of General Court*, 52–53 (defendant retained servant belonging to plaintiff).

9. *See* Parker v. DeLamaio, Gen. Ct. 1627/28, in *Minutes of General Court*, 167; Yardley v. Rastill, Gen. Ct. 1626, in *Minutes of General Court*, 109; Gainy v. Asson, Gen. Ct. 1626/27, in *Minutes of General Court*, 131–132. *Accord*, Waters v. Kennedy, Gen. Ct. 1626/27, in *Minutes of General Court*, 134–135.

10. *See* Darker v. Ward, Gen. Ct. 1626, in *Minutes of General Court*, 119; Edwards v. Harvie, Gen. Ct. 1626, in *Minutes of General Court*, 115; Treherne v. Carter, Gen. Ct. 1626, in *Minutes of General Court*, 126; Petition of Preene, Gen. Ct. 1626/27, in *Minutes of General Court*, 144.

11. *See, e.g.*, Luscam v. Perse, Gen. Ct. 1623/24, in *Minutes of General Court*, 9 (wages); Petition of Hunter, Northampton County Ct. 1661, in *Northampton County Virginia Record Book, 1657–1664*, ed. Howard Mackey (Rockport, Me.: Picton Press, 2002), 223 (seaman ordered to complete voyage); Gookin v. Kensam, Gen. Ct. 1623/24, in *Minutes of General Court*, 10 (seaworthiness); Bennet v. Preene, Gen. Ct. 1628, in *Minutes of General Court*, 170 (damage to goods in transit). *Cf.* Petition of Derickson, Northampton County Ct. 1660, in *Northampton Record Book, 1657–1664*, 145–146 (Dutch seaman removed from vessel in Virginia in order to comply with Navigation Act held entitled to pay and passage for voyage from Virginia to Europe).

12. *A Briefe Declaration of the Plantation of Virginia*, in *Journals of the House of Burgesses of Virginia, 1619–1658/59*, ed. H. R. McIlwaine (Richmond: Colonial Press, Va., 1915), 28, 36; Statement of Hamer, Gen. Ct. 1624, in *Minutes of General Court*, 31; *The Laws of Virginia Now in Force*, ed. Francis Moryson and Henry Randolph (London, 1662), 2.

13. Powell v. Matthews, Gen. Ct. 1625, in *Minutes of General Court*, 65 (emphasis added); Taylor v. Wormley, Gen. Ct. 1640, in *Minutes of General Court*, 470; Geney v. Whittakers, Gen. Ct. 1624, in *Minutes of General Court*, 31–32; Poore v. Withe, Gen. Ct. 1625, in *Minutes of General Court*, 64. *Accord*, Grymes v. Godlington, York County Ct. Dec. 29, 1662 (microfilm in Library of Virginia) (litigant must obtain appropriate documentary evidence).

14. *See Minutes of General Court*, 104 (July 28, 1626).

15. Pelteere v. Rastill, Gen. Ct. 1626, in *Minutes of General Court*, 109; Order re Debts, Gen. Ct. 1627, in *Minutes of General Court*, 483; Staffuerton v. Flint, Gen. Ct. 1628, in *Minutes of General Court*, 180; Rex v. Sweat, Gen. Ct. 1640, in *Minutes of General Court*, 477. The General Court had been reconstituted on July 28, 1626. Compare *Minutes of General Court*, 104 (July 28, 1626), with *Minutes of General Court*, 102 (May 8, 1626).

16. Kemp v. Panton, Gen. Ct. 1634, in *Minutes of General Court*, 481. *See* Panton v. Kemp, Gen. Ct. 1639/40–1640, in *Minutes of General Court*, 494–497.

17. Panton v. Kemp, *supra* n. 16, in *Minutes of General Court*, 496–497. For a later case similarly criticizing parties who "made themselves Judge (contrary to law and equity)," *see* Petition of Benthall, Northampton County Ct. 1656, in *Northampton County Virginia Record Book, 1654–1655*, ed. Howard Mackey (Rockport, Me.: Picton Press, 1999), 232–233.

18. Coleman v. Robins, Northampton County Ct. 1643, in *County Court Records of Accomack-Northampton, Virginia, 1640–1645*, ed. Susie Ames (Charlottesville: University Press of Virginia, 1973), 288. *But see* Boston v. Robins, Northampton County Ct. 1645, in *Records of Accomack-Northampton, 1640–1645*, 453, where a different jury found that a second servant sold along with Coleman under identical circumstances should have the year subtracted from his term. The *Coleman* case obviously was a troublesome one, for it took the jury two days to decide it after "having searched into it to the utmost of our endeavors." *Records of Accomack-Northampton, 1640–1645*, 288. It is unclear what the jury understood the law to be, and perhaps its understanding was wrong. What matters is that it believed the law to be controlling.

19. Gerard v. Ingle, Northampton County Ct. 1647, in *Northampton County Virginia Record Book: Orders, Deeds, Wills, 1645–1651*, ed. Howard Mackey (Rockport, Me.: Picton Press, 2000), 186; Lockey v. Lockey, York County Ct. Oct. 27, 1668 (microfilm in Library of Virginia).

20. Rex v. Watts, Northampton County Ct. 1661, in *Northampton Record Book, 1657–1664*, 159–160; Motion of Stringer, Northampton County Ct. 1660, in *Northampton Record Book, 1657–1664*, 120; Carter v. Williams, Northampton County Ct. 1655, in *Northampton Record Book, 1654–1655*, 287.

21. Scarburgh v. Williams, Northampton County Ct. 1649, in *Northampton Record Book, 1645–1651*, 374; Bennett v. Carpenter, Northumberland County Ct. July 20, 1656 (microfilm in Library of Virginia); Yardley v. Moore, Northampton County Ct. 1646/47, in *Northampton Record Book, 1645–1651*, 141–142. *See also* Harrington v. Beard, Northampton County Ct. 1649, in *Northampton Record Book, 1645–1651*, 336 (Beard to be "legally…possessed").

22. Inhabitants v. Cololough, Northumberland County Ct. Oct. 20, 1658 (microfilm in Library of Virginia).

23. York County Ct. Aug. 26, 1661 (microfilm in Library of Virginia); Complaint of Perque, Northampton County Ct. 1647/48, in *Northampton Record Book, 1645–1651*, 247.

24. Rex v. Epps, Gen. Ct. 1626/27–1627, in *Minutes of General Court*, 140–142, 148.

25. Rex v. Garret, Gen. Ct. 1627, in *Minutes of General Court*, 154; Commonwealth v. Scarborough, Grand Assembly 1654/55, in *Northampton Record Book, 1654–1655*, 77; Commonwealth v. Suthorne, Northampton County Ct. 1657, in *Northampton Record Book, 1657–1664*, 49.

26. Commonwealth v. Molesworthy, Charles City County Ct. Oct. 3, 1656 (microfilm in Library of Virginia); Commonwealth v. Charlton, Northampton County Ct. 1654, in *Northampton Record Book, 1654–1655*, 30; Rex v. Reade, Gen. Ct. 1627/28, in *Minutes of General Court*, 183–184.

27. Rex v. Martiau, Gen. Ct. 1627, in *Minutes of General Court*, 156. Kings of England had claimed the throne of France and occupied much of France at various times during the Middle Ages. They did not give up their theoretical claim to the French throne until the Congress of Vienna in 1815.

28. Rex v. Flint, Gen. Ct. 1628, in *Minutes of General Court*, 176–177; Rex v. Wilkinson, Gen. Ct. 1640, in *Minutes of General Court*, 469; Rex v. Reekes, Gen. Ct. 1640, in *Minutes of General Court*, 476; Commonwealth v. Johnson, Northampton County Ct. 1654, in *Northampton Record Book, 1654–1655*, 30–31, 40. *Accord*, Rex v. Elston, Gen. Ct. 1640, in *Minutes of General Court*, 476; Rex v. Ford, Northampton County Ct. 1637, in *County Court Records of Accomack-Northampton, Virginia, 1632–1640*, ed. Susie M. Ames (Washington, D.C.: American Historical Association, 1954), 82. *See also* Rex v. Cugley, Gen. Ct. 1630, in *Minutes of General Court*, 479. Although the penalty in the *Cugley* case was mild, harsh penalties remained the norm in some early 1630s cases. *See* three unnamed cases in *Minutes of General Court*, 480 (Feb. 23, 1630—loss of ears for perjury; March 25, 1630—pillory for lying about Lord Baltimore; Oct. 6, 1631—laid neck & heels "for nicknaming houses abusing men & their wives & night walking"); Nute v. Halloway, Northampton County Ct. 1634, in *Records of Accomack-Northampton, 1632–1640*, 24 (laid neck & heels for "contempt" in not answering suit).

29. Rex v. Walker, Northampton County Ct. 1645/46, in *Northampton Record Book, 1645–1651*, 40; Rex v. Parks, Northampton County Ct. 1645, in *Northampton Record Book, 1645–1651*, 8; Rex v. Walker, Northampton County Ct. 1649, in *Northampton Record Book, 1645–1651*, 377–378. *Accord*, Commonwealth v. Cartwright, Charles City County Ct. April 20, 1658 (microfilm in Library of Virginia). For another political case from the Civil War era, involving a prosecution for treason against Oliver Cromwell, the Lord Protector, *see* an unnamed entry in *Minutes of General Court*, 506 (June 12, 1658). No record survives of the outcome of this prosecution. For cases in the 1640s and 1650s challenging the fairness or authority of judges, *see* Commonwealth v. Parker, Northampton County Ct. 1655, in *Northampton Record Book, 1654–1655*, 292; Commonwealth v. Foxe, Northampton County Ct. 1654, in *Northampton Record Book, 1654–1655*, 110; Commonwealth v. Hudson, Northampton County Ct. 1654, in *Northampton Record Book, 1654–1655*, 44; Rex v. Berry, Northampton County Ct. 1649/50, in *Northampton Record Book, 1645–1651*, 395; Rex v. Gibbons, Northampton County Ct. 1649, in *Northampton Record Book, 1645–1651*, 344, 346; Rex v. Johnson, Northampton County

Ct. 1644/45, in *Records of Accomack-Northampton, 1640–1645*, 398–399. In none of these cases was a defendant required to do anything other than give a bond for good behavior or future appearance or "promise[] to demean himself with respect." Commonwealth v. Williams, Northampton County Ct. 1654, in *Northampton Record Book, 1654–1655*, 29. Of course, an individual who "continued her incorrigible demeanor...and affront[ed] the Commissioners with menacing abusive language" would receive corporal punishment. Commonwealth v. Holte, Northampton County Ct. 1654, *Northampton Record Book, 1654–1655*, 58.

30. Unnamed entry in *Minutes of General Court*, 505 (June 2, 1657); Commonwealth v. Robinson, Northampton County Ct. 1658, in *Northampton Record Book, 1657–1664*, 22.

31. Commonwealth v. Thruston, Gen. Ct. 1657, in *Minutes of General Court*, 506; Laws of March 1659/60, Act VI, in Hening, *Statutes*, I: 532. *See* Proceedings against Quakers, Gen. Ct. 1662, in *Minutes of General Court*, 507; Rex v. Comondo, Charles City County Ct. Feb. 3, 1663/64 (microfilm in Library of Virginia) (fined for contempt and allowing Quakers to meet at his house); Rex v. Colbourne, Northhampton County Ct. 1660/61, in *Northampton Record Book, 1657–1664*, 149 (fined £100 sterling "for entertaining Quakers"); Commonwealth v. Jackson, Northumberland County Ct. June 26, 1660 (microfilm in Library of Virginia) (20 lashes plus fine of £100 sterling); Rex v. Chisman, York County Ct. Aug. 26, 1661 (microfilm in Library of Virginia) (Quaker woman meeting in the woods with "Negroes"); Order re Quakers York County Ct. Sept. 10, 1659 (microfilm in Library of Virginia) (directing sheriff and constables to attend meetings of "several dangerous persons now in this county called Quakers" and to warn of their activities).

32. *See* Taylor v. Taylor, York County Ct. Oct. 26, 1657 (microfilm in Library of Virginia); King v. Storkey, Northampton County Ct. 1641, in *Records of Accomack-Northampton, 1640–1645*, 117.

33. *See* Kathleen M. Brown, *Good Wives, Nasty Wenches, and Anxious Patriarchs: Gender, Race, and Power in Colonial Virginia* (Chapel Hill: University of North Carolina Press, 1998), 189–190; Starche v. Gettings, Northampton County Ct. 1642/43, in *Records of Accomack-Northampton, 1640–1645*, 236; Rex v. Sweat, Gen. Ct. 1640, in *Minutes of General Court*, 477.

34. For the only known prosecution of sodomy, which resulted in a sentence of death, *see* Rex v. Cornish, Gen. Ct. 1624–1625/26, in *Minutes of General Court*, 34, 42, 47, 81, 85. It seems probable that the crime was prosecuted only because its victim was an unwilling servant, who was not himself prosecuted. For the only known prosecution of bestiality, for which there is no record of a trial, *see* King v. Moore, Northampton County Ct. 1644, in *Records of Accomack-Northampton, 1640–1645*, 371–372, 376. For the Epps case, which

is discussed above, *see* Rex v. Epps, Gen. Ct. 1626/27–1627, in *Minutes of General Court*, 140–42, 148. For two prosecutions for premarital intercourse, *see* Commonwealth v. Harrys, Lancaster County Ct. Jan. 25, 1659/60 (microfilm in Library of Virginia); Mary Beth Norton, *Founding Mothers and Fathers: Gendered Power and the Forming of American Society* (New York: Alfred A. Knopf, 1996), 67–68. *See also* Laws of March 13, 1657/58, Act XIV, in Hening, *Statutes*, I: 438. Mary Beth Norton agrees that Virginia courts, especially in comparison with those of New England, showed little interest in prosecuting sexual offenses other than bastardy. *See* Norton, *Founding Mothers and Fathers*, 66–69, 346, 354–357. *But see* Brown, *Good Wives, Nasty Wenches, and Anxious Patriarchs*, 188–193, who sees a shift around 1660 from prosecution of sexual misconduct as sinful to its prosecution merely as an economic crime. However, the only evidence that Brown presents of the prosecution of sex as sin is four cases in which women convicted of bastardy were made to do public penance, in addition to whatever other penalties were imposed. At least in comparison with the vast body of evidence that exists for New England, these four cases provide thin support for Brown's conclusion.

35. Confession of Willmote, Northampton County Ct. 1649, in *Northampton Record Book, 1645–1651*, 347. The case has been the subject of a book by John R. Pagan, *Anne Orthwood's Bastard: Sex and Law in Early Virginia* (New York: Oxford University Press, 2003).

36. Confession of Willmote, Northampton County Ct. 1649, in *Northampton Record Book, 1645–1651*, 347.

37. Ibid., 347–348.

38. Ibid.

39. *See* Complaint of Baily, Northampton County Ct. 1649, in *Northampton Record Book, 1645–1651*, 369.

40. *See* Order re Land Boundaries, Gen. Ct. 1640, in *Minutes of General Court*, 471.

41. Proclamation of Francis Wyatt, Northampton County Ct. 1641, in *Records of Accomack-Northampton, 1640–1645*, 125–126.

42. Laws of Feb. 17, 1644/45, Act XIV, in Hening, *Statutes*, I: 296; Rubin v. Dirrickson, Northampton County Ct. 1643, in *Records of Accomack-Northampton, 1640–1645*, 288.

43. Deposition of William Munns, Northampton County Ct. 1644/45, in *Records of Accomack-Northampton, 1640–1645*, 405–406; Laws of Feb. 17, 1644/45, Act XV, in Hening, *Statutes*, I: 296.

44. *See* Laws of September 4, 1632, Act XVIII, in Hening, *Statutes*, I: 185–186; A Remonstrance of the Grand Assembly, Apr. 1642, in Hening, *Statutes*, I: 236–237; Rex v. Francke and Clarke, Gen. Ct. 1622/23, in *Minutes of General Court*, 4–5.

45. Such as "nisi prius," Order re Company's Rents, Gen. Ct. 1624, in *Minutes of General Court*, 34; "bill of exchange," Tutchin v. Gyles, Gen. Ct. 1624/25, in *Minutes of General Court*, 40; Smith v. Orley, Northumberland County Ct. March 12, 1663 (microfilm in Library of Virginia); "nuncupative" will, Estate of Lightfoote, Gen. Ct. 1628/29, in *Minutes of General Court*, 181; "quietas est," Petition of Johnson, York County Ct. Dec. 21, 1657 (microfilm in Library of Virginia); "consideration," Condemnation against Nuttall, Northampton County Ct. 1643, in *Records of Accomack-Northampton, 1640–1645*, 265; "executor," Complaint of Bell, Northampton County Ct. 1654, in *Northampton Record Book, 1654–1655*, 6; "administrator," Petition of Jones, Northampton County Ct. 1655, in *Northampton Record Book, 1654–1655*, 293–294 (In the absence of a close relative, the "greatest creditor" of the estate would be appointed administrator, *see* Estate of Portins, Lancaster County Ct., May 14, 1662 [microfilm in Library of Virginia]); "adm. cum testamento annexo," Wheeler v. Huberd, York County Ct., Jan. 25, 1657/58 (microfilm in Library of Virginia); "fee simple," Broomfield v. Crumpe, Grand & Gen. Assembly March 24, 1654/55, in Hening, *Statutes*, I: 405; "feoffees in trust," Scarborough v. Pett, Northampton County Ct. 1645, in *Records of Accomack-Northampton, 1640–1645*, 430–431; "conversion," Hookins v. Johnson, Northampton County Ct. 1644/45, in *Records of Accomack-Northampton, 1640–1645*, 411 (actual word used was "converted"); and "nihil dicit." Mountney v. Fisher, Northampton County Ct. 1645, in *Northampton Record Book, 1645–1651*, 9.

46. Anonymous, Gen. Ct. 1657/58, in *Minutes of General Court*, 506; Evans v. Evans, Gen. Ct. 1654, in *Minutes of General Court*, 503.

47. *See* Rex v. Francke and Clarke, Gen. Ct., 1622/23, in *Minutes of General Court*, 4–5; Order re Company's Rents, Gen. Ct. 1624, in *Minutes of General Court*, 34 (jury of eighteen members); Inquest into Death of George Pope, Gen. Ct., 1624, in *Minutes of General Court*, 38. For legislation securing the right to trial by jury, *see* Laws of March 2, 1642/43, Act LVII, in Hening, *Statutes*, I: 273.

48. *See* Laws of Virginia, Nov. 20, 1645, Act X, in Hening, *Statutes*, I: 303; Rex v. Wilkins, Northampton County Ct. 1645, in *Northampton Record Book, 1645–1651*, 2 (Wilkins fined for refusing to serve as jury foreman after being "chosen" by sheriff). *See also* Order re Jurymen, Gen. Ct. 1676/77, in *Minutes of General Court*, 457, permitting only "free holders & house keepers" to serve on juries. This order apparently was required to reverse or clarify prior practice.

49. Gates v. Martin, Gen. Ct. 1627, in *Minutes of General Court*, 150; Weede v. Johnson, Northampton County Ct. 1643, in *Records of Accomack-Northampton, 1640–1645*, 318. *Accord*, Elyott v. Droight, Lancaster County Ct. June

9, 1662 (microfilm in Library of Virginia); Earle v. Lord, Northumberland County Ct. Sept. 21, 1657 (microfilm in Library of Virginia); Bibby v. Sprigge, Northampton County Ct. 1654, in *Northampton Record Book, 1654–1655,* 12. *See also* Slaighton v. Pope, Northumberland County Ct. Jan. 20, 1652/53 (microfilm in Library of Virginia) (plea of "non est factum"). On the common law forms of action in Virginia, *see generally* Pagan, *Anne Orthwood's Bastard,* 68–70.

50. *See* Laws of 1657/58, Act CXIX, in Hening, *Statutes,* I: 486; Warren M. Billings, "Pleading, Procedure, and Practice: The Meaning of Due Process of Law in Seventeenth Century Virginia," *Journal of Southern History,* 47 (1981): 569, 582–584. For examples of the informality of procedure by bill, *see* Petition of Henman, Northampton County Ct. 1646/47, in *Northampton Record Book, 1645–1651,* 129; Answer of Culpepper, Northampton County Ct. 1646/47, in *Northampton Record Book, 1645–1651,* 131.

51. Preamble to Laws of March 13, 1657/58, in Hening, *Statutes,* I: 432.

52. *See, e.g.,* Laws of March 2, 1642/43, Act LV, in Hening, *Statutes,* I: 270; Laws of March 2, 1642/43, Act LVI, in Hening, *Statutes,* I: 272; Laws of March 1645/46, Act XI, in Hening, *Statutes,* I: 344; Laws of October 5, 1646, Act XIII, in Hening, *Statutes,* I: 331; Laws of March 13, 1657/58, Act XXXVI, in Hening, *Statutes,* I: 449; Stubbing v. West, Northampton County Ct. 1645, in *Records of Accomack-Northampton, 1640–1645,* 432.

53. *See, e.g.,* Laws of Feb. 21, 1631/32, Act II, in Hening, *Statutes,* I: 155; Laws of Sept. 4, 1632, Act XXVI, in Hening, *Statutes,* I: 192; Laws of Aug. 21, 1633, Act X, in Hening, *Statutes,* I: 219; Laws of March 2, 1642/43, Act XI, in Hening, *Statutes,* I: 248. For cases dealing with statutory crimes, *see, e.g.,* Edwards v. Bigg, Gen. Ct. 1675, in *Minutes of General Court,* 410; Rex v. Johnson, Gen. Ct. 1628, in *Minutes of General Court,* 178; Mallory v. Alwyn, Charles City County Ct. Aug. 4, 1673 (microfilm in Library of Virginia); Rex v. Wells, Lancaster County Ct. Jan. 20, 1662/63 (microfilm in Library of Virginia); Rex v. Colbourne, Northampton County Ct. 1660/61, in *Northampton Record Book, 1657–1664,* 149; Cornish v. Holland, Northumberland County Ct. March 5, 1665/66 (microfilm in Library of Virginia); Rex v. Marriott, Surrey County Ct. Sept. 4, 1672 (microfilm in Library of Virginia); Rex v. Costian, York County Ct. Aug. 24, 1675 (microfilm in Library of Virginia); Rex v. Wills, York County Ct. Dec. 8, 1668 (microfilm in Library of Virginia).

54. *See* Laws of January 1639/40, Act XX, in Hening, *Statutes,* I: 227 (ecclesiastical offenses); Laws of March 1645/46, Act I, in Hening, *Statutes,* I: 309 (ecclesiastical offenses); Laws of March 13, 1657/58, Act XXX, in Hening, *Statutes,* I: 446 (probate jurisdiction); Act of Nov. 20, 1645, Act X, in Hening, *Statutes,* I: 303 (chancery jurisdiction); Underwood v. Hothersall, York County Ct. Dec. 20, 1661 (microfilm in Library of Virginia) (suit in chancery

commenced in county court). *See also* Page v. Effard, York County Ct. June 24, 1662 (microfilm in Library of Virginia) (cross suits at law and in chancery).

55. Notice of Court Meetings, Gen. Ct. 1623/24, in *Minutes of General Court*, 12.

56. Order for Commission at Accomack, Gen. Ct. 1624/25, in *Minutes of General Court*, 50. The term "small cause" was left undefined.

57. Order for Commission at Accomack, Gen. Ct. 1624/25, in *Minutes of General Court*, 50; Order re Court at Accomack, Gen. Ct. undated, in *Minutes of General Court*, 483 (giving Accomack a more extensive civil jurisdiction than other local courts possessed); Order re Courts at Charles Hundred and Elizabeth City, Gen. Ct. 1626, in *Minutes of General Court*, 106, responding to Laws of March 5, 1623/24 sec. 12, in Hening, *Statutes*, I: 125.

58. Order re By-Laws, Northampton County Ct. 1665, in *Northampton County Virginia Record Book, 1664–1674*, ed. Howard Mackey (Rockport, Me.: Picton Press, 2003), 19. *See* Petition of Blaze, Northampton County Ct. 1670, in *Northampton Record Book, 1664–1674*, 234 (granting 400 lb. tobacco reimbursement from public funds to anyone who "shall entertain the said poor man in their house"); Petition of Justices, Northampton County Ct. 1673, in *Northampton Record Book, 1664–1674*, 454 (petition to governor for appointment of named individual to bench granted); Petition of Justices, Northampton County Ct. 1669, in *Northampton Record Book, 1664–1674*, 197 (ibid.).

59. Order re Erroneous Judgment, Gen. Ct. undated, in *Minutes of General Court*, 482.

60. Order re Controversies, Gen. Ct. 1628/29, in *Minutes of General Court*, 193; Commission for Monthly Courts, Gen. Ct. 1631/32, in *Minutes of General Court*, 484; Order re Shires, Gen. Ct. 1634, in *Minutes of General Court*, 481.

61. *See* Jon Kukla, "Order and Chaos in Early America: Political and Social Stability in Pre-Restoration Virginia," *American Historical Review*, 90 (1985): 275. In citing Kukla, I do not intend to express a judgment on the issue whether Virginia was a stable or anarchic, or for that matter, a good or bad society. Any such judgment would reflect personal taste, not historical description.

62. *See* Laws of March 13, 1657/58, Act XVI, in Hening, *Statutes*, I: 440; Order re Church, Northampton County Ct. 1661/62, in *Northampton Record Book, 1657–1664*, 216 (double-time); Order re David, Northumberland County Ct. July 22, 1661 (microfilm in Library of Virginia) (double-time); Order re Clarke, Lancaster County Ct. Nov. 1, 1663 (microfilm in Library of Virginia) (1 year extra service for 2-month absence at height of crop); Order re Bradley, Northumberland County Ct. Dec. 10, 1663 (microfilm in Library of Virginia) (2 years extra service for 7-month absence plus recovery of costs of £5 sterling); Order against Gill, York County Ct. Oct. 25, 1662 (microfilm in Library of Virginia) (whipping). A servant who ran away a second time would be branded with the letter "R." *See* Laws of March 10, 1655/56, Act

XI, in Hening, *Statutes*, I: 401. Free men, of course, had the right to move to a new locale, even in another colony, provided there were no outstanding claims, civil or criminal, against them. *See* Complaint of Hack, Northampton County Ct. 1663/64, in *Northampton Record Book, 1664–1674*, 9–10. Earlier, there had been legislation to the contrary. *See* Laws of Sept. 4, 1632, Act LVI, in Hening, *Statutes*, I: 200. Of course, harboring runaway servants was a crime. *See* Laws of March 2, 1642/43, Act XXI, in Hening, *Statutes*, I: 253.

63. *See* Laws of March 2, 1642/43, Act LX, in Hening, *Statutes*, I: 274; Rex v. Ehert, Lancaster County Ct. Sept. 10, 1662 (microfilm in Library of Virginia); Bernard v. Finch, York County Ct. May 24, 1660 (microfilm in Library of Virginia); Rex v. Clutton, York County Ct. Jan. 24, 1661/62 (microfilm in Library of Virginia).

64. *See* Order re Watts, Northumberland County Ct. Oct. 20, 1664 (microfilm in Library of Virginia) (20 lashes for "scandaliz[ing] his master"); Order re Lowell, Northumberland County Ct. Aug. 20, 1663 (microfilm in Library of Virginia) (female servant gets one year extra service for striking mistress); Harrys v. Merryman, Lancaster County Ct. Nov. 24, 1658 (microfilm in Library of Virginia) (servant warned not to engage in future offenses against master); Harman v. Beale, York County Ct. Dec. 20, 1658 (microfilm in Library of Virginia) (whipping after unproved claim).

65. Earle v. Cole, Northumberland County Ct. July 21, 1662 (microfilm in Library of Virginia).

66. *See* Laws of March 2, 1642/43, Act XXII, in Hening, *Statutes*, I: 254; Knight v. Cole, Northumberland County Ct. Oct. 20, 1664 (microfilm in Library of Virginia).

67. *See, e.g.*, Verdict of Jury of Inquest, Northampton County Ct. 1659/60, in *Northampton Record Book, 1657–1664*, 106; Order Impanelling Jury of Inquest, Northumberland County Ct. Apr. 20, 1664 (microfilm in Library of Virginia). *But cf.* Rex v. Wally, Northampton County Ct. 1662, in *Northampton Record Book, 1657–1664*, 246 (master of dead servant whom he had abused required to give bond for good behavior); Commonwealth v. Hunt, York County Ct. June 24, 1658 (microfilm in Library of Virginia) (bond to keep the peace toward complaining servant).

68. Parker v. Holden, Northampton County Ct. 1660, in *Northampton Record Book, 1657–1664*, 121–122, 134.

69. *See, e.g.*, Hasley v. Fitzgerald, Charles City County Ct. Oct. 27, 1656 (microfilm in Library of Virginia); Order re McCrite, Northumberland County Ct. Feb. 10, 1662/63 (microfilm in Library of Virginia) ("Irish woman" freed because "upwards of twenty-three years of age"); Petition of John Negro, York County Ct. Sept. 11, 1660 (microfilm in Library of Virginia).

70. *See* Laws of March 2, 1642/43, Act XXII, in Hening, *Statutes*, I: 254; Rex v. Cornish, Gen. Ct. 1624–1625/26, in *Minutes of General Court*, 34, 42, 47, 81,

85 (capital punishment for sodomy committed on unwilling servant); Order re Garman, Lancaster County Ct. May 25, 1659 (microfilm in Library of Virginia) (servant "shall not work in the ground at any hard labor"); Balfour v. Hawley, Northumberland County Ct. Sept. 20, 1658 (microfilm in Library of Virginia) (new master inheriting apprentice from deceased master must give bond to teach trade of tailor).

71. *See* Anonymous, Gen. Ct. Dec. 1, 1657, in *Minutes of General Court*, 506 (medical care); Petition of Wells, York County Ct. Oct. 26, 1657 (microfilm in Library of Virginia) (medical care); Order re Tyler, York County Ct. Dec. 21, 1657 (microfilm in Library of Virginia) (necessities); Sale to Starling, Northampton County Ct. 1660, in *Northampton Record Book, 1657–1664*, 113–114. *Cf.* Rex v. Watts, Northampton County Ct. 1661, in *Northampton Record Book, 1657–1664*, 159–160 (master has duty not to provide incompetent medical assistance from which servant dies). *See also* Calvert v. Netsin, Northampton County Ct. 1662, in *Northampton Record Book, 1657–1664*, 229 (servant obligated to reimburse master for any medical care for which master has paid).

72. *See, e.g.*, Williams v. Nash, Lancaster County Ct. Feb. 10, 1663/64 (microfilm in Library of Virginia); Lockwitt v. Werber, Northumberland County Ct. Feb. 10, 1662/63 (microfilm in Library of Virginia). *See generally* Richard B. Morris, *Government and Labor in Early America* (New York: Columbia University Press, 1946), 429–431, 454–457, 468–469, 484–491. For a discussion of post-1660 legislation designed to protect female servants from being impregnated by their masters, *see* Pagan, *Anne Orthwood's Bastard*, 84–85.

73. York County Ct. May 18, June 25, and Aug. 24, 1658 (microfilm in Library of Virginia).

74. Lockolur v. Diggs, York County Ct. June 24, 1660 (microfilm in Library of Virginia). *See* Laws of March 13, 1657/58, Act XVIII, in Hening, *Statutes*, I: 441–442.

75. *See* Laws of March 31, 1655, Act VI, in Hening, *Statutes*, I: 411; Carrawill v. Harman, York County Ct. Feb. 26, 1660/61 (microfilm in Library of Virginia).

76. Resolution of General Court, Dec. 4, 1627, in *Minutes of General Court*, 483.

77. *See* Laws of March 2, 1642/43, Act XII, in Hening, *Statutes*, I: 248; Laws of March 2, 1642/43, Act II, in Hening, *Statutes*, I: 243; Petition of Daly, Northumberland County Ct. Jan., 1651/52 (microfilm in Library of Virginia); Brittaine v. Kendall, Northampton County Ct. 1659, in *Northampton Record Book, 1657–1664*, 95.

78. *See* Laws of Feb. 17, 1644/45, Act XI, in Hening, *Statutes*, I: 294; Laws of March 13, 1657/58, Act XLIII, in Hening, *Statutes*, I: 453; Petition of Warder, Northampton County Ct. 1647/48, in *Northampton Record Book, 1645–1651*, 244.

79. *See* Saunders v. Popeley, Gen. Ct. 1628/29, in *Minutes of General Court*, 189; Percy v. Waters, Gen. Ct. 1625/26, in *Minutes of General Court*, 87; Adventurers of the Magazine v. Persey, Gen. Ct. 1626, in *Minutes of General Court*, 118; Gunnery v. Jackson, Gen. Ct. 1627/28, in *Minutes of General Court*, 161.

80. In Accomack/Northampton County, for example, litigation increased sixfold between 1632 and 1638, from 40 to 249 cases, and some 80 percent of the cases in the latter year were for debt collection. *See* Kukla, "Order and Chaos," 287; George B. Curtis, "The Colonial County Court, Social Forum and Legislative Precedent: Accomack County, Virginia, 1633–1639," *Virginia Magazine of History and Biography*, 85 (1977): 274. This percentage is consistent with my own analysis of the rate of debt collection cases in Accomack/Northampton for the decade of the 1640s, which found that, out of a total of 1682 case entries for the years 1641–1650, 1294, or 76.9 percent, were for debt collection. The analysis is reported in greater detail in chapter 3, note 82.

81. Matthews v. Tillghman, Northampton County Ct. 1655, in *Northampton Record Book, 1654–1655*, 255; Complaint of Dolby, Northampton County Ct. 1655/56, in *Northampton Record Book, 1654–1655*, 260; Cornelius v. Tilghman, Northampton County Ct. 1655, in *Northampton Record Book, 1654–1655*, 229.

82. *See* Billings, "Pleading, Procedure, and Practice," 583; Laws of November 20, 1645, Act XI, in Hening, *Statutes*, I: 304; Laws of March 13, 1657/58, Acts XXXII and XLVII, in Hening, *Statutes*, I: 447, 455.

83. *See, e.g.*, Pryse v. Perry, Charles City County Ct. June 4, 1660 (microfilm in Library of Virginia); Bushrod v. White, Northampton County Ct. 1647/48, in *Northampton Record Book, 1645–1651*, 240. *See also* Harloe v. Lydall, Gen. Ct. 1671, in *Minutes of General Court*, 276 (rejecting plea of statute of limitations since demands had been made between the time of the initial judgment and the subsequent suit thirteen years later).

84. For some of the few who were, *see, e.g.*, Wigg v. Hutchenson, Gen. Ct. 1628/29, in *Minutes of General Court*, 188; Stubbins v. Jacob, Northampton County Ct. 1640/41, in *Court Records of Northampton, 1640–1645*, 65.

85. Petition of Perque, Northampton County Ct. 1647/48, in *Northampton Record Book, 1645–1651*, 239. For a suit against such a person, *see* Walton v. Hudson, Northumberland County Ct. Sept. 20, 1652 (microfilm in Library of Virginia). Cases brought by individuals who had given security for the appearance of others are not specially noted in the court records; they are recorded like all other cases of debt.

86. Feeding prisoners was an expensive proposition; one court entry directed the sheriff to "allow" food worth 150 lb. tobacco per month for a prisoner, *see* Motion of Sheriff, Northhampton County Ct. 1663, in *Northampton Record*

Book, 1657–1664, 300, in a context in which most debt actions involved claims in a range of 1,000 lb. tobacco or less.

87. *See, e.g.*, Elyott v. Droight, Lancaster County Ct. June 9, 1662 (microfilm in Library of Virginia); Littlepage v. Anderson, York County Ct. Jan. 25, 1662 (microfilm in Library of Virginia). *Cf.* Order re Sheriff, Northumberland County Ct. Feb. 10, 1662/63 (microfilm in Library of Virginia) ("ordered that the Sheriff shall have attachments against the estates of all those persons arrested to this Court who failed in their appearances by which their defaults judgment passed against the said Sheriff").

88. *But cf.* Order for Payment to Sheriff, Lancaster County Ct. Oct. 23, 1661 (microfilm in Library of Virginia) (granting proceeds of a fine of 30 lb. tobacco to sheriff "toward his great losses [and] long service performed to this County").

89. *See* Anthony S. Parent Jr., *Foul Means: The Formation of a Slave Society in Virginia, 1660–1740* (Chapel Hill: University of North Carolina Press, 2003), 1–4, 105–114. Of course, slavery has been a subject of a vast historiographic debate, growing most recently out of Edmund Morgan, *American Slavery, American Freedom*. Morgan argues that seventeenth-century Virginia was so characterized by chaotic, widespread class conflict among whites that the colonists turned to slavery to achieve a measure of social and economic stability. Others, like Elizabeth Haight, frame their studies in opposition to Morgan's, finding stability and compassion where he found chaos. Elizabeth Stanton Haight, "Heirs of Tradition/Creators of Change: Law and Stability on Virginia's Eastern Shore, 1633–1663 (Ph.D. dissertation, University of Virginia, 1987), 14. Without entering the fray on issues of stability vs. chaos or the relationship between black slavery and white freedom, it is enough to note that while Morgan employed legal sources, he never tried to understand law as a system of internalized norms and procedures, and he was not concerned with evaluating how changes in legal procedure and decision-making interacted with Virginia society during his period. Ironically, the few pages that Morgan devotes to the county courts themselves are animated by an obsession with establishing their connections with English courts—an obsession, that is, with the old subject of reception, which this study is striving to avoid. *See* Morgan, *American Slavery*, 149–153, 178.

Suffice it to say, Morgan's treatment of the origins of slavery in Virginia is not the only one. For a well-documented, persuasive dissenting view emphasizing the centrality of Anglo-American racism, *see* Winthrop Jordan, *White over Black: American Attitudes toward the Negro, 1550–1812* (Chapel Hill: University of North Carolina Press, 1968). As Jordan and Morgan show, the central issue in the modern historiography of seventeenth-century Virginia is whether economics or racism was the chief factor in the rise of slavery as the defining institution of the American South. At the heart of both Jordan's and Morgan's accounts is a broad definition of the motives of seventeenth-century Virginia society. Were Virginians, as in Morgan's account, so focused on achieving a society of independent, property-owning citizens that they were willing to divide people into two classes based on race? Or were they so racist that they were willing to consign their fellow man to the unremitting cruelty of slavery? It is not hard to imagine how these differing accounts might shape our perception of the type of legal system that seventeenth-century Virginians built. But it would ignore the defining elements of that system. For an excellent review essay that puts Jordan's and Morgan's work in the context of Eric Williams, *Capitalism and Slavery* (Chapel Hill: University of North Carolina Press, 1944), see Barbara Solow and Stanley Engerman, "British Capitalism and Caribbean Slavery: The Legacy of Eric Williams: An Introduction," in Barbara Solow and Stanley Engerman, eds., *British Capitalism and Caribbean Slavery* (Cambridge: Cambridge University Press, 1987). *See also* the sources cited in the Introduction, note 10.

CHAPTER 3

1. I have nothing new to add to the scholarly disagreements about the nature of Puritanism, and thus I see no point in discussing my understanding of the subject at great length. I remain heavily influenced, perhaps more so than I appreciate, by the work of Perry Miller, especially by *The New England Mind: The Seventeenth Century* (New York: Macmillan, 1939) and by his collection of essays, *Errand Into the Wilderness* (Cambridge, Mass.: Harvard University Press, 1956). Since Miller's work, however, important scholarship has proceeded in diverse directions. The reader can gain a sense of the vastness and diversity of the scholarship from the bibliography in Francis J. Bremer, *The Puritan Experiment: New England Society from Bradford to Edwards*: revised edition (Hanover, N.H.: University Press of New England, 1995), 234–247. I have found James F. Cooper Jr., *Tenacious of Their Liberties: The Congregationalists in Colonial Massachusetts* (New York: Oxford University Press, 1999), especially helpful for its understanding of church government as parallel to my understanding of secular law and government. Other recent books that I found particularly helpful in understanding the Puritan impulse are Virginia DeJohn Anderson, *New England's Generation: The Great Migration and the Formation of Society and Culture in the Seventeenth Century* (New York: Cambridge University Press, 1991); Stephen Innes, *Creating the Commonwealth: The Economic Culture of Puritan New England* (New York: W.W. Norton, 1995); Michael P. Winship, *Making Heretics: Militant Protestantism*

and Free Grace in Massachusetts, 1636–1641 (Princeton: Princeton University Press, 2002).

2. The two most important books on seventeenth-century Massachusetts law are George Lee Haskins, *Law and Authority in Early Massachusetts: A Study in Tradition and Design* (New York: Macmillan, 1960), and David Thomas Konig, *Law and Society in Puritan Massachusetts: Essex County, 1629–1692* (Chapel Hill: University of North Carolina Press, 1979). There are numerous other books and articles, among the most valuable of which are Daniel R. Coquillette ed., *Law in Colonial Massachusetts, 1630–1800* (Boston: Colonial Society of Massachusetts, 1984), which contains a wealth of bibliographical information; David H. Flaherty, *Privacy in Colonial New England* (Charlottesville: University Press of Virginia, 1972); Edgar J. McManus, *Law and Liberty in Early New England: Criminal Justice and Due Process, 1620–1692* (Amherst: University of Massachusetts Press, 1993); Edwin Powers, *Crime and Punishment in Early Massachusetts, 1620–1692: A Documentary History* (Boston: Beacon Press, 1966); and Julius Goebel Jr., "King's Law and Local Custom in Seventeenth Century New England," *Columbia Law Review*, 31 (1931), 416.

3. *See* Colony v. Starr, Ct. Asst. Jan. 1637/38, *Records of the Court of Assistants of the Colony of Massachusetts Bay, 1630–1692*, 3 vols. (Boston: Suffolk County, 1901–1928), II: 73, where a man was fined and ordered to confess his fault before the General Court for refusing to obey an order about swine because "he said the law was against God's law." Starr's conviction occurred only two months after the General Court had banished Anne Hutchinson for, among other things, claiming to have received direct personal revelations from God. *See* William K. B. Stoever, *'A Faire and Easie Way to Heaven': Covenant Theology and Antinomianism in Early Massachusetts* (Middletown, Conn.: Wesleyan University Press, 1978), 32–33. For detailed explorations of the balance and complexity, *see* Stephen Foster, *The Long Argument: English Puritanism and the Shaping of New England Culture, 1570–1700* (Chapel Hill: University of North Carolina Press, 1991); Winship, *Making Heretics*.

4. John Winthrop, *A Model of Christian Charity* (1630), in *Collections of the Massachusetts Historical Society*, 7 (Boston, 3d ser. 1838): 31, 33–34, 46.

5. John Cotton, *An Exposition Upon the Thirteenth Chapter of the Revelation* (London: Livewel, Chapman, 1655), 71–73.

6. Winthrop, "Model of Christian Charity," 34. The position stated in the preceding two paragraphs is elaborated, with extensive analysis of the primary sources, in Stephen Foster, *Their Solitary Way: The Puritan Social Ethic in the First Century of Settlement in New England* (New Haven: Yale University Press, 1971), 67–73.

7. Anderson, *New England's Generation*, 100. *Accord*, Innes, *Creating the Commonwealth*, 6–13. On the profit motive, *see generally* Stephen Innes,

Labor in a New Land: Economy and Society in Seventeenth-Century Spring-field (Princeton: Princeton University Press, 1983); John Frederick Martin, *Profits in the Wilderness: Entrepreneurship and the Founding of New England Towns in the Seventeenth Century* (Chapel Hill: University of North Carolina Press, 1991).

8. *See* Bremer, *Puritan Experiment*, 47, 102–103.

9. *See* Colony v. Clenton, Quarterly Ct. Salem 1670, in *Records and Files of the Quarterly Courts of Essex County, Massachusetts*, 8 vols. (Salem, Mass.: Essex Institute, 1911–1921), IV: 269, where a man was ordered personally to hand his wife two shillings per week, "to live with her, as duty binds him, and at least to lodge with her one night in a week." She, in turn, "was enjoined to entertain him as her husband whenever he comes." And, when Mr. Clenton disobeyed the Court's order, he was sent to the House of Correction. Clenton v. Clenton, Quarterly Ct. Ipswich 1671, in *Records of Essex*, IV: 425. *Accord,* Colony v. Johnson, Middlesex County Ct. Oct. 6, 1663 (microfilm in possession of Genealogical Society of Utah).

10. *See* Drury v. Drury, Ct. Asst. 1677, in *Records of Assistants,* I: 91; Colony v. Ball, Middlesex County Ct. Dec. 28, 1658 (microfilm in possession of Genealogical Society of Utah). One man was even prosecuted "for lying from his wife these many years," although he was not convicted when "[h]is answer satisfied the court." Colony v. Hethersay, Quarterly Ct. Salem 1643, in *Records of Essex*, I: 58. Another man, whose wife claimed he was impotent, was ordered "to take counsel of physicians forthwith, follow their advice, and report to court." Colony v. Rolinson, Quarterly Ct. Ipswich 1651, in *Records of Essex*, I: 221. *Accord,* White v. White, Quarterly Ct. Salem 1662/63, in *Records of Essex*, III: 110, where a wife complained about her husband's "insufficiency concerning the marriage state." Initially, the Court of Assistants "advised" the couple "to a more loving & suitable cohabitation one with the other & that all due physical means may be used," White v. White, Ct. Asst. 1662, in *Records of Assistants*, III: 131, but later the Quarterly Court ruled "that it would not be offensive...for her...to marry another man." White v. White, Quarterly Ct. Salem 1663, in *Records of Essex,* III: 110.

11. *See* Colony v. Barefoot, Ct. Asst. 1671, in *Records of Assistants*, III: 211–212; Colony v. Iron, Middlesex County Ct. Aug. 7, 1651 (microfilm in possession of Genealogical Society of Utah); Colony v. Crown, Suffolk County Ct. 1674, in *Records of the Suffolk County Court, 1671–1680,* 2 vols. (Boston: Colonial Society of Massachusetts, 1933), I: 425. Indeed, a man who claimed that his wife had died in England was "ordered...to repair to the last place of her abode or bring certificate that she is dead." *See* Colony v. Hall, Suffolk County Ct. 1671, in *Records of Suffolk*, I: 23. However, a man would not be required to return to England if he could prove that he had tried to bring his wife

to Massachusetts and that she had "a comfortable estate to live upon and maintain herself in England." Colony v. Bayley, Quarterly Ct. Salem 1654, in *Records of Essex*, I: 359.

12. Colony v. Atherton, Suffolk County Ct. 1676, in *Records of Suffolk*, II: 720.

13. *See* Colony v. Turell, Ct. Asst. 1672, in *Records of Assistants*, III: 223 (colony treasurer ordered to pay for transportation of impoverished wife and children to Virginia); Colony v. Luffe, Quarterly Ct. Salem 1648/49, in *Records of Essex*, I: 158 (selectmen ordered to find work for husband).

14. Colony v. Littleale, Quarterly Ct. Hampton 1672, in *Records of Essex*, V: 104. *Accord*, Colony v. Henshaw, Middlesex County Ct., Apr. 4, 1672 (microfilm in possession of Genealogical Society of Utah). Parents had an obligation to their children "to educate & bring them up as they ought to be," Colony v. Mansfield, Middlesex County Ct. Dec. 30, 1656 (microfilm in possession of Genealogical Society of Utah), and not in a "rude, irreligious, profane, and barbarous manner contrary to the word of God." Colony v. Dunton, Middlesex County Ct. Apr. 7, 1674 (microfilm in possession of Genealogical Society of Utah). A father who neglected his obligation could be prosecuted "for neglect of family government." Colony v. Dickerman, Middlesex County Ct. Dec. 19, 1676 (microfilm in possession of Genealogical Society of Utah). *Accord*, Colony v. Blond, Middlesex County Ct. Dec. 18, 1678 (microfilm in possession of Genealogical Society of Utah) (prosecution "for letting his daughter...escape, who was accused of having a bastard"). Children would be removed from a family by court order if a father "by reason of the misgovernment of himself & wife" proved unable to meet his obligation. Colony v. Mansfield, *supra. Accord*, Colony v. Dunton, *supra. Cf.* Colony v. Dickerman, *supra*, where the father avoided conviction by proving that he had bound out his misbehaving daughter. In addition, individuals under family government were subject to correction by the head of the family at court order. *See* Colony v. Hunt, Quarterly Ct. Ipswich 1674, in *Records of Essex*, IV, 306. Indeed, in one case a court ordered a father and mother to whip their son and daughter, respectively, "in their own house in the presence of the constable." Colony v. Chandler, Suffolk County Ct. 1674, in *Records of Suffolk*, I: 478–479. Children guilty of "stubborn and wicked carriages towards...parents" would be sent to the House of Correction. Colony v. Gale, Middlesex County Ct., Oct. 4, 1671 (microfilm in possession of Genealogical Society of Utah).

15. Colony v. Wilson, Middlesex County Ct., Apr. 7, 1685 (microfilm in possession of Genealogical Society of Utah). On the importance of requiring people to live together as families, *see* Mary Beth Norton, *Founding Mothers and Fathers: Gendered Power and the Forming of American Society* (New York: Alfred A. Knopf, 1996), 38–42.

16. *See* James Horn, *A Land as God Made It: Jamestown and the Birth of America* (New York: Basic Books, 2005), 245–246; Edmund S. Morgan, *American Slavery, American Freedom: The Ordeal of Colonial Virginia* (New York: W.W. Norton, 1975), 141–142 n.32; Haskins, *Law and Authority*, 88.

17. Answer of Pratt, Ct. Asst. 1635, in *Records of Assistants*, II: 109–112. *See* Bremer, *Puritan Experiment*, 101–120.

18. *See* Order re Town Meeting about School, Quarterly Ct. Salem 1641, in *Records of Essex*, I: 25; Bremer, *Puritan Experiment*, 117–119. *See generally* James Axtell, *The School upon a Hill: Education and Society in Colonial New England* (New Haven: Yale University Press, 1974); Robert Middlekauff, *Ancients and Axioms: Secondary Education in Eighteenth-Century New England* (New Haven: Yale University Press, 1963).

19. *See* Francis J. Bremer, *John Winthrop: America's Forgotten Founding Father* (New York: Oxford University Press, 2003); Bremer, *Puritan Experiment*, 102–103. On the power of magnates in England, *see* Carl Bridenbaugh, *Vexed and Troubled Englishmen, 1590–1642* (New York: Oxford University Press, 1968), 240–248, 263.

20. The Body of Liberties of 1641, in Powers, *Crime and Punishment in Early Massachusetts*, 533. The most recent scholar to discuss the *Humfry* case and to take note of earlier scholarly discussions is John Phillip Reid, *Rule of Law: The Jurisprudence of Liberty in the Seventeenth and Eighteenth Centuries* (DeKalb: Northern Illinois University Press, 2004), 47–50. The most important earlier discussion is in Haskins, *Law and Authority*, 150–151. Reid also notes that explicit authorization for recourse to the law of God went back at least to the Body of Liberties of 1641. *See* Reid, *Rule of Law*, 37.

21. Colony v. Jeanison, Ct. Asst. 1669, in *Records of Assistants*, III: 199. *See also* Colony v. Basto, Ct. Asst. 1676, in *Records of Assistants*, I: 74 (African-American slave guilty of rape on three-year-old daughter of master, in aftermath of legislation prohibiting rape of minors, sentenced to death). The *Jeanison* case is discussed in Reid, *Rule of Law*, 49–50.

22. *See* Gardiner v. Nevard, Middlesex County Ct. June 15, 1675 and Dec. 19, 1676 (microfilm in possession of Genealogical Society of Utah); Colony v. Stuart, Suffolk County Ct. 1673/74, in *Records of Suffolk*, I: 405–408. *Cf.* Stanton v. Trott, Suffolk County Ct. 1673, in *Records of Suffolk*, I: 242 (suit by father on behalf of daughter for failure to pay money to support child the defendant begot).

23. *See, e.g.,* Colony v. Hutchinson, Ct. Asst. 1641, in *Records of Assistants*, II: 109 (banished); Colony v. Ratliffe, Ct. Asst. 1631, in *Records of Assistants*, II: 16 (whipped, ears cut off, and banished); Colony v. Goult, Quarterly Ct. Salem 1642, in *Records of Essex*, I: 49 (whipped); Colony v. Buet, Ct. Asst. 1640, in *Records of Assistants*, II: 101 (banished for heresy); Colony v. Redknape,

Quarterly Ct. Salem 1644, in *Records of Essex*, I: 70 (ordered to baptize child). *Cf.* Colony v. Tomlins, Ct. Asst. 1641, in *Records of Assistants*, II: 105 (discharged after "retracting his opinions against singing in the churches"). On Hutchinson and Williams, *see* Bremer, *Puritan Experiment*, 62–70; Winship, *Making Heretics*, 79–80, 169–185, 197–209.

24. *See, e.g.,* Colony v. Penyon, Quarterly Ct. Salem 1647, in *Records of Essex*, I: 134 (missing church); Colony v. Scott, Quarterly Ct. Salem 1642/43, in *Records of Essex*, I: 51 (sleeping in church and "striking him who awakened him"); Colony v. Hacklinton, Springfield Ct. 1661, in Joseph H. Smith, ed., *Colonial Justice in Western Massachusetts (1639–1702): The Pynchon Court Record* (Cambridge, Mass.: Harvard University Press, 1961), 255 (carrying bricks on Sunday). *Cf.* Colony v. Veren, Quarterly Ct. Salem 1663, in *Records of Essex*, III: 111 (one hour in stocks "for disowning the country's power, in open court, about forcing any to come to the public worship").

25. Colony v. Ledra, Ct. Asst. 1660/61, in *Records of Assistants*, III: 93–94. *See* Bremer, *Puritan Experiment*, 155–156.

26. *See* Colony v. Davis, Ct. Asst. 1659, in *Records of Assistants*, III: 68–69 (banished); Colony v. Robbinson, Ct. Asst. 1659, in *Records of Assistants*, III: 68 (whipped); Colony v. Hadlock, Quarterly Ct. Salem 1668, in *Records of Essex*, IV: 74 (whipped); Colony v. Brend, Quarterly Ct. Salem 1658, in *Records of Essex*, II: 103–104 (jailed); Colony v. Phelps, Quarterly Ct. Salem 1658, in *Records of Essex*, II: 103–104 (fined); Colony v. Bowers, Middlesex County Ct. Oct. 16, 1663 (microfilm in possession of Genealogical Society of Utah) (fined).

27. Colony v. Shattuck, Quarterly Ct. Ipswich 1658, in *Records of Essex*, II: 118.

28. *See* Bremer, *Puritan Experiment*, 154–156.

29. *The Book of the General Lawes and Libertyes Concerning the Inhabitants of the Massachusetts* (Cambridge, Mass.: 1648), ed. Richard S. Dunn (San Marino, Cal.: Huntington Library, 1998), 20. *See* Allen Carden, *Puritan Christianity in America: Religion and Life in Seventeenth-Century Massachusetts* (Grand Rapids, Mich.: Baker Book House, 1990), 105–108; Cooper, *Tenacious of Their Liberties*, 68–79.

30. *See* Giddings v. Brown, Essex County Ct. 1657, in Mark DeWolfe Howe, ed., *Readings in American Legal History* (Cambridge, Mass.: Harvard University Press, 1949), 232; Konig, *Law and Society*, 93–95; Howe ed., *Readings*, 240 n. 7.

31. *See* Howe ed., *Readings*, 137, 144–179; Winship, *Making Heretics*, 79–80, 168–185, 197–209; Day v. Blinman, Quarterly Ct. Salem 1649, in *Records of Essex*, I: 173.

32. Roger Thompson, *Sex in Middlesex: Popular Mores in a Massachusetts County, 1649–1699* (Amherst: University of Massachusetts Press, 1986), 36. McManus, *Law and Liberty*, 201–204, shows that there were a few more prosecutions

for fornication than even for drunkenness. I do not understand that my conclusion about the comparatively high rate of prosecution for fornication in Massachusetts is at all inconsistent with Thompson's findings, *see* Thompson, *Sex in Middlesex*, 17, 54, 70, about the comparatively low frequency with which fornication actually occurred. On the contrary, our findings are totally consistent: the junction between law and religion both nurtured and enforced religious norms and induced the populace to obey them. When the norms were breached, the law was quickly and effectively brought to bear to enforce them. *See* ibid., 198.

33. *See, e.g.*, Colony v. Bull, Ct. Asst. 1642/43, in *Records of Assistants*, II: 121. *Cf.* Colony v. Hobell, Springfield Ct. 1640/41, in *Pynchon Court Record*, 209 (man whipped for obtaining promise of marriage from woman "after both he and she had been prohibited by her father several times" and they had attempted fornication, "though as far as we can discern…the act was not done"). *See generally* Norton, *Founding Mothers and Fathers*, 69–72.

34. *See* Colony v. Bridges, Quarterly Ct. Ipswich 1657, in *Records of Essex*, II: 53. The birth of an illegitimate child was not a prerequisite for a fornication prosecution. *See* Colony v. Starr, Middlesex County Ct. Apr. 2, 1661 (microfilm in possession of Genealogical Society of Utah).

35. Colony v. Wyar, Ct. Asst. 1642/43, in *Records of Assistants*, II: 121. The good people of Massachusetts were so eager to prevent illicit sex, even when no human was involved, that the Court of Assistants adopted the following ordinance:

> [I]f any ram goat be found among ewe goats between the first of July and the tenth of November it shall be lawful for any man to seize on him before witnesses & to convey him to some safe place till the said tenth of November & then half of him is to go to the public & the other half to the party that seizes on him.

Order re Rams, Ct. Asst. 1633, in *Records of Assistants*, II: 34.

36. *See* Order re Adultery, Ct. Asst. 1631, in *Records of Assistants*, II: 19; *Lawes and Libertyes of 1648*, 6; Colony v. Brittaine, Ct. Asst. 1643/44, in *Records of Assistants*, II: 139 (man and woman executed for adultery). No one else was ever executed for adultery, as those who were accused were either acquitted or found guilty of lesser offenses such as lying in bed together or suspicion of incontinency. *See* Norton, *Founding Mothers and Fathers*, 342–343.

37. *See Lawes and Libertyes of 1648*, 5; Colony v. Cuppie, Ct. Asst. 1657, in *Records of Assistants*, III: 67 (man accusing another of bestiality whipped because his accusation "had it been true would have endangered" the accused's "life"); Colony v. Pitfold, Ct. Asst. 1657, in *Records of Assistants*, III: 66 (not guilty);

Colony v. Ocrimi, Ct. Asst. 1642/43, in *Records of Assistants*, II: 121 (guilty only of attempt).

38. *See Lawes and Libertyes of 1648*, 5; Colony v. Johnson, Quarterly Ct. Salem 1642, in *Records of Essex*, I: 44; Colony v. Burrell and Legg, Quarterly Ct. Salem 1638, in *Records of Essex*, I: 8. *See also* Norton, *Founding Mothers and Fathers*, 354–357.

39. Colony v. Trotter, Quarterly Ct. Ipswich 1653, in *Records of Essex*, I: 305; Colony v. Terry, Springfield Ct. 1650, in *Pynchon Court Record*, 224.

40. On alcohol, *see, e.g.*, Order Requiring Licenses for Sale of Alcoholic Beverages, Ct. Asst. 1633, in *Records of Assistants*, II: 33; Colony v. Hamon, Ct. Asst. 1632, in *Records of Assistants*, II: 26; Colony v. Davis, Middlesex County Ct. Dec. 27, 1659 (microfilm in possession of Genealogical Society of Utah). On cards and dice, *see, e.g.*, Order To Throw Away Cards and Dice, Ct. Asst. 1630/31, in *Records of Assistants*, II: 12; Colony v. Miller, Springfield Ct. 1661/62, in *Pynchon Court Record*, 257. On singing, etc., *see, e.g.*, Colony v. Waters, Ct. Asst. 1638, in *Records of Assistants*, II: 75; Colony v. Owls, Quarterly Ct. Salem 1641, in *Records of Essex*, I: 37. On tobacco, *see, e.g.*, Order re Tobacco, Ct. Asst. 1632, in *Records of Assistants*, II: 28; Colony v. Harris, Quarterly Ct. Salem 1652, in *Records of Essex*, I: 274. On the sumptuary laws, *see, e.g.*, Colony v. Kippin, Quarterly Ct. Salem 1652, in *Records of Essex*, I: 273. *See generally* Flaherty, *Privacy in New England*, 179–188.

41. Colony v. Clark, Quarterly Ct. Salem 1643, in *Records of Essex*, I: 58; Colony v. Greenfeild, Quarterly Ct. Salisbury 1649, in *Records of Essex*, I: 166. *Accord*, Colony v. Wilson, Quarterly Ct. Ipswich 1654, in *Records of Essex*, I: 365. *Cf.* Colony v. Lovell, Ct. Asst. 1636/37, in *Records of Assistants*, II: 65 ("light & whorish behavior"); Colony v. Bridges, Quarterly Ct. Ipswich 1667, in *Records of Essex*, III: 448 ("uncivil carriages and suspicions of the act of uncleanness"); Colony v. Osier, Quarterly Ct. Salem 1664, in *Records of Essex*, III: 226 ("lascivious carriages towards the maids of the house"); Colony v. Plumb, Suffolk County Ct. 1672, in *Records of Suffolk*, I: 185 ("lascivious carriage"); Colony v. Longhorne, Colony v. Liman, Springfield Ct. 1660, in *Pynchon Court Record*, 248 ("gross lascivious carriage").

42. *See* Order re Prices, Ct. Asst. 1633, in *Records of Assistants*, II: 39; Haskins, *Law and Authority*, 52, 90, 126; Innes, *Creating the Commonwealth*, 160–191. *See also* Order re Purchases off Ships, Ct. Asst. 1631, in *Records of Assistants*, II: 16 (prohibiting all purchases from vessels in harbor without license from governor or court). Innes's argument that the Bay Colony had accepted a free market economy by the end of the 1630s is overstated in light of the regulatory efforts of that and later decades. He is correct, however, in emphasizing the relationship between just price and market price, although, contrary perhaps

to his intentions, he shows that Puritan thinkers had not worked out the precise contours of that relationship.

43. *See* Order re Corn, Ct. Asst. 1633, in *Records of Assistants*, II: 38; Order re Corn, Ct. Asst. 1634, in *Records of Assistants*, II: 43. *See also* Order re Swine, Ct. Asst. 1633, in *Records of Assistants*, II: 38 (unlawful to feed corn to swine); Order re Swine, Ct. Asst. 1633, in *Records of Assistants*, II: 34 (lawful to kill pigs who invade corn fields).

44. *See* Colony v. Fuller, Ct. Asst. 1639, in *Records of Assistants*, II: 85; Colony v. Hunt, Ct. Asst. 1641, in *Records of Assistants*, II: 106; Colony v. Payne, Quarterly Ct. Ipswich 1658, in *Records of Essex*, II: 118.

45. *See* Colony v. Knopp, Ct. Asst. 1630/31, in *Records of Assistants*, II: 11; Colony v. Keesar, Quarterly Ct. Salem 1647/48, in *Records of Essex*, I: 137; Order re Sudbury Mill, Ct. Asst. 1643, in *Records of Assistants*, II: 135.

46. *See Lawes and Libertyes of 1648*, 38; Order re Workmen's Wages, Ct. Asst. 1633, in *Records of Assistants*, II: 36; Rates for Workmen, Ct. Asst. 1630, in *Records of Assistants*, II: 5, *repealed by* Workmen's Wages at Liberty, Ct. Asst. 1630/31, in *Records of Assistants*, II: 12. For prosecutions, *see, e.g.*, Colony v. Applefourd, Quarterly Ct. Ipswich 1659, in *Records of Essex*, II: 152; Colony v. Goodhue, Quarterly Ct. Ipswich 1658, in *Records of Essex*, II: 119; Colony v. Dixie, Quarterly Ct. Salem 1636, in *Records of Essex*, I: 3. The early study on this subject, Richard B. Morris, *Government and Labor in Early America* (New York: Columbia University Press, 1946), 55–78, remains unsurpassed.

47. Colony v. Boutwell, Quarterly Ct. Salem 1640, in *Records of Essex*, I: 20.

48. *See* Idleness to be Punished, Ct. Asst. 1633, in *Records of Assistants*, II: 37. For prosecutions, *see, e.g.*, Colony v. Ellen, Ct. Asst. 1639, in *Records of Assistants*, II: 84; Colony v. Brumfield, Ct. Asst. 1637, in *Records of Assistants*, II: 70; Colony v. Oddingsall, Quarterly Ct. Salem 1641, in *Records of Essex*, I: 34; Colony v. Daniel, a Scotchman, Springfield Ct. 1654, in *Pynchon Court Record*, 231. *Cf.* Horton v. Merricke, Springfield Ct. 1639/40, in *Pynchon Court Record*, 205 (civil suit "for not doing a sufficient day's work for the wages of a day").

49. Complaint of Lancaster Selectmen, Middlesex County Ct. Oct. 1, 1672 (microfilm in possession of Genealogical Society of Utah) (language in court order concerning treatment of illegitimate infant for whom the selectmen assumed no responsibility); Colony v. Adames, Quarterly Ct. Salem 1640, in *Records of Essex*, I: 21.

50. *See generally* Morris, *Government and Labor*, 390–512.

51. *See, e.g.*, Order re Runaways, Ct. Asst. 1634, in *Records of Assistants*, II: 43; Colony v. Robinson, Quarterly Ct. Salem 1653, in *Records of Essex*, I: 286; Colony v. Williams, Quarterly Ct. Salem 1659, in *Records of Essex.*, II: 161–162. But, if a man were prosecuted as a runaway when he was in fact free, he could maintain an action for damages. *See* Deane v. Wade, Quarterly

Ct. Ipswich 1658, in *Records of Essex*, II: 62. Of course, if a servant failed to prove his claim of freedom, he would remain in service. *See* Edwards v. Palfrey, Quarterly Ct. Salem 1649, in *Records of Essex*, I: 181.

52. *See, e.g.*, Colony v. Legge, Ct. Asst. 1631, in *Records of Assistants*, II: 14 (whipping for assault); Colony v. Mickenna, Middlesex County Ct. Nov. 3, 1653 (microfilm in possession of Genealogical Society of Utah) (whipping plus two months additional service for resistance).; Colony v. Perry, Ct. Asst. 1631, in *Records of Assistants*, II: 18 (whipping for speaking); Colony v. Cokar, Ct. Asst. 1634, in *Records of Assistants*, II: 51 (assisting escape).

53. *See, e.g.*, Colony v. Wilson, Ct. Asst. 1639, in *Records of Assistants*, II: 86 (extra service); Colony v. Legge, Ct. Asst. 1631, in *Records of Assistants*, II: 14 (whipping); Colony v. Spencer, Quarterly Ct. Ipswich 1665, in *Records of Essex*, III: 254 (whipping and treble damages). *Cf.* Colony v. Scarlett, Ct. Asst. 1635, in *Records of Assistants*, II: 60 (master ordered to sell servant, a thief, out of the country).

54. *See Lawes and Libertyes of 1648*, 38; Order re Servants, Ct. Asst. 1630, in *Records of Assistants*, II: 5.

55. *See* Colony v. Androws, Ct. Asst. 1638, in *Records of Assistants*, II: 78; Colony v. Stevens, Ct. Asst. 1640, in *Records of Assistants*, II: 100; Colony v. Cooke, Quarterly Ct. Salem 1640, in *Records of Essex*, I: 20.

56. *See Lawes and Libertyes of 1648*, 38; Colony v. Staughton, Ct. Asst. 1639, in *Records of Assistants*, II: 84. *Cf.* Colony v. Batte, Ct. Asst. 1640, in *Records of Assistants*, II: 100 (prosecution "for selling servant his time" referred to county court). Morris, *Government and Labor*, 390, attributes the rule against manumission to a concern that servants not become public charges. In view of the shortage of labor in the earliest years of the Bay Colony, such a concern was unfounded, although the Colony's leaders may have had the concern if they were still functioning in an English mindset, which assumed an excess supply of labor.

57. *See Lawes and Libertyes of 1648*, 39; Colony v. Graunt, Ct. Asst. 1640/41, in *Records of Assistants*, II: 103; Colony v. Poole, Ct. Asst. 1638, in *Records of Assistants*, II: 80. But at least one servant who complained of abuse and failed to prove his claim was whipped. *See* Complaint of Carey, Quarterly Ct. Salem 1650, in *Records of Essex*, I: 204.

58. *See* Sharratt v. Hiskeas, Quarterly Ct. Ipswich 1654, in *Records of Essex*, I: 339; Colony v. Hogges, Ct. Asst. 1638/39, in *Records of Assistants*, II: 81; Colony v. Betts, Ct. Asst. 1652/53, in *Records of Assistants*, III: 24.

59. *See* Shadow v. Jay, Middlesex County Ct. Feb. 3, 1655 (microfilm in possession of Genealogical Society of Utah); Burton v. Rowden, Quarterly Ct. Salem 1649/50, in *Records of Essex*, I: 185; Legate v. Fullar, Quarterly Ct. Ipswich 1646, in *Records of Essex*, I: 111. *Cf.* Colony v. Urselton, Quarterly Ct.

Ipswich 1660, in *Records of Essex*, II: 247 (parents admonished for "leaving their children alone in the night in a lonely house, far from neighbors"). *See also* Colony v. Perry, Quarterly Ct. Ipswich 1650, in *Records of Essex*, I: 188.

60. *See* Osbourne v. Hook, Ct. Asst. 1649/50, in *Records of Assistants*, III: 23.

61. *See* Order re Servants, Ct. Asst. 1631, in *Records of Assistants*, II: 15; Colony v. Phelps, Quarterly Ct. Salem 1645, in *Records of Essex*, I: 79. *Accord*, Whithare v. Gray, Quarterly Ct. Salem 1656, in *Records of Essex*, I: 424 (master must return plaintiff's son from Virginia). On the ability of families to protect servant kin, *see* Axtell, *School upon a Hill*, 130–131.

62. *See* Konig, *Law and Society*, 70–74. On the need for permission, *see Laws and Libertyes of 1648*, 49.

63. *See* Haskins, *Law and Authority*, 34. *But see* Gifford v. Savage, Quarterly Ct. Hampton, 1653, in *Records of Essex*, I: 309–310 (upholding objection to calling of special court).

64. *See* Saggamore John v. Saltonstall, Ct. Asst. 1630/31, in *Records of Assistants*, II: 11; Order Prohibiting Employment of Indians as Servants, Ct. Asst. 1630/31, in *Records of Assistants*, II: 11; Order Prohibiting Trade with Indians, Ct. Asst. 1630/31, in *Records of Assistants*, II: 10; Miller v. Jones, Springfield Ct. 1650, in *Pynchon Court Record*, 223 (15 lashes for assault on Indian).

65. *See* Haskins, *Law and Authority*, 154; *Lawes and Libertyes of 1648*, 53–54; Estate of Averill, Quarterly Ct. Ipswich 1655, in *Records of Essex*, I: 387.

66. *See* Order re John and Elizabeth Mansfield, Middlesex County Ct. Dec. 30, 1656 (microfilm in possession of Genealogical Society of Utah), concerning eight-year-old twins placed in service. John was placed "for ten years next ensuing, three whereof to be kept at school, and the other seven at any honest trade or employment, and the daughter likewise for ten years," because their father was "not capable…to educate & bring them up as they ought to be." The word "likewise" is somewhat ambiguous in this court order, but, especially in light of the subsequent word "educate," it should be read as providing three years of school for Elizabeth, not merely ten years in a trade. On Harvard, *see* Axtell, *School upon a Hill*, 176–179, 199–244; Robert Middlekauff, *Ancients and Axioms*, 15, 70–74, 104–109.

67. *See* Norton, *Founding Mothers and Fathers*, 73–74, 88; Colony v. Portor, Quarterly Ct. Salem 1661, in *Records of Essex*, II: 335 (abusive son committed to house of correction); Colony v. White, Quarterly Ct. Ipswich 1657, in *Records of Essex*, II: 39 (whipping for son who resisted chastisement by father).

68. *See* Norton, *Founding Mothers and Fathers*, 91–94; Clarke v. Clarke, Ct. Asst. 1643/44, in *Records of Assistants*, II: 138.

69. On the legislation, *see* Norton, *Founding Mothers and Fathers*, 73–74, 78. For prosecutions of husbands, *see, e.g.*, Colony v. Reynolds, Quarterly Ct. Salem 1648/49, in *Records of Essex*, I: 158; Colony v. Draper, Middlesex County Ct. June

16, 1657 (microfilm in possession of Genealogical Society of Utah). *Cf.* Colony v. Browne, Quarterly Ct. Salem 1641, in *Records of Essex*, I: 25 (wife whipped for assaulting husband); Colony v. Miller, Springfield Ct. 1655/56, in *Pynchon Court Record*, 235 (ibid.). For a wife excused from living with her husband, *see* Colony v. Ellis, Quarterly Ct. Salem 1647/48, in *Records of Essex*, I: 135.

70. *See, e.g.*, Colony v. Walford, Ct. Asst. 1631, in *Records of Assistants*, II: 14 (general contempt); Colony v. Jennison, Ct. Asst. 1634, in *Records of Assistants*, II: 48 (disappointed litigant); Colony v. Gregory, Springfield Ct. 1640, in *Pynchon Court Record*, 207 (ibid.).

71. Colony v. Dexter, Ct. Asst. 1632/33, in *Records of Assistants*, II: 30–31; Colony v. Lee, Ct. Asst. 1634, in *Records of Assistants*, II: 49; Colony v. Starr, Ct. Asst. 1637/38, in *Records of Assistants*, II: 73.

72. *See, e.g.*, Colony v. Holland, Ct. Asst. 1640, in *Records of Assistants*, II: 102; Colony v. Palmer, Ct. Asst. 1633, in *Records of Assistants*, II: 35; Colony v. Kent, Quarterly Ct. Ipswich 1654, in *Records of Essex*, I: 362; Colony v. Cooper, Ct. Asst. 1643/44, in *Records of Assistants*, II: 138; Colony v. Goffe, Middlesex County Ct. Feb. 4, 1654 (microfilm in possession of Genealogical Society of Utah).

73. Order about Counsel, Ct. Asst. 1649, in *Records of Assistants*, III: 21.

74. *See* Colony v. Knower, Ct. Asst. 1632, in *Record of Assistants*, II: 21; Colony v. Lynn, Ct. Asst. 1631, in *Records of Assistants*, II: 19; Colony v. Norman, Ct. Asst. 1639, in *Records of Assistants*, II: 82. *But see* Petition of Gibones, Ct. Asst. 1645, in *Records of Assistants*, III: 11 (case involving ship seized as enemy of King and Parliament referred to High Court of Admiralty in England).

75. *See, e.g.*, Colony v. Williams, Ct. Asst. 1637, in *Records of Assistants*, II: 69 (murder); Colony v. Perry, Quarterly Ct. Salem 1654, in *Records of Essex*, I: 360 (assault); Colony v. West, Quarterly Ct. Salem 1657, in *Records of Essex*, II: 48 (burglary); Colony v. Hill, Ct. Asst. 1630, in *Records of Assistants*, II: 9 (stealing bread); Colony v. Holgrave, Quarterly Ct. Salem 1642/43, in *Records of Essex*, I: 50 (perjury).

76. *See* McManus, *Law and Liberty*, 201–204.

77. *See, e.g.*, Colony v. Fogge, Quarterly Ct. Salem 1649, in *Records of Essex*, I: 185; Colony v. Farrington, Quarterly Ct. Salem 1649, in *Records of Essex*, I: 171; Johnson v. Carter, Middlesex County Ct. Dec. 28, 1658 (microfilm in possession of Genealogical Society of Utah).

78. Stiles v. Bennet, Springfield Ct. 1655, in *Pynchon Court Record*, 236. For other cases of sexual slander, *see, e.g.*, Colony v. Vinson, Quarterly Ct. Salem 1649, in *Records of Essex*, I: 174; Page v. Flemmin, Middlesex County Ct. Feb. 2, 1650 (microfilm in possession of Genealogical Society of Utah).

79. Gifford v. Webb, Quarterly Ct. Ipswich 1658, in *Records of Essex*, II: 71.

80. Haskins, *Law and Authority*, 91.

81. Elmer v. Holton, Springfield Ct. 1658, in *Pynchon Court Record*, 238.

82. This conclusion is based on a comparison of the proportion of debt collection cases in the printed court records for Accomack/Northampton counties in Virginia and Essex County, Massachusetts, for the decade of the 1640s. Even the printed records do not, unfortunately, always specify as clearly as one might like whether a case is one for debt collection, and thus it was necessary to develop arbitrary categorization rules that could be applied uniformly in both jurisdictions; for example, all writs of debt were counted as debt collection cases, even though occasional ones might have been suits to recover penalties. Cases too ambiguous to fit within any strict rule were counted as debt cases in Essex and nondebt cases in Accomack/Northampton—a methodology tending to undercount debt cases in Accomack/Northampton and overcount them in Essex. Out of a total of 1682 case entries for Accomack/Northampton for the years 1641–1650, 1294, or 76.9 percent, were for debt collection. In Essex County for the same years, 255 out of 1073 filings or 238 percent, were debt collection cases Using standard tests of statistical significance, it is possible to state with a 95 percent level of confidence that these results were not random.

83. *See Lawes and Libertyes of 1648*, 2–3.

84. *See* Order re Bills, Ct. Asst. 1631, in *Records of Assistants*, II: 18; *Lawes and Libertyes of 1648*, 4.

85. *See, e.g.*, Company of Seamen v. Risbie, Ct. Asst. 1648, in *Records of Assistants*, III: 16; Foote v. Foxcroft, Ct. Asst. 1645, in *Records of Assistants*, III: 12; Broune v. Armestrong, Ct. Asst. 1661, in *Records of Assistants*, III: 129. *Cf.* Bartholomew v. Knight, Quarterly Ct. Ipswich 1647, in *Records of Essex*, I: 127 (suit on bill of exchange payable in London).

86. *See* Hakins v. Gooden, Ct. Asst. 1659/60, in *Records of Assistants*, III: 86.

87. Of course, there were occasional commercial cases in the courts serving interior towns, especially those like Springfield that were commercial in character. *See, e.g.*, Colony v. Sackett, Springfield Ct. 1662, in *Pynchon Court Record*, 260 (fine for trading unlawfully in skins).

88. *See, e.g.*, Assurance of Lands, Ct. Asst. 1634, in *Records of Assistants*, II: 45; Colony v. Ipswich, Ct. Asst. 1639, in *Records of Assistants*, II: 90; Order re Town Meeting, Quarterly Ct. Salem 1641, in *Records of Essex*, I: 25; Simes v. Broughton, Middlesex County Ct. June 16, 1657 (microfilm in possession of Genealogical Society of Utah). On the development of the recording system, *see generally* Haskins, *Law and Authority*, 172–174.

89. *See, e.g.*, Colony v. Dedham, Ct. Asst. 1639, in *Records of Assistants*, II: 90; Colony v. Cambridge, Ct. Asst. 1639, in *Records of Assistants*, II: 90; Colony v. Cambridge, Ct. Asst. 1639, in *Records of Assistants*, II: 85; License of Palfrey, Middlesex County Ct. Apr. 20, 1654 (microfilm in possession of Genealogical Society of Utah).

90. Colony v. Lee, Ct. Asst. 1634, in *Records of Assistants*, II: 49.

91. For title cases, *see, e.g.*, Dexter v. Layton, Ct. Asst. 1657, in *Records of Assistants*, III: 46; Hammond v. Bridge, Middlesex County Ct. Aug. 5, 1652 (microfilm in possession of Genealogical Society of Utah). For damage cases, *see, e.g.*, Tayler v. King, Ct. Asst. 1646, in *Records of Assistants*, III: 13; Symonds v. Story, Quarterly Ct. Ipswich 1647, in *Records of Essex*, I: 124; Bliss v. Dorchester, Springfield Ct. 1653/54, in *Pynchon Court Record*, 230.

92. *See generally* Innes, *Labor in a New Land*; Martin, *Profits in the Wilderness*.

93. Thompson, *Sex in Middlesex*, 200.

CHAPTER 4

1. *See* Barbara A. Black, "The Judicial Power and the General Court in Early Massachusetts (1634–1686)" (Ph.D. diss.: Yale University, 1975), 5–8, 12–15.

2. *See* George Lee Haskins, *Law and Authority in Early Massachusetts: A Study in Tradition and Design* (New York: Macmillan, 1960), 9–12, 23–26.

3. *See* Haskins, *Law and Authority*, 28–31.

4. The seminal work on the negative remains Mark deWolfe Howe and Louis F. Eaton, Jr., "The Supreme Judicial Power in the Colony of Massachusetts Bay," *New England Quarterly*, 20 (1947): 291. *See also* Black, "Judicial Power," 269–346; Haskins, *Law and Authority*, 38–39.

5. The jurisdiction of the various Massachusetts courts is best set out in Joseph H. Smith, "Legal and Historical Introduction to the Pynchon Court Record," in Joseph H. Smith, ed., *Colonial Justice in Western Massachusetts (1639–1702): The Pynchon Court Record* (Cambridge, Mass.: Harvard University Press, 1961), 1, 65–88. *See also* Haskins, *Law and Authority*, 32–35; Black, "Judicial Power," 76–137.

6. *See* Smith, "Introduction," 83–98. Even in later years, for example, the General Court, *see* Hough v. Hill, Middlesex County Ct. Oct. 6, 1685 (microfilm in possession of Genealogical Society of Utah), and the Court of Assistants, *see* Deane v. Hubbard, Suffolk County Ct. 1677, in *Records of the Suffolk County Court, 1671–1680*, 2 vols. (Boston: Colonial Society of Massachusetts, 1933), II: 788, sometimes intervened in pending litigation, even at the county level.

7. Complaint of Woodbridge, Ct. Asst. 1673, in *Records of the Court of Assistants of the Colony of the Massachusetts Bay*, 3 vols. (Boston: County of Suffolk, 1901–1928), III: 252. At other times, however, courts did enforce jurisdictional limitations. *See* Milles v. Read, Middlesex County Ct. Feb. 3, 1655 (microfilm in possession of Genealogical Society of Utah) (action "by law is not triable in this Court").

8. *See* Stone v. Broughton, Middlesex County Ct. Oct. 2, 1655 (microfilm in possession of Genealogical Society of Utah) (appeal to "next Quarter Court

to be held at Boston"). Prior to 1649, the Court of Assistants was also known as the Great Quarter Court, but in that year its sittings were reduced to two per year. *See* Smith, "Introduction," 68. Thus, I conclude that the appeal was to the County Court at Boston, not the Court of Assistants, but perhaps that conclusion is wrong. If so, the *Stone* case still makes the point that seventeenth-century language usage made jurisdictional bounds permeable and imprecise.

9. *See* Smith, "Introduction," 72, 76; Black, "Judicial Power," 129; Hutchinson v. Bacon, Middlesex County Ct. Apr. 2, 1661 (microfilm in possession of Genealogical Society of Utah) (appeal directly from county court to General Court).

10. *See* Smith, "Introduction," 33–34, 75–76; *Pynchon Court Record*, 245; Order re Nominations for County Court, Quarterly Ct. Salisbury 1674, in *Records and Files of the Quarterly Courts of Essex County, Massachusetts*, 8 vols. (Salem, Mass.: Essex Institute, 1911–1921), V: 298. Smith's observation about the lengthy service of John Pynchon is confirmed by perusal of the records of the Court of Assistants and County Courts, which shows that the same judges sat year after year.

11. *Pynchon Court Record*, 203.

12. *See* Smith, "Introduction," 16–19.

13. Order re Justices, Ct. Asst. Aug. 1630, in *Records of Assistants*, II: 3.

14. The Body of Liberties of 1641, in Edwin Powers, *Crime and Punishment in Early Massachusetts, 1620–1692: A Documentary History* (Boston: Beacon Press, 1966), 533, 536.

15. F. W. Maitland, *The Forms of Action at Common Law: A Course of Lectures* (Cambridge: Cambridge University Press, 1909).

16. *See, e.g.*, Edwards v. Hams, Middlesex County Ct. Aug. 3, 1654 (microfilm in possession of Genealogical Society of Utah) (case on bond); Hildreth v. Eldred, Middlesex County Ct. Aug. 7, 1651 (microfilm in possession of Genealogical Society of Utah) (case for trespass); Coale v. Shippie, Middlesex County Ct. Oct. 25, 1655 (microfilm in possession of Genealogical Society of Utah) (case for assault); Mud v. Painter, Middlesex County Ct. Aug. 5, 1652 (microfilm in possession of Genealogical Society of Utah) (debt on unsealed instrument).

17. Horton v. Mericke, Springfield Ct. 1639/40, in *Pynchon Court Record*, 205; Allin v. Bliss, Springfield Ct. 1659, in *Pynchon Court Record*, 242; Blanchard v. Blanchard, Middlesex County Ct. June 16, 1663 (microfilm in possession of Genealogical Society of Utah).

18. *See* Haskins, *Law and Authority*, 163–169. *See generally* David Grayson Allen, *In English Ways: The Movement of Societies and the Transferal of English Local Law and Custom to Massachusetts Bay in the Seventeenth Century* (Chapel Hill: University of North Carolina Press, 1981).

19. Zechariah Chafee, Jr., "Introduction," in *Records of the Suffolk County Court, 1671–1680*, 2 vols. (Boston: Colonial Society of Massachusetts, 1933), I: xvii, l–lvi, shows that the conclusion of Barbara Black, *see* Black, "Judicial Power," 151–157, that granting equitable relief was primarily a function of the General Court and that the lower courts, including the Court of Assistants, enjoyed only very limited equitable powers is wrong. Black does not cite Chafee's work in the section of her bibliographic essay dealing with equity. *See* Black, "Judicial Power," 370. Moreover, the magistrates themselves claimed they possessed broad chancery powers. *See* Howe and Eaton, Jr., "Supreme Judicial Power," 310.

20. *See, e.g.*, Foote v. Foxcroft, Ct. Asst. 1645, in *Records of Assistants*, III: 12; Ridgway v. Nash, Middlesex County Ct. Oct. 25, 1655 (microfilm in possession of Genealogical Society of Utah).

21. *See* Makefashion v. Lenard, Quarterly Ct. Ipswich 1673, in *Records of Essex*, V:130: Thayer v. Paine, Suffolk County Ct. 1675, in *Records of Suffolk*, II: 563; Baker v. Johnson, Suffolk County Ct. 1673/74, in *Records of Suffolk*, I: 392–393; Coleman v. Swift, Ct. Asst. 1640, in *Records of Assistants*, II: 96.

22. Matter of Woburn Election, Ct. Asst. 1663/64, in *Records of Assistants*, III: 147; Ely v. Leonard, Hampshire County Ct., in *Pynchon Court Record*, 268; Davis v. Hutchins, Quarterly Ct. Salisbury 1665, in *Records of Essex*, III: 249–250.

23. "To Our Beloved Brethren and Neighbors," in *The Book of the General Lawes and Libertyes Concerning the Inhabitants of the Massachusetts* (Cambridge, Mass.: 1648), ed. Richard S. Dunn (San Marino, Cal.: Huntington Library, 1998), unnumbered introductory page.

24. Haskins, *Law and Authority*, 124. *See generally ibid.*, 119–140.

25. *See ibid.*, 137.

26. *Lawes and Libertyes of 1648*, 23.

27. *See* Haskins, *Law and Authority*, 130, 135–136.

28. *Lawes and Libertyes of 1648*, 32.

29. The Body of Liberties of 1641, in Powers, *Crime and Punishment*, 533, 536.

30. *Lawes and Libertyes of 1648*, 32.

31. *See, e.g.*, Colony v. Pope, Quarterly Ct. Salem 1667, in *Records of Essex*, III: 434. Even a man accused of fathering a bastard could obtain a jury trial if he demanded one. *See* Colony v. Wright, Springfield Court 1654/55, in *Pynchon Court Record*, 230. But the courts would grant a bench trial if both parties desired one. *See* Johnson v. Town of Woburn, Middlesex County Ct. Apr. 1, 1662 (microfilm in possession of Genealogical Society of Utah).

32. *Pynchon Court Record*, 203.

33. Order re Lechford, Ct. Asst. 1639, in *Records of Assistants*, II: 87; Order re Jury of Six, Springfield Ct., in *Pynchon Court Record*, 203; Roby v. Fulsham,

Quarterly Ct. Hampton 1668, in *Records of Essex*, IV: 64. *But cf.* Shepard v. Town of Rowley, Quarterly Ct. Ipswich 1677, in *Records of Essex*, VI: 338 (new trial ordered when court learned after trial that only eleven jurors had sat on case).

34. *See* Colony v. Morton, Ct. Asst. 1630, in *Records of Assistants*, II: 4; Colony v. Ratliffe, Ct. Asst. 1631, in *Records of Assistants*, II: 16; Haskins, *Law and Authority*, 200–201, 207.

35. Colony v. Aleworth, Ct. Asst. 1630/31, in *Records of Assistants*, II: 10; Colony v. Caleb, Ct. Asst. 1676, in *Records of Assistants*, I: 76. *But see, e.g.,* Colony v. John, Ct. Asst. 1675, in *Records of Assistants*, I: 53 (Native American acquitted by jury).

36. Colony v. Lorphelin, Ct. Asst. 1679, in *Records of Assistants*, I: 145; Petition of Town of Boston, Ct. Asst. 1681, in *Records of Assistants*, I: 197.

37. Colony v. Compton, Ct. Asst. 1679, in *Records of Assistants*, I: 145; Colony v. Waters, Ct. Asst. 1679, in *Records of Assistants*, I: 158; Colony v. Fuller, Ct. Asst. 1683, in *Records of Assistants*, I: 228.

38. Colony v. Parsons, Springfield Ct. 1649, in *Pynchon Court Record*, 219. On the subsequent accusation, *see* Smith, "Introduction," 21–22.

39. Colony v. Terry, Springfield Ct. 1650, in *Pynchon Court Records*, 224. *Cf.* Colony v. Thurlay, Quarterly Ct. Ipswich 1669, in *Records of Essex*, IV: 126 (defendant discharged since indictment not "in the compass of the law of pernicious lying, but being the occasion of much trouble," defendant ordered to pay witness fees).

40. *See* Haskins, *Law and Authority*, 200–201.

41. The Body of Liberties of 1641, in Powers, *Crime and Punishment*, 533, 537. The Code of 1648 clarified the provision by substituting the word "differ" for "suffer." *See Lawes and Libertyes of 1648*, 32. After 1660, bench-jury disagreements in the county courts resulted in cases going to the Court of Assistants and, only if a further bench-jury disagreement occurred there, to the General Court. *See* Black, "Judicial Power," 329–330.

42. *Lawes and Libertyes of 1648*, 32.

43. *See, e.g.,* Wincoll v. Joanes, Middlesex County Ct. Apr. 6, 1658 (microfilm in possession of Genealogical Society of Utah).

44. Colony v. Sawser, Ct. Asst. 1654, in *Records of Assistants*, III: 34; Colony v. Parker, Ct. Asst. 1669, in *Records of Assistants*, III: 201; Colony v. Upton, Quarterly Ct. Salem 1665, in *Records of Essex*, III: 264–265; Bellingham v. Wilkins, Quarterly Ct. Salem 1666, in *Records of Essex*, III: 322.

45. Howe and Eaton, "Supreme Judicial Power," 292–293, quoting the statute.

46. Barbara Black thinks it did, *see* Black, "Judicial Power," 275–284, but Mark Howe thought it did not. *See* Howe and Eaton, "Supreme Judicial Power," 299–300.

47. Howe and Eaton, "Supreme Judicial Power," 292–293, quoting the statute. After the 1649 legislation, the two chambers continued to meet separately when voting on cases unless disagreement or some other reason necessitated a joint meeting. *See* Colony v. Sawser, Ct. Asst. 1654, in *Records of Assistants*, III: 34, 37, where the deputies, after their separate vote, reported that they were evenly divided and wished to have the case decided "by the whole Court together."

48. Howe and Eaton, "Supreme Judicial Power," 292, 302.

49. *But see* Black, "Judicial Power, 329–330, who without any citation to evidence claims that, when the magistrates in the Court of Assistants faced a bench-jury disagreement, "they simply rejected the jury verdict and decided the case as they, the bench, thought fit." *Ibid.*, 330. My own examination of the published Court of Assistants records indicates, on the contrary, that every bench-jury disagreement in that court was forwarded to the General Court.

50. Pateshall v. Gerardy, Ct. Asst. 1656, in *Records of Assistants*, III: 42. For other instances of special verdicts, *see, e.g.*, Gifford v. Kayne, Quarterly Ct. Ipswich 1655, in *Records of Essex*, I: 398.

Chapter 5

1. Cornelia H. Dayton, *Women Before the Bar: Gender, Law, and Society in Connecticut, 1639–1789* (Chapel Hill: University of North Carolina Press, 1995), 21. *See* generally ibid., 27–30.

2. Order re Source of Law, New Haven Gen. Ct. 1639, in *Records of the Colony and Plantation of New Haven,* 3 vols. (Hartford: Case, Tiffany & Co., 1857–1858), I: 21; Appointment of Winthrop, Conn. Gen. Ct. 1647, in *The Public Records of the Colony of Connecticut,* 15 vols. (Hartford: Brown & Parsons, 1850–1858), I: 157; Smith v. Town of Wethersfield, Conn. Particular Ct. 1639/40, in *Records of the Particular Court of Connecticut, 1639–1663* (Hartford: Connecticut Historical Society, 1928), 9.

3. Order re Judicial Laws, New Haven Gen. Ct. 1644, in *New Haven Colony Records,* I: 130; Order re Sabbath, New Haven Gen. Ct. 1647/48, in *New Haven Colony Records,* I: 358.

4. Colony v. Heardman, New Haven Magis. Ct. 1659, in *New Haven Colony Records,* III: 271; Colony v. Bell, New Haven Magis. Ct. 1645, in *New Haven Colony Records,* I: 173; Colony v. Bussaker, Conn. Particular Ct. 1648, in *Records of Connecticut,* I: 168; Colony v. Allen, Ply. Gen. Ct. 1651/52, in *Records of the Colony of New Plymouth,* ed. Nathaniel B. Shurtleff, 12 vols. (Boston: William White, 1855–1861), III: 4; Colony v. Williams, Plymouth Ct. Asst. 1635, in *Records of Plymouth,* I: 35. For underlying legislation, *see* General Laws and Liberties of Connecticut Colony, 1672, in John D. Cushing

ed., *The Earliest Laws of the New Haven and Connecticut Colonies, 1639–1673* (Wilmington, Del.: Michael Glazier, 1977), 95–96; New Haven's Settling in New England and Some Lawes for Government, in Cushing ed., *Earliest Laws*, 29–30.

5. Act of June 5, 1655, in *Records of Plymouth*, XI: 64; Colony v. Willerd, Ply. Gen. Ct. 1641, in *Records of Plymouth*, II: 17; Colony v. Hazell, Ply. Gen. Ct. 1650, in *Records of Plymouth*, II: 162; Colony v. Kirby, Ply. Gen. Ct. 1655/56, in *Records of Plymouth*, III: 96; Colony v. Kirby, Ply. Gen. Ct. and Ply. Ct. Asst. 1656/57, in *Records of Plymouth*, III: 111–112. For additional legislation, *see* Acts of June 10, 1650, in *Records of Plymouth*, XI: 57–58.

6. *See, e.g.*, Colony v. Troughton, Conn. Magis. Ct. 1654, in *Records of Particular Court*, 128 (missing church); Colony v. Blayden, New Haven Magis. Ct. 1647, in *New Haven Colony Records*, I: 322, 324 (missing church); Colony v. Gutteridge, Conn. Particular Ct. 1650, in *Records of Particular Court*, 88 (violating Sabbath); Colony v. Adey, Ply. Gen. Ct. 1638, in *Records of Plymouth*, I: 86 (violating Sabbath); Colony v. Veare, Conn. Particular Ct. 1640, in *Records of Connecticut*, I: 50 (profanity); Colony v. Hall, Ply. Gen. Ct. 1640/41, in *Records of Plymouth*, II: 9 (profanity). For underlying legislation, *see* Laws of Connecticut, in Cushing ed, *Earliest Laws*, 96, 132; Lawes of New Haven, in Cushing ed., *Earliest Laws*, 30, 47–48; Act of March 3, 1639/40, in *Records of Plymouth*, XI: 33, 57–58; Laws...of His Majestys Colony of Rhode-Island, 1662, in John D. Cushing ed., *The Earliest Acts and Laws of the Colony of Rhode Island and Providence Plantations, 1640–1719* (Wilmington, Del.: Michael Glazier, Inc., 1977), 147.

7. Colony v. King, New Haven Magis. Ct. 1646/47, in *New Haven Colony Records*, I: 293; Colony v. Ledra, Ply. Gen. Ct. 1659/60, in *Records of Plymouth*, III: 184.

8. Colony v. Norton, Ply. Gen. Ct. 1657, in *Records of Plymouth*, III: 123. *Accord*, Colony v. Barnes, New Haven Magis. Ct. 1659, in *New Haven Colony Records*, III: 276.

9. *See* Colony v. Smith, New Haven Magis. Ct. 1659, in *New Haven Colony Records*, III: 292 (whipped); Colony v. Copeland, Ply. Gen. Ct. 1657/58, in *Records of Plymouth*, III: 127 (whipped). *Cf.* Colony v. Crabb, New Haven Magis. Ct. 1658, in *New Haven Colony Records*, III: 242 (fined for concealing Quaker books plus other miscarriages).

10. Laws of September 29, 1658, in *Records of Plymouth*, XI: 100; Order for Day of Fasting and Humiliation, Ply. Gen. Ct. 1658, in *Records of Plymouth*, III: 151. Connecticut also legislated against Quakers. *See* Laws of Connecticut, in Cushing ed., *Earliest Laws*, 102.

11. Colony v. Mallery, New Haven Magis. Ct. 1648/49, in *New Haven Colony Records*, I: 435. For the statutory basis of fornication prosecutions, *see* Laws

of Connecticut, in Cushing ed., *Earliest Laws*, 100; Lawes of New Haven, in Cushing ed., *Earliest Laws*, 32; Acts of November 13, 1636 and Act of June 4, 1645, in *Records of Plymouth*, XI: 12, 46; Laws of Rhode Island, 1662, in Cushing ed., *Acts and Laws of Rhode Island*, 7.

12. *See, e.g.*, Colony v. Richmond, R.I. Ct. Trials 1658, in *Rhode Island Court Records: Records of the Court of Trials of the Colony of Providence Plantations, 1647–1670*, 2 vols. (Providence: Rhode Island Historical Society, 1920–1922), I: 46; Colony v. Galpin, New Haven Ct. Magis. 1647, in *New Haven Colony Records*, I: 327. In Plymouth after 1645, a husband could be cleared of premarital intercourse with his wife by paying a fine. *See* Act of June 4, 1645, in *Records of Plymouth*, XI: 46; Colony v. Winter, Ply. Gen. Ct. 1648, in *Records of Plymouth*, II: 135.

13. Colony v. Hoskings, New Haven Magis. Ct. 1642, in *New Haven Colony Records*, I: 75, 77; Colony v. Harding, New Haven Magis. Ct. 1642/43, in *New Haven Colony Records*, I: 84; Colony v. Badger, New Haven Magis. Ct. 1641/42, in *New Haven Colony Records*, I: 61; Colony v. Linnet, Ply. Gen. Ct. 1652, in *Records of Plymouth*, III: 11; Colony v. Powell, Ply. Gen. Ct. 1655, in *Records of Plymouth*, III: 91.

14. Colony v. French, Ply. Gen. Ct. 1659, in *Records of Plymouth*, III: 165, 176.

15. *See* Colony v. Baldwin, New Haven Magis. Ct. 1658–1659, in *New Haven Colony Records*, III: 263, 290 (court delays judgment on accused father until mother gives birth "to see what the providence of God will discover concerning him" and eventually concludes that "the main thing charged be not proved"). For a case of a man acquitted by a jury, *see* Colony v. Mott, R.I. Ct. Trials 1659/60, in *Rhode Island Court Records*, I: 65.

16. Colony v. Uffoote, New Haven Magis. Ct. 1657, in *New Haven Colony Records*, III: 201. Upon further investigation, the court declared the divorce "a horrible sin" for which the wife was responsible because "she did refuse her duty and befooled him…to force herself out of his hand." The court also announced that "were the thing fully proved, it could be no less than death," but that on the present proof the former wife, now remarried, deserved only a fine. Colony v. Beard, New Haven Magis. Ct. 1657, in *New Haven Colony Records*, III: 209.

17. Colony v. Richardson, New Haven Magis. Ct. 1654, in *New Haven Colony Records*, III: 122.

18. *See* Lawes of New Haven, in Cushing ed., *Earliest Laws*, 19. Lesser penalties, such as whipping or branding with the letter "A," were imposed in the other colonies. *See* Laws of Connecticut, in Cushing ed., *Earliest Laws*, 76–77; Act of Nov. 15, 1636 and Act of Sept. 29, 1658, in *Records of Plymouth*, XI: 19, 95; Laws of Rhode Island, 1662, in Cushing ed., *Acts and Laws of Rhode Island*, 65.

19. Colony v. Mendame, Ply. Gen. Ct. 1639, in *Records of Plymouth*, I: 132; Colony v. Turtall, Ply. Gen. Ct. 1655/56, in *Records of Plymouth*, III: 97; Colony v. Winter, Ply. Gen. Ct. 1651/52, in *Records of Plymouth*, III: 5. Another case in which the punishment was whipping and the wearing of a badge was Colony v. Bray, Ply. Gen. Ct. 1641, in *Records of Plymouth*, II: 28.

20. Colony v. Granger, Ply. Gen. Ct. 1642, in *Records of Plymouth*, II: 44; Colony v. Robinson, New Haven Magis. Ct. 1654/55, in *New Haven Colony Records*, III: 132. The dog also was ordered to "be killed in his sight" immediately prior to his hanging. *Accord*, Colony v. Potter, New Haven Magis. Ct. 1662, in *New Haven Colony Records*, III: 440; Colony v. Spencer, New Haven Gen. Ct. 1641/42–1642, in *New Haven Colony Records*, I: 62–73; Colony v. Chasemore, R.I. Ct. Trials 1656/57, in *Rhode Island Court Records*, I: 26.

21. Colony v. Starke, Conn. Particular Ct. 1640–1643, in *Records of Particular Court*, 13, 20 (defendant pleads guilty to attempt and is whipped and sold into servitude); Colony v. Newberry, Conn. Particular Ct. 1647, in *Records of Particular Court*, 48, 49 (penalty unspecified); Colony v. Ferris, New Haven Magis. Ct. 1657, in *New Haven Colony Records*, III: 223. *See also* Colony v. Starke, Conn. Particular Ct. 1640–1643, in *Records of Connecticut*, I: 55, 84 (penalty of whipping plus indefinite servitude).

22. For one, *see* Colony v. Knight, New Haven Magis. Ct. 1655, in *New Haven Colony Records*, III: 137. New Haven's extraordinary statute, which made sodomy a capital offense, also made it a crime for a man "in the sight of others [to] spill his own seed"—an act that, in its view, "tend[ed] to the sin of sodomy, if it be not one kind of it"; a man committing the crime was to be "punished according to the nature of the offense; or if the case considered with the aggravating circumstances, shall according to the mind of God revealed in his word require it, he shall be put to death." Lawes of New Haven, in Cushing ed., *Earliest Laws*, 19. Of course, sodomy also was a capital offense in Connecticut, Plymouth, and Rhode Island. *See* Laws of Connecticut, in Cushing ed., *Earliest Laws*, 9, 83; Act of Nov. 15, 1636 and Act of Sept. 29, 1658, Ply. Gen. Ct. 1636 and 1658, in *Records of Plymouth*, XI: 12, 95; Acts of May 19–21, 1647, in Cushing ed., *Acts and Laws of Rhode Island*, 6.

23. Colony v. Mitchell, Ply. Gen. Ct. 1641/42, in *Records of Plymouth*, II: 35; Colony v. Williams, Conn. Particular Ct. 1654, in *Records of Particular Court*, 137; Colony v. Alexander and Roberts, Plymouth Ct. Asst. 1637, in *Records of Plymouth*, I: 64; Colony v. Norman, Ply. Gen. Ct. 1650, in *Records of Plymouth*, II: 163. *Accord*, Colony v. Rickard, Ply. Gen. Ct. 1660/61, in *Records of Plymouth*, III: 210 (woman convicted of "lascivious and unnatural practices").

24. Order re Sex Offenses, Conn. Gen. Ct. 1642, in *Records of Connecticut*, I: 78; Colony v. Brunson, Conn. Particular Ct. 1640, in *Records of Connecticut*, I: 45; Colony v. Wiberd, Conn. Particular Ct. 1651, in *Records of Particular*

Court, 105. It is not entirely clear whether this case involved sexual offenses, failure to pay debts, or misconduct by servants.

25. *See* Colony v. Hogg, New Haven Magis. Ct. 1646/47, in *New Haven Colony Records*, I: 295; Colony v. Atkins, Ply. Gen. Ct. 1660, in *Records of Plymouth*, III: 199–200; Colony v. Bundy, Ply. Ct. Asst. 1637, in *Records of Plymouth*, I: 65; Colony v. Peck, Ply. Gen. Ct. 1654/55, in *Records of Plymouth*, III: 75.

26. Colony v. Heywood, New Haven Magis. Ct. 1647, in *New Haven Colony Records*, I: 306. *Accord, e.g.*, Colony v. Latimer, Conn. Gen. Ct. 1639, in *Records of Connecticut*, I: 29; Colony v. Holmes, Ply. Ct. 1633, in *Records of Plymouth*, I: 12; Colony v. Parker, Aquidneck Quarter Ct. 1641, in Howard M. Chapin, *Documentary History of Rhode Island*, 2 vols. (Providence: Preston & Rounds, 1919), II: 133. The crime of drunkenness was sufficiently important in Plymouth to warrant a jury trial if a defendant demanded one. *See* Colony v. Sampson, Ply. Gen. Ct. 1646/47, in *Records of Plymouth*, II: 111, which is the first instance in which a criminal jury trial was recorded.

27. *See, e.g.*, Colony v. Eaton, Ply. Gen. Ct. 1651, in *Records of Plymouth*, II: 174; Colony v. Dammon, Ply. Gen. Ct. 1640, in *Records of Plymouth*, II: 4; Colony v. Adey, Ply. Gen. Ct. 1638, in *Records of Plymouth*, I: 87.

28. *See* Laws of Connecticut, in Cushing ed., *Earliest Laws*, 55; Lawes of New Haven, in Cushing ed., *Earliest Laws*, 43; Colony v. Barnes, Ply. Gen. Ct. 1640, in *Records of Plymouth*, II: 5 (selling rye purchased at 4s. per barrell for 5s.); Colony v. Clark, Ply. Gen. Ct. 1639, in *Records of Plymouth*, I: 137 (fined 30s. for selling boots purchased for 10s. at 15s.); Colony v. Hopkins, Ply. Gen. Ct. 1638, in *Records of Plymouth*, I: 87 (selling mismeasured beer); Colony v. Ford, Ply. Gen. Ct. 1646/47, in *Records of Plymouth*, II: 112 (admonished for first offense).

29. Order re English Commodities, New Haven Gen. Ct. 1640, in *New Haven Colony Records*, I: 35; Colony v. Hurlbut, Conn. Particular Ct. 1642/43, in *Records of Particular Court*, 19.

30. Order re Indian Corn, Conn. Gen. Ct. 1638, in *Records of Connecticut*, I: 18 (fixing price of corn); Order Making Corn Legal Tender, Conn. Gen. Ct. 1640/41, in *Records of Connecticut*, I: 61 (all debts payable in corn at specified price for corn); Colony v. Pynchon, Conn. Gen. Ct. 1638, in *Records of Connecticut*, I: 19; Order re Wages and Prices, Conn. Gen. Ct. 1649/50, in *Records of Connecticut*, I: 205.

31. *See* Act of June 4, 1639, in *Records of Plymouth*, XI: 32; Order re Wages, Conn. Gen. Ct. 1641, in *Records of Connecticut*, I: 65; Order re Rates, New Haven Gen. Ct. 1641, in *New Haven Colony Records*, I: 52; Colony v. Reader, New Haven Magis Ct. 1640/41, in *New Haven Colony Records*, I: 51; Colony v. Mowers, Ply. Gen. Ct. 1643, in *Records of Plymouth*, II: 60.

32. Ward v. Company of Merchants of New Haven, New Haven Magis. Ct. 1647, in *New Haven Colony Records*, I: 329; Rayner v. Olda, Conn. Gen. Ct. 1636, in

Records of Connecticut, I: 3. The classic study remains Richard B. Morris, *Government and Labor in Early America* (New York: Columbia University Press, 1946), 78–84.

33. *See, e.g.*, Colony v. Brian, Plymouth Ct. 1632/33, in *Records of Plymouth*, I: 7; Order re Servants, Conn. Gen. Ct. 1644, in *Records of Connecticut*, I: 105; Agreement of Bishop, Ply. Gen. Ct. 1639, in *Records of Plymouth*, I: 128.

34. *See, e.g.*, Colony v. Smoolt, New Haven Magis. Ct. 1647, in *New Haven Colony Records*, I: 308; Colony v. Tanner, New Haven Magis. Ct. 1639, in *New Haven Colony Records*, I: 26. For a case of a man who said "I will be the death of" whoever "taketh me servant," *see* Westcott v. Crooke, R.I. Ct. Trials 1658, in *Rhode Island Court Records*, I: 41. *But see* Colony v. Thurston, Ply. Gen. Ct. 1644, in *Records of Plymouth*, II: 73 (whipping remitted in return for commitment for good behavior "upon a petition exhibited by the young men of Plymouth").

35. *See* Order against Incorrigibles, Conn. Gen. Ct. 1642, in *Records of Connecticut*, I: 78; Colony v. Coles, Conn. Particular Ct. 1644/45, in *Records of Connecticut*, I: 124. *See also* Colony v. Coles, Conn. Particular Ct. 1644/45, in *Records of Particular Court*, 33 (servant sent to House of Correction for "rebellious carriage" toward mistress).

36. *See* Colony v. Chapman, Conn. Particular Ct. 1653/54, in *Records of Particular Court*, 124; Turner v. Gennings, New Haven Magis. Ct. 1643, in *New Haven Colony Records*, I: 105.

37. Lawes of New Haven, in Cushing ed., *Earliest Laws*, 43. *Cf.* Colony v. Emerson, Ply. Gen. Ct. 1638/39, in *Records of Plymouth*, I: 118 (entertaining other men's servants unlawfully).

38. *See* Colony v. Wood, New Haven Magis. Ct. 1656, in *New Haven Colony Records*, III: 187 (theft); Colony v. Anthony, New Haven Magis. Ct. 1647, in *New Haven Colony Records*, I: 335 (drunkenness); Colony v. Chapman, Conn. Particular Ct. 1653/54, in *Records of Particular Court*, 124 ("family discipline"); Act of June 4, 1639, in *Records of Plymouth*, XI: 33.

39. Smith v. Dowty, Ply. Ct. 1633/34, in *Records of Plymouth*, I: 23. *Cf.* Complaint of Baker, Ply. Ct. 1632/33, in *Records of Plymouth*, I: 7 (master ordered to provide clothing or give servant to another).

40. *See* Hercules v. Hatch, Ply. Gen. Ct. 1643/44, in *Records of Plymouth*, II: 69; Wheadon v. Meigs, New Haven Magis. Ct. 1658, in *New Haven Colony Records*, III: 242. *Cf.* Sprout v. Briggs, Ply. Ct. Asst. 1658, in *Records of Plymouth*, III: 133 (servant at end of term may recover compensation provided by indenture).

41. *See* Colony v. Messenger, Conn. Particular Ct. 1653, in *Records of Particular Court*, 119; Colony v. Huckens, Ply. Gen. Ct. 1654, in *Records of Plymouth*, III: 51; Colony v. Crocker, Ply. Gen. Ct. 1639/40, in *Records of Plymouth*, I: 141.

42. Colony v. Latham, Ply. Gen. Ct. 1654/55, in *Records of Plymouth*, III: 73; Colony v. Ballard, Aquidneck Quarter Ct. 1641, in *Rhode Island History*, II: 134:

Davis v. Wilks, New Haven Ct. Magis. 1640, in *New Haven Colony Records*, I: 47. *See* Order re Sale of Servants, New Haven Gen. Ct. 1656, in *New Haven Colony Records*, III: 169.

43. *See* Order re Stiles, Conn. Gen. Ct. 1637, in *Records of Connecticut*, I: 8 (suit by apprentice); Hall v. Baker, Ply. Gen. Ct. 1655, in *Records of Plymouth*, III: 83, 88 (suit by father against master for abusing servant; son returned to father upon payment to master). *Cf.* North v. Goodale, Conn. Quarter Ct. 1660, in *Records of Particular Court*, 218, where a father recovered damages against a skipper for "abusing" and "cruel[ly] beating" his son.

44. Colony v. Frost, New Haven Gen. Ct. 1656, in *New Haven Colony Records*, III: 169. On the law regulating servants, *see* Morris, *Government and Labor*, 402–405, 416–419, 437–441, 464–466, 472–477, who concurs that the law of servitude was less harsh in New England than in the Chesapeake, *see ibid.*, 472, 482, although he does not attribute the difference to New England's religiosity. In my view, Morris long underestimated the impact of New England's religious values on its law. *See* Richard B. Morris, "Book Review," *American Journal of Legal History*, XXI (1977), 86, 90, *reviewing* William E. Nelson, *Americanization of the Common Law: The Impact of Legal Change on Massachusetts Society, 1760–1830* (Cambridge, Mass.: Harvard University Press, 1975), 44–45.

45. *See* Colony v. Larebe, New Haven Magis. Ct. 1647, in *New Haven Colony Records*, I: 338; Laws of Connecticut, in Cushing ed., *Earliest Laws*, 111. *Cf.* Acts of May 19–21, 1647, in Cushing ed., *Acts and Laws of Rhode Island*, 9 (subjecting foreigners to equal customs duties); Act of Nov. 15, 1636, Ply. Gen. Ct. 1636, in *Records of Plymouth*, XI: 11 (requiring equality of taxation).

46. *See* Goodhart v. VarLeet, Conn. Magis. Ct. 1657, in *Records of Particular Court*, 183; Colony v. Peach, Ply. Gen. Ct. 1638, in *Records of Plymouth*, I: 96–97; Colony v. Woodcock, Ply. Gen. Ct. March 1654/55, in *Records of Plymouth*, III: 74; Colony v. David the Jew, Conn. Gen. Ct. 1659, in *Records of Connecticut*, I: 343.

47. Will of Tomson, Conn. Magis. Ct. 1656, in *Records of Particular Court*, 163; Colony v. Marsh, New Haven Magis. Ct. 1645, in *New Haven Colony Records*, I: 180. An outstanding book, Dayton, *Women Before the Bar*, focuses entirely on the role of women in Connecticut's legal system. For the role of women in colonial America more generally, *see* Mary Beth Norton, *Founding Mothers and Fathers: Gendered Power and the Forming of American Society* (New York: Alfred A. Knopf, 1996), another excellent book. Neither Dayton nor Norton disagrees with my main conclusion here that Chesapeake law was harsher than New England law on women and other underclasses. I have tried to adhere to their understanding about the relationship of seventeenth-century women to the law—a subject that they address in far greater detail than I possibly can within the scope of this book.

48. *See* Townsmen of Hartford v. Lord, Conn. Gen. Ct. 1651, in *Records of Connecticut*, I: 224; Colony v. Pell, New Haven Magis. Ct. 1647, in *New Haven Colony Records*, I: 334.
49. Colony v. Egleston, Conn. Particular Ct. 1645, in *Records of Connecticut*, I: 127.
50. *See* Lawes of New Haven, in Cushing ed., *Earliest Laws*, 28; Complaint of Beckwith, Conn. Gen. Ct. May 1655, in *Records of Connecticut*, I: 275; Andrews v. Andrews, New Haven Magis. Ct. 1661, in *New Haven Colony Records*, III: 425. *Cf.* Wade v. Wade, Conn. Gen. Ct. 1657, in *Records of Connecticut*, I: 301 (divorce granted husband whose wife "slighted & rejected" him and "disown[ed] him & fellowship with him").
51. *See* Colony v. Clemens, Conn. Gen. Ct. 1660, in *Records of Connecticut*, I: 351.
52. *See* Colony v. Cheesbrooke, Conn. Gen. Ct. 1650/51, in *Records of Connecticut*, I: 216; Order re Young Men, Conn. Gen. Ct. 1636/37, in *Records of Connecticut*, I: 8; Order re Young Men, New Haven Gen. Ct. 1641/42, in *New Haven Colony Records*, I: 70; Colony v. Bessie, Ply. Gen. Ct. 1638/39, in *Records of Plymouth*, I: 118. For a case of a man presented by a grand jury for living alone, *see* Colony v. Colfax, Conn. Particular Ct. 1650/51, in *Records of Particular Court*, 94.
53. Colony v. Ramsden, Ply. Ct. Asst. 1652, in *Records of Plymouth*, III: 6–7; Order re Land, Ply. Gen. Ct. 1636, in *Records of Plymouth*, I: 45. *See also* Land Grants, Ply. Ct. Asst. 1636, in *Records of Plymouth*, I: 45.
54. *See* Laws of Connecticut, in Cushing ed., *Earliest Laws*, 80; Lawes of New Haven, in Cushing ed., *Earliest Laws*, 16; Edwards v. Fellows, Conn. Particular Ct. 1657/58, in *Records of Particular Court*, 187 (case involving assigned bill); Colony v. Herriman, Conn. Gen. Ct. 1651, in *Records of Connecticut*, I: 219 (Dutch vessel seized for unlawfully trading with Indians at Saybrook); Evans v. Charles, New Haven Magis. Ct. 1646/47, in *New Haven Colony Records*, I: 281; Evans v. Peirce, New Haven Magis. Ct. 1649, in *New Haven Colony Records*, I: 467 (sailors win).
55. Palmer v. Beech, New Haven Magis. Ct. 1645, in *New Haven Colony Records*, I: 170; Meggs v. Gregory, New Haven Magis. Ct. 1647, in *New Haven Colony Records*, I: 345.
56. *See* Laws of Connecticut, in Cushing ed., *Earliest Laws*, 78. In the decade of the 1670s in the relatively commercial county of New Haven, which had then become part of Connecticut, there were only 38 debt cases, or less than four per year, which constituted 45.8 percent of the total of 83 civil cases. Seven decades later, debt litigation had grown 44 times to 1676 cases. Other litigation had increased only tenfold, with the result that debt in the 1740–1749 decade constituted 78.4 percent of all litigation. *See* Dayton, *Women Before*

the Bar, 84–85. The Connecticut data also needs to be compared with data from the decade of the 1640s in Essex County, Massachusetts, where 23.8 percent of litigation was to collect debts, and Northampton County, Virginia, where 76.9 percent was for debt.

Despite the relative insignificance of debt litigation, Connecticut did enact some legislation designed to assist creditors. *See* Order re Land Subject to Debts, Conn. Gen. Ct. 1647, in *Records of Connecticut*, I: 151, subjecting land to debts if personalty was not sufficient to pay and further providing that, if a debtor was known to be insolvent, the court could "call in all the creditors in a short time, and set an equal and indifferent way how that creditors shall be paid." *See also* Order re Payment of Debts, Conn. Gen. Ct. 1660, in *Records of Connecticut*, I: 349, providing that creditors due payment in special pay, such as corn, could attach any asset available.

For early debt collection cases in another colony, Plymouth, *see* Carver v. Hiller, Ply. Ct. Asst. 1642, in *Records of Plymouth*, II: 43, which was submitted to arbitration. Another case led to a judgment for the creditor by the Court of Assistants, to which the debtor engaged to "enter his traverse" at the next General Court. *See* Starr v. Clark, Ply. Ct. Asst. 1642/43, in *Records of Plymouth*, II: 50. No further record of the case appeared. In a third case, where the debtor had left the jurisdiction, his assets were divided among creditors in proportion to their claims. *See* Estate of Hall, Ply. Gen. Ct. 1652/53, in *Records of Plymouth*, III: 21.

57. *See* Acts 4 and 5, Ply. Ct. 1633/34, in *Records of Plymouth*, I: 22.

58. *See* Order re Recording of Land Bargains and Mortgages, Conn. Gen. Ct. 1643, in *Records of Connecticut*, I: 83; Order re Town Land Registers, Conn. Gen. Ct. 1639, in *Records of Connecticut*, I: 37; Order re Alienations of Land, New Haven Gen. Ct. 1642, in *New Haven Colony Records*, I: 83; Order re Brett, Ply. Ct. Asst. 1652, in *Records of Plymouth*, III: 20. *Cf.* Acknowledgment of Hatherley, Ply. Gen. Ct. 1647, in *Records of Plymouth*, II: 118 (record of wife giving assent to husband's sale of land).

59. *See, e.g.*, Order re Highway between Windsor and Hartford, Conn. Gen. Ct. 1645, in *Records of Connecticut*, I: 125; Order re Causeway, New Haven Gen. Ct. 1640, in *New Haven Colony Records*, I: 44; Order re Highways, Ply. Ct. Asst. 1637, in *Records of Plymouth*, I: 58–60; License of Deane, Ply. Ct. 1632/33, in *Records of Plymouth*, I: 8; License of Rogers, Ply. Gen. Ct. 1635/36, in *Records of Plymouth*, I: 39; Order re Pounds and Stocks, Ply. Gen. Ct. 1637, in *Records of Plymouth*, I: 61; Order re Measures, Ply. Ct. 1633/34, in *Records of Plymouth*, I: 23. *Cf.* Inhabitants of the Eel River v. Town of Sandwich, Ply. Ct. Asst. 1652, in *Records of Plymouth*, III: 20 (jury verdict for failure to build bridge).

60. *See, e.g.*, Pope v. Shirtlife, Ply. Ct. Asst. 1659, in *Records of Plymouth*, III: 169; Soule v. Thomas, Ply. Gen. Ct. 1636/37, in *Records of Plymouth*, VII: 4;

Washburne v. Dowty, Ply. Ct. Asst. 1632/33, in *Records of Plymouth*, I: 6; Bonney v. Willis, Ply. Ct. Asst. 1646, in *Records of Plymouth*, II: 107. *Cf.* Hopkins v. Stiles, Conn. Gen. Ct. 1639, in *Records of Connecticut*, I: 34 (breach of contract for sale of land). *See also* Colony v. Fugill, New Haven Magis. Ct. 1646, in *New Haven Colony Records*, I: 262–264 (criminal prosecution for "unrighteousness in taking in & detaining of the town's land").

61. Smyths v. Beach, New Haven Magis. Ct. 1643, in *New Haven Colony Records*, I: 88. *See also* Barnes v. Dighton, New Haven Magis. Ct. 1645, in *New Haven Colony Records*, I: 162, where the court concluded that a boy watching cattle was "innocent" of the death of a cow, the foot of which got stuck between the bank of a stream and the root of a tree and which therefore died from "an afflicting providence of God" rather than from "neglect" of the boy.

62. *See* Allen v. Lewis, Conn. Particular Ct. 1644, in *Records of Particular Court*, 26; Chambers v. Hoar, Ply. Ct. Asst. 1653/54, in *Records of Plymouth*, VII: 69; King v. Cuthbert, Ply. Ct. Asst. 1653, in *Records of Plymouth*, III: 42. At least some of these agrarian cases presented sophisticated legal issues, such as the rules for making gifts. *See* Tompson v. Estate of Roberts, New Haven Magis. Ct. 1656, in *New Haven Colony Records*, III: 198 (no gift found because court did not "judge it rational that he [i.e., the purported donor] should give away his estate in such a manner").

63. Colony v. Sheather, New Haven Magis. Ct. 1662, in *New Haven Colony Records*, III: 439; Colony v. Smith, R.I. Ct. Trials 1662, in *Rhode Island Court Records*, II: 6. *See also* Colony v. Bull, R.I. Ct. Trials 1655/56, in *Rhode Island Court Records*, I: 16 (contempt of subpoena).

64. Colony v. Gorton, Ply. Gen. Ct. 1638, in *Records of Plymouth*, I: 105; Colony v. Stockbridge, Ply. Gen. Ct. 1638, in *Records of Plymouth*, I: 87; Colony v. North, Ply. Gen. Ct. 1643/44, in *Records of Plymouth*, II: 70. *But see* Colony v. Calkins, Conn. Particular Ct. 1655, in *Records of Particular Court*, 149 (defendant acquitted because of conflict among witnesses as to exactly what he had said).

65. Colony v. Dexter, R.I. Ct. Trials 1657, in *Rhode Island Court Records*, I: 34; Colony v. Crooke, R.I. Ct. Trials 1658, in *Rhode Island Court Records*, I: 43; Colony v. Tyler, Aquidneck Quarter Ct. 1643, in *Rhode Island History*, II: 142; Colony v. Gorton, Aquidneck Quarter Ct. 1646, in *Rhode Island History*, II: 164; Colony v. Tomlinson, New Haven Gen. Ct. 1660, in *New Haven Colony Records*, III: 367. For another example of the importance that the New England colonies attached to maintaining harmony with each other, *see* Order re Wills, Conn. Gen. Ct. 1648/49, in *Records of Connecticut*, I: 179, which, on a proposal from the Commissioners of United Colonies, directed that wills proved in other colonies be automatically admitted to probate in Connecticut.

66. *See, e.g.*, Colony v. Dawes, Conn. Gen. Ct. 1653, in *Records of Connecticut*, I:
242; Complaint of Winslow, Ply. Gen. Ct. 1645, in *Records of Plymouth*, II: 85;
Colony v. Earl, R.I. Ct. Trials 1656, in *Rhode Island Court Records*, I: 18; Colony v. Bernard, Conn. Particular Ct. 1648, in *Records of Connecticut*, I: 174;
Colony v. Finney, Ply. Gen. Ct. 1653, in *Records of Plymouth*, III: 42; Colony
v. Olney, R.I. Ct. Trials 1655, in *Rhode Island Court Records*, I: 13; Colony v.
Gilson, Ply. Gen. Ct. 1637, in *Records of Plymouth*, I: 67; Colony v. Roberts,
R.I. Ct. Trials 1658/59, in *Rhode Island Court Records*, I: 51. The Rhode Island
cases show that Quakers in the colony were not excused from jury service
because they could not take the usual oath; they were permitted to affirm.
67. *See* Colony v. Lord, Conn. Particular Ct. 1644/45, in *Records of Connecticut*,
I: 123.
68. *See* Brenton v. Coddington, R.I. Ct. Trials, 1656, in *Rhode Island Court
Records*, I: 19 (recusal); Colony v. Russell, Conn. Particular Ct. 1654, in
Records of Particular Court, 126 (perjury). *Cf.* Colony v. Berry, Ply. Gen.
Ct. 1649/50, in *Records of Plymouth*, II: 148 (whipped for falsely accusing
another of sodomy).
69. Colony v. Bynxe, Conn. Particular Ct. 1651/52, in *Records of Particular
Court*, 108.
70. For homicide prosecutions, *see* Colony v. Allyn, Conn. Particular Ct. 1651,
in *Records of Particular Court*, 107; Colony v. Bishop, Ply. Gen. Ct. 1648, in
Records of Plymouth, II: 134; Colony v. Waumaion, R.I. Ct. Trials 1660/61,
in *Rhode Island Court Records*, I: 71. For assault, *see* Colony v. Taylor, Conn.
Particular Ct. 1655, in *Records of Particular Court*, 144; Colony v. Dotey,
Ply. Gen. Ct. 1637/38, in *Records of Plymouth*, I: 75. For burglary, *see* Col-
ony v. Eams, Conn. Particular Ct. 1654, in *Records of Particular Court*, 136.
For larceny, *see* Colony v. Bedle, Conn. Particular Ct. 1644, in *Records of
Connecticut*, I: 115; Colony v. Dickinson, New Haven Magis. Ct. 1642, in
New Haven Colony Records, I: 77; Colony v. Till, Ply. Gen. Ct. 1639/40, in
Records of Plymouth, I: 143; Colony v. Tibbets, R.I. Ct. Trials 1658, in *Rhode
Island Court Records*, I: 42. For arson, *see* Colony v. Buckly, Conn. Particu-
lar Ct. 1654, in *Records of Particular Court*, 133; Colony v. Bridges, Hart-
ford County Ct. 1667 (ms. in Connecticut State Library). For witchcraft, *see*
Colony v. Gilbert, Conn. Particular Ct. 1654, in *Records of Particular Court*,
131; Colony v. Carrington, Conn. Particular Ct. 1650/51, in *Records of Particular Court*, 93; Colony v. Jonson, Conn. Particular Ct. 1648, in *Records of
Connecticut*, I: 171; Colony v. Garlick, Conn. Magis. Ct. 1658, in *Records of
Particular Court*, 188. For a list of what she considers the most important
New England cases of witchcraft, *see* Carol F. Karlsen, *The Devil in the Shape
of a Woman: Witchcraft in Colonial New England* (New York: W.W. Norton
1987), 259–263.

71. *See, e.g.*, Law v. Mead, New Haven Magis. Ct. 1656, in *New Haven Colony Records*, III: 164; Kimberly v. Fish, New Haven Magis. Ct. 1655, in *New Haven Colony Records*, III: 150; Farnyseed v. Bonney, Ply. Gen. Ct. 1645/46, in *Records of Plymouth*, II: 97. *Cf.* Colony v. Gray, Conn. Particular Ct. 1654, in *Records of Particular Court*, 134 (criminal prosecution for falsely accusing a couple of adultery).

72. Colony v. Till, Ply. Gen. Ct. 1639, in Records of Plymouth, I: 132; Barlow v. Burgis, Ply. Gen. Ct. 1660, in *Records of Plymouth*, VII: 97; Staples v. Ludlow, New Haven Magis. Ct. 1654, in *Records of New Haven*, III: 77.

73. Order re Sex Offenses, Conn. Gen. Ct. 1642, in *Records of Connecticut*, I: 78; Complaint against Train Band of Scituate, Ply. Gen. Ct. 1655, in *Records of Plymouth*, III: 89; Order re House at Saybrook, Conn. Gen. Ct. 1649, in *Records of Connecticut*, I: 188; Petition of Inhabitants of Saybrook, Conn. Gen. Ct. 1649/50, in *Records of Connecticut*, I: 205–206; Order re Secrecy, Conn. Gen. Ct. 1639, in *Records of Connecticut*, I: 39.

74. *See* Dayton, *Women Before the Bar*, 28.

75. For writs of case for trespass, *see* Lyman v. Ford, Conn. Particular Ct. 1653, in *Records of Particular Court*, 120; Turner v. Besto, Ply. Gen. Ct. 1650, in *Records of Plymouth*, VII: 51; Cowdall v. Painter, R.I. Ct. Trials 1658, in *Rhode Island Court Records*, I: 40.. *Cf.* Ford v. Loomis, Hartford County Ct. June 4, 1663 (ms. in Connecticut State Library) (writ of case "for taking away a cow"); Willis v. Bradford, Ply. Gen. Ct. 1637/38, in *Records of Plymouth*, VII: 7 (case "for a lot of land"). For writs of debt on unsealed instruments, *see* Whiting v. Marshfield, Conn. Particular Ct. 1643, in *Records of Connecticut*, I: 88 (debt on bill of exchange); Turner v. Hamans, Ply. Gen. Ct. 1636/37, in *Records of Plymouth*, VII: 6. For writs of debt to balance accounts, *see* Bissell v. Lyman, Conn. Particular Ct. 1660, in *Records of Particular Court*, 211; Cranston v. Elton, R.I. Ct. Trials, 1655, in *Rhode Island Court Records*, I: 13.

76. Saull v. Cowdall, R.I. Ct. Trials 1658, in *Rhode Island Court Records*, I: 49; Earle v. Brenton, Aquidneck Quarter Ct. 1643, in *Rhode Island History*, II: 147.

77. Cotterell v. Havens, Aquidneck Quarter Ct. 1641/42, in *Rhode Island History*, II: 135; Barstow v. Palmer, Ply. Gen. Ct. 1656, in *Records of Plymouth*, VII: 80; Richmond v. Cowdall, R.I. Ct. Trials 1656, in *Rhode Island Court Records*, I: 22; Wadsworth v. Olmstead, Conn. Quarter Ct. 1655, in *Records of Particular Court*, 151; Cornell v. Bull, Aquidneck Quarter Ct. 1641/42, in *Rhode Island History*, II: 135.

78. Rushmer v. Webb, Conn. Particular Ct. 1654/55, in *Records of Particular Court*, 139; Gull v. Fellows, Conn. Magis. Ct. 1657, in *Records of Particular Court*, 176 (emphasis added); Cooke v. Barker, Ply. Gen. Ct. 1645, in *Records of Plymouth*, VII: 41 (emphasis in original).

79. *See* Peirson v. Sylvester, New Haven Magis. Ct. 1656, in *New Haven Colony Records*, III: 190; Mead v. Law, New Haven Magis. Ct. 1656, in *New Haven Colony Records*, III: 162, for early examples of writs. For an example of an incorrect form, *see* Glover v. Mills, New Haven Magis. Ct. 1661, in *New Haven Colony Records*, III: 392 (case for forfeiture of bond).

80. Brenton v. Coddington, R.I. Ct. Trials 1656, in *Rhode Island Court Records*, I: 19; Burnam v. Wright, Conn. Quarter Ct. 1658/59, in *Records of Particular Court*, 198. For other cases of hung juries, *see* Tilman v. Mott, R.I. Ct. Trials 1659/60, in *Rhode Island Court Records*, I: 64; Davis v. Ussell, R.I. Ct. Trials 1657, in *Rhode Island Court Records*, I: 31. Similarly, a Plymouth jury declined to consider a suit brought by a militiaman against a captain who had fined him "for not training, after the said captain had refused to let him train"; in the jury's view, the suit "belonge[d] to the council of war." Johnson v. Cudworth, Ply. Gen. Ct. 1657/58, in *Records of Plymouth*, VII: 87.

81. Order re Hartford Church, Conn. Gen. Ct. 1656/57, in *Records of Connecticut*, I: 290; Smith v. Motts, Conn. Magis. Ct. 1658, in *Records of Particular Court*, 196.

82. Act of Sept. 29, 1658, in *Records of Plymouth*, XI: 93. *Accord*, Laws of Connecticut, in Cushing ed., *Earliest Laws*, 111; Act of Nov. 15, 1636, in *Records of Plymouth*, XI: 12; Acts of Rhode Island, May 19–21, 1647, in Cushing ed., *Acts and Laws of Rhode Island*, 12. On the New Haven colony, *see* Dayton, *Women Before the Bar*, 28.

83. Colony v. Tilden, Ply. Gen. Ct. 1658–1658/59, in *Records of Plymouth*, III: 148–149, 156–157; Knight v. Dickens, R.I. Ct. Trials 1659/60, in *Rhode Island Court Records*, I: 63.

84. *See* Order re Juries, Conn. Gen. Ct. 1644/45, in *Records of Connecticut*, I: 117–119; Order re Juries, Conn. Gen. Ct. 1643, in *Records of Connecticut*, I: 84. The power of the court to impanel a second jury was codified in Laws of Connecticut, in Cushing ed., *Earliest Laws*, 111. For a case altering a jury verdict of damages, *see* Kelsy v. Edwards, Conn. Particular Ct. 1650, in *Records of Particular Court*, 91.

85. *See, e.g.*, Appeal of Wood, Conn. Gen. Ct. 1655, in *Records of Connecticut*, I: 275.

86. Allyn v. Allyn, Conn. Gen. Ct. 1650, in *Records of Connecticut*, I: 211. *Accord*, Lobdell v. Spencer, Conn. Gen. Ct. 1660/61, in *Records of Connecticut*, I: 360 (jury verdict for plaintiff affirmed, but damages increased). For an affirmance in a criminal case, *see* Colony v. Burnham, Conn. Gen. Assembly 1662/63, in *Records of Connecticut*, I: 394.

87. Barlowe v. Wheelers, Conn. Gen. Ct. 1651, in *Records of Connecticut*, I: 226; Alsop v. Foner, New Haven County Ct. June 10, 1668 (ms. in Connecticut State Library); Stanborough v. Cooper, Conn. Gen. Ct. 1652, in *Records of*

Connecticut, I: 231; Cone v. Lord, Hartford County Ct. Oct. 11, 1664 (ms. in Connecticut State Library).

88. *See* Lattimore v. Fellows, Conn. Quarter Ct. 1655, in *Records of Particular Court*, 155; Greene v. Easton, R.I. Ct. Trials 1659, in *Rhode Island Court Records*, I: 56.

89. *See* Order re Publication of Laws, Conn. Gen. Ct. 1639, in *Records of Connecticut*, I: 39; Order re Capital Laws, Conn. Gen. Ct. 1642, in *Records of Connecticut*, I: 77; Lawes of New Haven, in Cushing ed., *Earliest Laws*, 1; Act of Sept. 29, 1658, in *Records of Plymouth*, XI: 33, 57–58; Acts of May 19–21, 1647, in Cushing ed., *Acts and Laws of Rhode Island*, 1.

90. Acts of May 19–21, 1647, in Cushing ed., *Acts and Laws of Rhode Island*, 5, 12; Colony v. Parent, R.I. Ct. Trials 1658, in *Rhode Island Court Records*, I: 44. It did, however, put the defendant under bond to appear at the next General Court, which would "search the laws of England as touching the premises." Colony v. Parent, *supra*.

91. Colony v. Stephens, New Haven Gen. Ct. 1662, in *New Haven Colony Records*, III: 429, 431; Colony v. Betts, New Haven Magis. Ct. 1663, in *New Haven Colony Records*, III: 509; Colony v. Godman, New Haven Magis. Ct. 1655, in *New Haven Colony Records*, III: 151. For earlier inconclusive proceedings involving the same defendant, *see* Godman v. Larramore, New Haven Magis. Ct. 1653, in *New Haven Colony Records*, III: 29.

92. Jessup v. Crabb, New Haven Magis. Ct. 1657, in *New Haven Colony Records*, III: 204; Pell v. Persons, New Haven Magis. Ct. 1647/48, in *New Haven Colony Records*, I: 360; Colony v. Coggeshall, R.I. Ct. Trials 1656, in *Rhode Island Court Records*, I: 22; Colony v. Gould, R.I. Ct. Trials 1657/58, in *Rhode Island Court Records*, I: 36.

93. Order re Maintenance of Ministers, Conn. Gen. Ct. 1644, in *Records of Connecticut*, I: 111; Order re Maintenance of Scholars at Cambridge, Conn. Gen. Ct. 1644, in *Records of Connecticut*, I: 112.

94. Allen v. Church of Hartford, Conn. Gen. Ct. 1644, in *Records of Connecticut*, I: 106, 111; Hollister v. Church of Wethersfield, Conn. Gen. Ct. 1658/59, in *Records of Connecticut*, I: 330. In this latter case, the court required the defendant church to follow proper procedures in disciplining members.

95. Order re Church of Wethersfield, Conn. Gen. Ct. 1660/61, in *Records of Connecticut*, I: 363; Order re Stow, Conn. Gen. Ct. 1660, in *Records of Connecticut*, I: 356; Peirson v. Cowper, New Haven Magis. Ct. 1658, in *New Haven Colony Records*, III: 270.

96. *See* W. K. Jordan, *The Development of Religious Toleration in England from the Accession of James I to the Convention of the Long Parliament (1603–1640)* (Cambridge, Mass.: Harvard University Press, 1936), 216, 225.

97. Petition of Inhabitants of Rehoboth, Ply. Gen. Ct. 1655, in *Records of Plymouth*, III: 81.
98. Petition of Church of Marshfield, Ply. Gen. Ct. 1655, in *Records of Plymouth*, III: 81–82; Act of June 3, 1657, in *Records of Plymouth*, XI: 67; Order re Inhabitants of Yarmouth, Ply. Gen. Ct. 1658/59, in *Records of Plymouth*, III: 155.

CHAPTER 6

1. The preceding four paragraphs are based on Charles M. Andrews, *The Colonial Period of American History*, 4 vols. (New Haven: Yale University Press, 1936), II: 287–323; Russel Menard and Lois Green Carr, "The Lords of Baltimore and the Colonization of Maryland," in David B. Quinn ed., *Early Maryland in a Wider World* (Detroit, Mich.: Wayne State University Press, 1982), 167.
2. Act Concerning Religion, 1648, in *Archives of Maryland*, 72 vols. (Baltimore: Maryland Historical Society, 1883–1972), I: 244–247.
3. Proprietary v. Fitzherbert, Md. Prov. Ct. 1658–1661/62, in *Md. Archives*, XLI: 144, 566; Complaint of Lewis, Md. Prov. Ct. 1638, in *Md. Archives*, IV: 35; Proprietary v. Holt, Md. Prov. Ct. 1658/59, in *Md. Archives*, XLI: 244.
4. Proprietary v. Lumbrozo, Md. Prov. Ct. 1658/59, in *Md. Archives*, XLI: 203; Proprietary v. Thurston, Md. Prov. Ct. 1659, in *Md. Archives*, XLI: 286, 322. The dropping of the prosecution against Lumbrozo is discussed in Andrews, *Colonial Period*, II: 311 n. 2. *See also* Petition of Norwood, Md. Prov. Ct. 1658, in *Md. Archives*, LXV: 670 (petition of sheriff for reimbursement for apprehending Quakers).
5. *See* Proprietary v. Rogers, Kent County Ct. 1656, in *Md. Archives*, LIV: 59; Proprietary v. Price, Kent County Ct. 1655/56, in *Md. Archives*, LIV: 51.
6. Proprietary v. Palldin, Md. Prov. Ct. 1657/58, in *Md. Archives*, XLI: 14; Stratton v. Turner, Md. Prov. Ct. 1659, in *Md. Archives*, XLI: 291. *But see* Proprietary v. Wilkins, Kent County Ct. 1669, in *Md. Archives*, LIV: 264 (woman "not able to make appear who is the father" whipped for false accusation and ordered to support child by herself).
7. Petition of Taylor, Md. Prov. Ct. 1653/54, in *Md. Archives*, X: 337; Motion of Warren, Md. Prov. Ct. 1651, in *Md. Archives*, X: 80. For another man held liable for support on suspicion, *see* Grosse v. Scott, Md. Prov. Ct. 1657, in *Md. Archives*, X: 525.
8. One way for a man to establish his innocence was to sue the mother for slander. In one case where the court found that a servant had slandered her master by saying "he had use of her body," the court ordered her whipped. *See* Bradnox v. Mannering, Kent County Ct. 1657, in *Md. Archives*, LIV: 122.
9. Robinson v. Wennam, Charles County Ct. 1661, in *Md. Archives*, LIII: 133; Stratton v. Turner, Md. Prov. Ct. 1659, in *Md. Archives*, XLI: 291,

reversing Stratton v. Turner, Charles County Ct. 1658/59, *Md. Archives*, LIII: 30, 37 (jury verdict for Stratton on same evidence as on appeal). *See also* Proprietary v. Stratton, Charles County Ct. 1658, in *Md. Archives*, LIII: 28 (mother receives 30 lashes, but is unable to prove Turner the father). *Cf.* Proprietary v. Fairbank, Talbot County Ct. 1673, in *Md. Archives*, LIV: 571 (two witnesses assert defendant "went naked to bed" with another's servant girl; defendant required to give bond for good behavior).

10. Williams v. Smith, Charles County Ct. 1660, in *Md. Archives*, LIII: 78; Proprietary v. Hartwell, Kent County Ct. 1656, in *Md. Archives*, LIV: 78.

11. Proprietary v. Hudson, Md. Prov. Ct. 1651, in *Md. Archives*, X: 111; Proprietary v. Tomkins, Kent County Ct. Mar. 26, 1678 (ms. in Maryland State Archives). For another adultery conviction, *see* Order re Butler, Md. Prov. Ct. 1657, in *Md. Archives*, X: 515. For a presentment for adultery for which no judgment was recorded, *see* Proprietary v. Dunn, Charles County Ct. 1672, in *Md. Archives*, LX: 439.

12. Province v. Mitchell, Md. Prov. Ct. 1652, in *Md. Archives*, X: 182; Dickerson v. Winder, Somerset County Ct. 1674, in *Md. Archives*, LXXXVII: 364 (available online at http://aomol.net/megafile/msa/speccol/sc2908/000001/000087/html/am87–364.html). *Cf.* Proprietary v. Coppedge, Kent County Ct. 1652, in *Md. Archives*, LIV: 9 (man fined and woman whipped); Proprietary v. Watson, Somerset County Ct. 1673/74, in *Md. Archives*, LXXXVII: 327 (available online at http://www.aomol.net/000001/000087/html/am87–327.html) (man fined and woman whipped). *See also* Proprietary v. Robins, Md. Prov. Ct. 1657/58. in *Md. Archives*, XLI: 20, where a jury of six women found that the defendant had taken "savin" and thought she had a dead child in her. No final judgment was ever entered. Six months later, when Robert Robins failed to prove his claim that his wife's child was not his, he was ordered to "take the said Elisabeth his wife again, & provide for her & her children." Robins v. Robins, Charles County Ct. 1658, in *Md. Archives*, LII: 4. Subsequently, they "disclaime[d]" each other as husband and wife and agreed "never to molest or trouble" each other in the future. *See* Declarations of Robert and Elizabeth Robins, Charles County Ct. 1658/59, in *Md. Archives*, LIII: 33.

13. Hollis v. Boys, Md. Prov. Ct. 1642, in *Md. Archives*, IV: 149; Taylor v. Courtney, Md. Prov. Ct. 1661/62, in *Md. Archives*, XLI: 550.

14. Cannady v. Cannady, Md. Prov. Ct. 1656, in *Md. Archives*, X: 471. *Accord*, Declarations of Robert and Elizabeth Robins, Charles County Ct. 1658/59, in *Md. Archives*, LIII: 33.

15. *See* Bradley T. Johnson, *The Foundation of Maryland and the Origin of the Act Concerning Religion of April 21, 1649* (Baltimore: Maryland Historical Society, 1883), 34, 50–51.

16. *See* Marilyn L. Geiger, *The Administration of Justice in Colonial Maryland, 1632–1689* (New York: Garland Publishing, 1987), 44–54, 138–139.

17. Cornwallis v. Calvert, Md. Prov. Ct. 1643/44, in *Md. Archives*, IV: 243; Warr v. Harris, Md. Prov. Ct. 1651/52, in *Md. Archives*, X: 144, which held bills of exchange to be negotiable.

18. Probate of Will of John Smithson, Md. Prov. Ct. 1638, in *Md. Archives*, IV: 46; Letters of Administration to Thomas Gerard, Md. Prov. Ct. 1638/39, in *Md. Archives*, IV: 56; Hollingsworth v. Price, Md. Prov. Ct. 1664/65, in *Md. Archives*, XLIX: 396; Motion of Hatton, Md. Prov. Ct. 1653, in *Md. Archives*, X: 271; Calvert v. Dailey, Md. Prov. Ct. 1668/69, in *Md. Archives*, LVII: 424; Adams v. Land, Md. Prov. Ct. 1651/52, in *Md. Archives*, X: 123; Evett v. Brimington, Md. Prov. Ct. 1666, in *Md. Archives*, LVII: 122.

19. Petition of Eltonhead, Md. Prov. Ct. 1658, in *Md. Archives*, XLI: 178. The quotation in the text, stating the usual rule, was dictum, with the court holding that an oral will was acceptable in this case because of "the impossibility of obtaining pen, ink or paper to make a formal will."

20. Cordea v. Atwood, Md. Prov. Ct. 1680, in *Md. Archives*, LXIX: 187; Reynolds v. Hebb, Md. Prov. Ct. 1680/81, in *Md. Archives*, LXIX: 378. But suit could be maintained on a "bill" even without consideration. *See* Johnson v. Sly, Charles County Ct. 1662, in *Md. Archives*, LIII: 295.

21. *See* Simmons v. Bostooke, Charles County Ct. 1658, in *Md. Archives*, LIII: 14. *Cf.* Petition of Lovely, Kent County Ct. 1660/61, in *Md. Archives*, LIV: 204 (court returns to wife property belonging to her child that husband had unlawfully sold to one Bennett).

22. *See* Glover v. Lumbrozo, Charles County Ct. 1662/63, in *Md. Archives*, LIII: 318; Meeks v. Foulke, Charles County Ct. 1664, in *Md. Archives*, LIII: 492. *Cf.* Mee v. Douglas, Charles County Ct. 1665. in *Md. Archives*, LIII: 586 (plaintiff cannot sue administrator of husband for debt owed by estate of wife). *But see* Motion of Ward, Md. Prov. Ct. 1652/53, in *Md. Archives*, X: 228, granting a woman power to sell lands patented by her in fee simple.

23. *See* Colony v. Warren and Colony v. Smith, Md. Prov. Ct. 1637/38, in *Md. Archives*, IV: 22, 23. The charge in both cases was piracy.

24. *See* Ellison v. Hervey, Md. Prov. Ct. 1643/44, in *Md. Archives*, IV: 240; Colony v. Dandy, Md. Prov. Ct. 1643/44, in *Md. Archives*, IV: 260.

25. *See* Sturman v. Daynes, Md. Prov. Ct. 1651, in *Md. Archives*, X, 115. As to chancery, *see* Snow v. Gerrard, Md. Prov. Ct. 1664, in *Md. Archives*, XLIX: 279. If either party "desire[d] to be tried...in equity, & not by a jury," the court would determine the case. Smith v. Battin, Md. Prov. Ct. 1659/60, in *Md. Archives*, XLI: 369. As to admiralty, *see* Hudson v. Carver, Md. Prov. Ct. 1664, in *Md. Archives*, XLIX: 322 (argument of counsel).

26. Order re Jury, Md. Prov. Ct. 1648, in *Md. Archives*, IV: 379. *See* Price v. Harditch, Md. Prov. Ct. 1648, in *Md. Archives*, IV: 420, where a jury verdict was accepted when one juror dissented but failed to express his dissent in open court loudly enough to be heard. *See also* Hardwich v. Beane, Md. Prov. Ct. 1650, in *Md. Archives*, X: 26, where the foreman of the jury testified that the twelfth juror did give his consent in open court to the verdict.

27. *See, e.g.,* Hudson v. Anderson, Md. Prov. Ct. 1665, in *Md. Archives*, XLIX: 491.

28. Gerry v. Leitchworth, Md. Prov. Ct. 1668, in *Md. Archives*, LVII: 368. The special matter included evidence about the deceased defendant's handwriting and a claim of full administration of his estate, plus a legal claim that the debts were not in writing, were more than nine months old, and hence were no longer subject to suit.

29. Sturman v. Daynes, Md. Prov. Ct. 1651, in *Md. Archives*, X: 115. *Accord*, Blunt v. Copley, Md. Prov. Ct. 1651/52, in *Md. Archives*, X: 132.

30. *See* Blunt v. Copley, Md. Prov. Ct. 1651/52, in *Md. Archives*, X: 132; Hilliard v. Percy, Md. Prov. Ct. 1648, in *Md. Archives*, IV: 419.

31. Sturman v. Daynes, Md. Prov. Ct. 1651, in *Md. Archives*, X: 115; Wade v. Woodruff, Md. Prov. Ct. 1658, in *Md. Archives*, XLI: 72.

32. Blunt v. Copley, Md. Prov. Ct. 1651/52, in *Md. Archives*, X: 132; Daynes v. Anonymous, Md. Prov. Ct. 1651/52, in *Md. Archives*, X: 147; Taylor v. Brooke, Md. Prov. Ct. 1653, in *Md. Archives*, X: 273; Province v. Langworth, Md. Prov. Ct. 1651/52, in *Md. Archives*, X: 142.

33. *See* Lugar v. Fleet, Md. Prov. Ct. 1637/38, in *Md. Archives*, IV: 5; Cotton v. Cornwallis, Md. Prov. Ct. 1638, in *Md. Archives*, IV: 43; Throughgood v. Cornwallis, Md. Prov. Ct. 1638, in *Md. Archives*, IV: 44; Cornwallis v. Smith, Md. Prov. Ct. 1642, in *Md. Archives*, IV: 153.

34. Mitchell v. Dodd, Charles County Ct. 1663, in *Md. Archives*, LIII: 373; Morris v. Marrell, Md. Prov. Ct. 1658/59, in *Md. Archives*, XLI: 255. *Accord*, Dorman v. Stevens, Somerset County Ct. 1675, in *Md. Archives*, LXXXVII: 548 (available online at http://www.msa.md.gov/megafile/msa.md.gov/megafile/msa/speccol/sc2900/sc2908/000001/000087/html/am87-548.html).

35. Mitchell v. Cage, Charles County Ct. 1663, in *Md. Archives*, LIII: 372; Wells v. Glevin, Md. Prov. Ct. 1664/65-1665, in *Md. Archives*, XLIX: 416, 485.

36. Smyth v. Pennington, Md. Prov. Ct. 1667, in *Md. Archives*, LVII: 177; Brooks v. Commins, Md. Prov. Ct. 1648, in *Md. Archives*, IV: 393.

37. *See* Johnson, *Maryland and the Origin of the Act Concerning Religion.*

38. *See* Geiger, *Justice in Colonial Maryland*, 3-4; David Thomas Konig, "'Dale's Laws' and the Non-Common Law Origins of Criminal Justice in Virginia," *American Journal of Legal History*, 26 (1982), 354-375. For the Maryland charter, *see The Federal and State Constitutions, Colonial Charters, and Other*

Organic Laws of the States, Territories, and Colonies Now or Heretofore Form-ing the United States of America, 7 vols., ed. Francis Newton Thorpe (Wash-ington, D.C.: Government Printing Office, 1909), III: 1677–1686.

39. *See* Geiger, *Justice in Colonial Maryland*, 22–24.

40. *See* W. K. Jordan, *The Development of Religious Toleration in England from the Beginning of the English Reformation to the Death of Queen Elizabeth* (Cam-bridge, Mass.: Harvard University Press, 1932), 202–203, 373–374, 382–420; W. K. Jordan, *The Development of Religious Toleration in England from the Accession of James I to the Convention of the Long Parliament, 1603–1640* (Cambridge, Mass.: Harvard University Press, 1936), 505–521.

41. Smith v. Mitchell, Md. Prov. Ct. 1652, in *Md. Archives*, X: 164; Hinson v. Deere, Kent County Ct. 1659, in *Md. Archives*, LIV: 177; Motion of Ward, Md. Prov. Ct. 1652/53, in *Md. Archives*, X, 235; Lomax v. Packer, Charles County Ct. 1658, in *Md. Archives*, LIII: 13. *Cf.* Order re Grace, Charles County Ct. 1660, in *Md. Archives*, LIII: 93 (all contracts with any "infirm man…not capable of making any bargain…shall not be of any effect, unless…made in open court or before two Justices of the Peace"). For another case of hard dealing, *see* Tolson v. Stone, Md. Prov. Ct. 1660/61, in *Md. Archives*, XLI: 425. *See generally* Geiger, *Justice in Colo-nial Maryland*, 48.

42. *See* Vanderdunke v. Fendall, Charles County Ct. 1661, in *Md. Archives*, LIII: 145; Pinner v. Lindsey, Charles County Ct. 1662/63, in *Md. Archives*, LIII: 322. For a standard example of an appeal, *see* Clay v. Ward, Md. Prov. Ct. 1652/53, in *Md. Archives*, X: 235.

43. *See* Smith v. Mitchell, Md. Prov. Ct. 1652/53, in *Md. Archives*, X: 251; Corn-wallis v. Sturman, Md. Prov. Ct. 1652/53, in *Md. Archives*, X: 253.

44. Upton v. Cornwallis, Md. Prov. Ct. 1637/38, in *Md. Archives*, IV: 15 (issue of whether a prior owner of the tobacco had gotten it wet; after hearing two wit-nesses, court concluded that he had not and hence that the tobacco was good and merchantable, as warranted); Blunt v. Copley, Md. Prov. Ct. 1651/52, in *Md. Archives*, X: 132. *Accord*, Calloway v. Poier, Kent County Ct. 1655/56, in *Md. Archives*, LIV: 40.

45. *See, e.g.*, Wicks v. Owens, Md. Prov. Ct. 1659, in *Md. Archives*, XLI: 270 (peti-tion for breach of contract to deliver healthy servant); Eltonhead v. Potter, Md. Prov. Ct. 1651/52, in *Md. Archives*, X: 131 (no writ named); Briant v. Walker, Md. Prov. Ct. 1647, in *Md. Archives*, IV: 356 (no writ named). *But see, e.g.*, Grimes v. Wright, Md. Prov. Ct. 1660/61, in *Md. Archives*, XLI: 397 ("action of trespass"); Pakes v. Waring, Md. Prov. Ct. 1660/61, in *Md. Archives*, XLI: 396 ("summons in chancery").

46. *See* Philpot v. Heard, Charles County Ct. 1663, in *Md. Archives*, LIII: 372; Hopkins v. Morgan, Kent County Ct. 1658/59, in *Md. Archives*, LIV: 155.

47. Colony v. Cornwallis, Md. Prov. Ct. 1643/44, in *Md. Archives*, IV: 249; Clocker v. Gwyther, Md. Prov. Ct. 1659/60, in *Md. Archives*, XLI: 368.

48. Snow v. Gerrard, Md. Prov. Ct. 1662, in *Md. Archives*, XLI: 571; Calvert v. Cooke, Md. Prov. Ct. 1659/60, in *Md. Archives*, XLI: 346.

49. *See* Abington v. Whyte, Md. Prov. Ct. 1663/64, in *Md. Archives*, XLIX: 142; Hallowes v. Percy, Md. Prov. Ct. 1648, in *Md. Archives*, IV: 414. *Accord*, Lillie v. Turner, Charles County Ct. 1658, in *Md. Archives*, LIII: 15 (after defendant refuses to "swear upon the Evangelist," plaintiff does so swear and is granted judgment).

50. *See* Harditch v. Clarke, Md. Prov. Ct. 1648, in *Md. Archives*, IV: 382. *But see* Proprietary v. Naughnongis, Md. Prov. Ct. 1658, in *Md. Archives*, XLI: 186, where an Indian was convicted of theft on his own confession "notwithstanding the evidence" was "not pregnant against the prisoner."

51. Province v. Taylor, Md. Prov. Ct. 1653/54–1654, in *Md. Archives*, X: 339, 366; Washington v. Prescott, Md. Prov. Ct. 1659, in *Md. Archives*, XLI: 327. *See also* Deposition of Johnson and Deposition of Brome, Md. Prov. Ct. 1653, in *Md. Archives*, X: 280, 282.

52. *See, e.g.*, Clocker v. Cornwallis, Md. Prov. Ct. 1652/53, in *Md. Archives*, X: 238; Barber v. Morley, Md. Prov. Ct. 1662, in *Md. Archives*, XLI: 587; Robbins v. Dodd, Md. Prov. Ct. 1663/64, in *Md. Archives*, XLIX: 118; Sanford v. Fendall, Charles County Ct. 1662/63, in *Md. Archives*, LIII: 349.

53. Bayley v. Staplefort, Md. Prov. Ct. 1666, in *Md. Archives*, LVII: 38; Saffin v. Battin, Md. Prov. Ct. 1662, in *Md. Archives*, XLIX: 76; Cole v. True, Md. Prov. Ct. 1660/61, in *Md. Archives*, XLI: 425. *Accord*, Wicks v. Goodhard, Kent County Ct. Mar. 24, 1685/86 (ms. in Maryland State Archives) (nonsuit granted "for error in the declaration"). For a defense of improper joinder of claims, which was rejected by the court, *see* Slye v. Stagg, Md. Prov. Ct. 1681/83, in *Md. Archives*, LXX: 116.

54. Halfhead v. Nicculgutt, Md. Prov. Ct. 1664, in *Md. Archives*, XLIX: 237. The court ultimately ruled in defendant's favor. *See* Halfhead v. Nicculgutt, Md. Prov. Ct. 1664/65, in *Md. Archives*, XLIX: 380.

55. Gerrard v. Dent, Md. Prov. Ct. 1666/67, in *Md. Archives*, LVII: 154.

56. Cornwallis v. Brent, Md. Prov. Ct. 1643/44, in *Md. Archives*, IV: 217; Pheypo v. Hallowes, Md. Prov. Ct. 1647/48, in *Md. Archives*, IV: 361. *Accord*, Smith v. Beane, Md. Prov. Ct. 1650, in *Md. Archives*, X: 41.

57. Rex v. Walker, Northampton County Ct. 1645/46, in *Northampton County Virginia Record Book, 1645–1651*, ed. Howard Mackey (Rockport, Me.: Picton Press, 2000), 40; Province v. Mee, Md. Prov. Ct. 1651/52, in *Md. Archives*, X: 136.

58. Halfhead v. Nicculgutt, Md. Prov. Ct. 1664, in *Md. Archives*, XLIX: 237.

59. *See* Colony v. Brent, Md. Prov. Ct. 1642–1642/43, in *Md. Archives*, IV: 128, 140, 151–152, 156, 159–161, 164.

60. *See* Andrews, *Colonial Period,* II: 308; Colony v. Ingle, Md. Prov. Ct. 1643/44, in *Md. Archives,* IV: 237, 241, 245; Luger v. Ingle, Md. Prov. Ct. 1643/44, in *Md. Archives,* IV: 261. For a later case condemning a vessel for violating the Navigation Acts, *see* Proprietary v. Winslow, Md. Admiralty Ct. 1663, in *Md. Archives,* XLIX: 23.

61. Order re Administrator of Leonard Calvert, Md. Prov. Ct. 1647/48, in *Md. Archives,* IV: 358; Sharpe v. Brent, Md. Prov. Ct. 1648, in *Md. Archives,* IV: 379.

62. Brent v. Vaughan, Md. Prov. Ct. 1648, in *Md. Archives,* IV: 394; Application of Brent, Md. Prov. Ct. 1648, in *Md. Archives,* IV: 457.

63. Province v. Commins, Md. Prov. Ct. 1648, in *Md. Archives,* IV: 436; Attorney General v. Brent, Md. Prov. Ct. 1652, in *Md. Archives,* X: 164; Brent v. Brookes, Md. Prov. Ct. 1653/54, in *Md. Archives,* X: 335.

64. *See* Province v. Price, Md. Prov. Ct. 1655, in *Md. Archives,* X: 425 (fine reduced from 30,000 lb. tobacco to 10,000 lb. in return for immediate payment); Province v. Clarke, Md. Prov. Ct. 1655, in *Md. Archives,* X: 425; Petition of Clarke, Md. Prov. Ct. 1655/56, in *Md. Archives,* X: 441.

65. *See* Morgan v. Munday, Md. Prov. Ct. 1648, in *Md. Archives,* IV: 395; Colony v. Elkin, Md. Prov. Ct. 1642/43, in *Md. Archives,* IV: 177, 181; Proprietary v. Weston, Md. Prov. Ct. 1642, in *Md. Archives,* IV: 156.

66. Order re Mitchell, Md. Prov. Ct. 1657, in *Md. Archives,* XLI: 10. The court postponed consideration of Mitchell's case, and apparently Mitchell had died by next term of court. *See* Hall v. Estate of Mitchell, Md. Prov. Ct. 1658, in *Md. Archives,* XLI: 45.

67. Order re Respect of Magistrates, Kent County Ct. 1658, in *Md. Archives,* LIV: 139.

68. Metcalf v. Derrickson, Md. Prov. Ct. 1652, in *Md. Archives,* X: 166.

69. *See* Johnson v. Yardley, Md. Prov. Ct. 1653/54, in *Md. Archives,* X: 312: Proprietary v. Geley, Md. Prov. Ct. 1659, in *Md. Archives,* XXLI: 310.

70. Colony v. Elkin, Md. Prov. Ct. 1642/43, in *Md. Archives,* IV: 177, 180.

71. Colony v. Pye, Md. Prov. Ct. 1642/43, in *Md. Archives,* IV: 183; Colony v. Elkin, Md. Prov. Ct. 1642/43, in *Md. Archives,* IV: 177, 181.

72. Md. Prov. Ct. 1658–1661/62, in *Md. Archives,* XLI: 144, 566. *See* Andrews, *Colonial Period,* II: 321.

73. Cornwallis v. Gerrard, Md. Prov. Ct. 1653/54, in *Md. Archives,* X: 341.

74. Speed v. Edward Erbery & Co., Md. Prov. Ct. 1676, in *Md. Archives,* LXVI: 422; Colony v. Elkin, Md. Prov. Ct. 1642/43, in *Md. Archives,* IV: 177.

75. *See, e.g.,* Cadger v. Harlow, Md. Prov. Ct. 1653/54, in *Md. Archives,* X: 322; Colony v. White, Md. Prov. Ct. 1642/43, in *Md. Archives,* IV: 165 (defendant whipped for encouraging servant to attempt escape).

76. *See* Ployden v. Fletcher, Md. Prov. Ct. 1643/44, in *Md. Archives,* IV: 224. On the law of servitude generally, *see* Richard B. Morris, *Government and Labor*

in Early America (New York: Columbia University Press, 1946), 395, 398, 401, 409–410, 427–429, 453–454, 488–492, 502–503.

77. *See, e.g.,* Bradnox v. Mannering, Kent County Ct. 1657, in *Md. Archives,* LIV: 122; Province v. Smith, Md. Prov. Ct. 1653, in *Md. Archives,* X: 291; Taylor v. Bradnox, Kent County Ct. 1659, in *Md. Archives,* LIV: 178.

78. Hall v. Wynne, Md. Prov. Ct. 1664, in *Md. Archives,* XLIX: 318. *See also* Jones v. Eltonhead, Md. Prov. Ct. 1652, in *Md. Archives,* X: 191.

79. *See* Taylor v. Brodnax, Kent County Ct. 1661, in *Md. Archives,* LIV: 224; Ward v. Turner, Charles County Ct. 1663, in *Md. Archives,* LIII: 410. *See also* Frizell v. Goulson, Md. Prov. Ct. 1655, in *Md. Archives,* X: 416 (servant freed "because of…rigor").

80. *See* Proprietary v. Nevell, Md. Prov. Ct. 1661, in *Md. Archives,* XLI: 478; Proprietary v. Oversee, Md. Prov. Ct. 1658/59, in *Md. Archives,* XLI: 204; Proprietary v. Boadnox, Kent County Ct. 1652, in *Md. Archives,* LIV: 8. *But see* Proprietary v. Dandy, Md. Prov. Ct. 1657, in *Md. Archives,* X: 542 (master convicted by jury and sentenced to death for murdering servant). *Cf.* Parrott v. Brasse, Md. Prov. Ct. 1659, in *Md. Archives,* XLI: 296 (suit by master saying servant had defamed him by claiming excessive correction "with a great stick" dismissed on evidence servant was seriously injured).

81. Proprietary v. Ward, Kent County Ct. 1652, in *Md. Archives,* LIV: 9.

82. *See* Petition of Donovan, Md. Prov. Ct. 1683, in *Md. Archives,* LXX: 454; Hyde v. Starkey, Md. Prov. Ct. 1652/53, in *Md. Archives,* X: 247; Ashbiston v. Hatch, Md. Prov. Ct. 1648, in *Md. Archives,* IV: 447. *Cf.* Nelson v. Stockett, Md. Prov. Ct. 1661, in *Md. Archives,* XLI: 456 (servant given freedom on basis of letter signed by master prior to death). In such cases, the burden of proof was on the servant. *See* Holland v. Taylor, Md. Prov. Ct. 1656, in *Md. Archives,* X: 451.

83. *See* Pearce v. Watson, Charles County Ct. 1658, in *Md. Archives,* LIII: 14; Buttery v. Brooke, Md. Prov. Ct. 1649/50, in *Md. Archives,* X: 58; Warren v. Mitchell, Md. Prov. Ct. 1652, in *Md. Archives,* X: 185. *Cf.* Vaughan v. Trafford, Md. Prov. Ct. 1643, in *Md. Archives,* IV: 201 (plaintiff to recover 11 months of wages, even though there were "no wages agreed upon").

84. *See* Petition of Douglas, Md. Prov. Ct. 1681/82, in *Md. Archives,* LXX: 169; Williams v. Oversee, Md. Prov. Ct. 1659, in *Md. Archives,* XLI: 284.

85. *See* Custom of Country re Servants' Wages, Md. Prov. Ct. 1647/48, in *Md. Archives,* IV: 361; Sturman v. Daynes, Md. Prov. Ct. 1651, in *Md. Archives,* X: 115; Starkey v. Carrington, Md. Prov. Ct. 1652, in *Md. Archives,* X: 186. *See also* Norman v. Bowles, Md. Prov. Ct. 1654, in *Md. Archives,* X: 382, which reaffirmed the custom of the country but allowed it to be varied by provisions in a servant's indenture.

86. Md. Prov. Ct. 1661, in *Md. Archives,* XLI: 476.

87. Quigley v. Delaroche, Md. Prov. Ct. 1676, in *Md. Archives,* LXVI: 347; England v. Slye, Md. Prov. Ct. 1680/81, in *Md. Archives,* LXIX: 320 (argument of counsel).

88. *See* Hatton v. True, Md. Prov. Ct. 1654, in *Md. Archives*, X: 366.
89. *See* Williams v. Oversee, Md. Prov. Ct. 1659, in *Md. Archives*, XLI: 284; Harris v. Pott, Md. Prov. Ct. 1659/60, in *Md. Archives*, XLI: 369; Bushell v. Fenwick, Md. Prov. Ct. 1654, in *Md. Archives*, X: 365. *Cf.* Atwicks v. Lindsay, Charles County Ct. 1660, in *Md. Archives*, LIII: 83.
90. Information of the Governor, Md. Prov. Ct. 1673, in *Md. Archives*, LXV: 94.
91. *See* Departure of Henry Hare, Md. Prov. Ct. 1666, in *Md. Archives*, LVII: 80.
92. *See* Proprietary v. Sherman, Charles County Ct. 1660, in *Md. Archives*, LIII: 84 (profanity); Proprietary v. Holliday, Md. Prov. Ct. 1659, in *Md. Archives*, XLI: 316 (refusal to assist officer); Proprietary v. Greene, Md. Prov. Ct. 1664, in *Md. Archives*, XLIX: 234 (death penalty for infanticide).
93. *See* Proprietary v. Gibbons, Md. Prov. Ct. 1661, in *Md. Archives*, XLI: 457 (penalty of death); Proprietary v. Williams, Md. Prov. Ct. 1658/59, in *Md. Archives*, XLI: 221, 255 (penalty of death). Gibbons was pardoned in the same record by which he was sentenced, and Williams subsequently was pardoned. *See* Williams v. Oversee, Md. Prov. Ct. 1659, in *Md. Archives*, XLI: 284. *Cf.* Eliot v. Salter, Kent County Ct. 1655/56, in *Md. Archives*, LIV: 49, where the defendant was found guilty of suspicion of theft of hogs and ordered not to butcher any hogs in the future except in the presence of two honest neighbors. In a related case, Eliot v. Price, Kent County Ct. 1655/56, in *Md. Archives*, LIV: 51, a defendant was fined and, when unable to pay the fine, made to stand in open court with a paper on his breast declaring his offense. *See also* Province v. Takanine, Md. Prov. Ct. 1648, in *Md. Archives*, IV: 409 (jury verdict that Native Americans not guilty of theft).
94. *See* Province v. Howell, Md. Prov. Ct. 1648, in *Md. Archives*, IV: 445 (perjury); Province v. Goneere, Md. Prov. Ct. 1648, in *Md. Archives*, IV: 393 (perjury); Proprietary v. Bushell, Md. Prov. Ct. 1652, in *Md. Archives*, X: 202 (drunk); Proprietary v. Pickard, Kent County Ct. 1659, in *Md. Archives*, LIV: 172 (drunk); Province v. Battan, Md. Prov. Ct. 1652/53, in *Md. Archives*, X: 219 (unlawful sale); Proprietary v. Hull, Kent County Ct. 1658/59, in *Md. Archives*, LIV: 159 (insufficient corn).
95. *See* Haggat v. Wade, Charles County Ct. 1661, in *Md. Archives*, LIII: 131; Sturman v. Daynes, Md. Prov. Ct. 1651, in *Md. Archives*, X: 115.
96. *Cf.* Warr v. Harris, Md. Prov. Ct. 1651/52, in *Md. Archives*, X: 144 (plaintiff may collect on bill of exchange given in payment for a man thought by all parties to be a servant but actually a freeman, although court "in point of equity" allows collection of only one-half of face value of bill).
97. Fendall v. Baysey, Md. Prov. Ct. 1658/59, in *Md. Archives*, XLI: 249.
98. *See* Smith v. Mitchell, Md. Prov. Ct. 1651–1652, in *Md. Archives*, X: 78, 164; Metcalf v. Derrickson, Md. Prov. Ct. 1652, in *Md. Archives*, X: 166; Beach v. Adams, Md. Prov. Ct. 1649, in *Md. Archives*, IV: 530.

Index